PENGUIN BOOKS

FROM COLD WAR TO HOT PEACE

Anthony Parsons is the former Ambassador to Iran and former UK Permanent Representative to the United Nations, as well as former Special Adviser on foreign affairs to Margaret Thatcher. He is currently a Research Fellow at the University of Exeter.

Anthony Parsons is married with four children and lives in Devon.

To John Koumoulides with
best wishes from the
author.

Anthony Parsons
Jan 1996

From Cold War to Hot Peace

UN INTERVENTIONS 1947–1995

ANTHONY PARSONS

PENGUIN BOOKS

PENGUIN BOOKS

Published by the Penguin Group
Penguin Books Ltd, 27 Wrights Lane, London W8 5TZ, England
Penguin Books USA Inc., 375 Hudson Street, New York, New York 10014, USA
Penguin Books Australia Ltd, Ringwood, Victoria, Australia
Penguin Books Canada Ltd, 10 Alcorn Avenue, Toronto, Ontario, Canada M4V 3B2
Penguin Books (NZ) Ltd, 182–190 Wairau Road, Auckland 10, New Zealand

Penguin Books Ltd, Registered Offices: Harmondsworth, Middlesex, England

First published by Michael Joseph 1995
Published in Penguin Books 1995
1 3 5 7 9 10 8 6 4 2

Printed in England by Clays Ltd, St Ives plc

CONTENTS

ACKNOWLEDGEMENTS

When I embarked on this book, my principal anxieties related to research, availability of up-to-date information, and the presentation of the manuscript to the publishers in a legible form. Being fully retired, I have no administrative back-up and my personal technology does not extend beyond the use of a fountain pen and a bottle of ink.

I could not have written the case studies without the massive supply of historical and current UN documents which the UN Information Centre in London provided. I put the staff of the Centre, particularly the Director, Graeme Warner, his assistant, Adrienne de Doncker, and the Librarian, Alexandra McLeod, to a great deal of trouble, and am correspondingly grateful to them for the speed and efficiency with which they kept me supplied. I also owe a debt of gratitude to Mrs Sally Morphet and her colleagues in the Research and Analysis Department of the FCO. They were always ready to answer my questions on matters of fact and their summaries of Security Council resolutions are a goldmine. Needless to say, all the opinions in the book are mine alone. Finally my warmest thanks go to my son Rupert Parsons and my son-in-law Rob Wisnovsky, not only for their magical performance in putting the manuscript on disc but also for their encouragement and comments on the substance of the text.

PREFACE

I brooded long before deciding to write this book. In recent years there has been an abundance of collections of essays and articles about the United Nations, to some of which I have contributed. Why produce another one? Was there a genuine gap to be filled and, if so, were there not many people better qualified than me to produce it? I enjoy writing but my private demon reminded me that I was happier looking after my garden without pressure than sitting at my desk writing tens of thousands of words to a rigorous deadline.

My younger daughter, herself an academic, tipped my scale. She told me that I must write the book so long as it was one which only I could write, not another rehash of known historical facts and interpretations. I wondered what quality I possessed which would entitle me to write about the United Nations from a perspective peculiar to myself. It occurred to me that I was, perhaps more than most of my former colleagues, the embodiment of Decolonization Man. Since 1945 I had never held a job which was not related in some way to the decolonization of the British Empire, or to the immediate aftermath of decolonization, or to withdrawal from spheres of influence which had marched with imperial territories. My overseas posts had comprised eight countries of the Middle East and North Africa, from Palestine in the last years of the British Mandate to Iran in the last days of the Pahlavi monarchy thirty years later. In addition I had served twice in the British Mission to the United Nations in New York, first as Counsellor and Head of Chancery and latterly as Permanent Representative. Anyone familiar with the UN knows that, although created by the wartime Alliance against the Axis powers to deter and, if necessary, to punish aggressors, i.e. to prevent a Third World War, it has been for most of its life a decolonization machine, its halls echoing with slogans such as 'national liberation', 'self-determination', 'anti-imperialism' and 'neo-colonialism'. The Security Council, the focus of this book, grappled only indirectly with the Cold War, the competition between American-led capitalism and Soviet-led communism. The Council's agenda was instead dominated by conflicts and crises arising out of decolonization – Palestine, Southern Rhodesia, apartheid in South

Africa, the Congo, Cyprus, the Lebanon, Kashmir, India and Pakistan being some examples.

The United Nations is above all else a forum for public diplomacy. Speeches are made in public, votes are taken in public and, in my time, so-called confidential consultations were leaked so instantaneously to the waiting press corps as to render their privacy meaningless. This configuration brought out the worst in governments. National statements of policy, addressed more often than not to an invisible audience back home, were redolent with self-righteousness. Votes were cast with an eye to pressure groups in domestic politics, to bilateral relations with important states, or as cynical horse trades; hypocrisy was seldom absent from the proceedings when it came to scoring off opponents. A multiple, rather than a double standard prevailed. The parable about the mote and the beam found a ready echo.

And yet, beneath the miasma of suffocating boredom at the gush of routine and repetitive rhetoric in the 'awesome organ': (the Security Council), still more in the 'august body' (the General Assembly), the 'distinguished' representatives succeeded in accomplishing serious business, notwithstanding the exasperating injection of frequently gratuitous Cold War rivalry as East and West competed for the hearts and minds of the newly independent, so-called 'non-aligned' majority. The fulminatory and fatuous rhetoric, the resolutions so painstakingly negotiated and so clearly destined for the dustbin, frequently acted as a safety-valve alternative to more drastic action: the UN on many occasions deployed its peacemaking and peacekeeping capabilities to help Great Powers descend a ladder from the backs of dangerously high horses that their national policies had led them to mount. The UN defused many crises, separated combatants, set the stage for negotiations. The one thing it could not do, and was never intended to do, was to solve underlying disputes. That could only be done by the parties themselves. Hence, for all the absurdities and the insufferable longueurs, the failures and the disillusionments, the UN has always been more than 'the best poker game in the world, played for matchsticks', as an old friend of mine, a skilful and devoted negotiator, once characterized it.

As I have suggested, the UN was for decades a home from home for Decolonization Man, the despair of 'conviction politicians' with their narrowly focused certainties about right and wrong. Endless patience and the ability to absorb and understand a multiplicity of points of view without instant value judgements are the characteristics of Decolonization Man. He or she does not use terms like 'mindless' or 'irrational' when describing acts or policies which have to be rejected or opposed. The psychopathic killer, whether in a balaclava or a neatly pressed uniform, is abhorrent but the motives which lie behind those who direct such monsters are often understandable. Can it be that Decolonization Man is exposed to so many conflicting views of events that he loses touch with his own direction? It is only too easy to succumb to the tendency to say, 'If I were an Afrikaner, an Israeli, a Palestinian, a Northern Irish Catholic or Protestant, I would . . .'. I do not regard this as intellectual decadence, rather as the foundation of good diplomacy. However, when engaged in negotiation, the important thing is to focus unrelentingly on the task at hand rather than explore motives frequently obscured by the darkness of centuries. These are for reflection at leisure.

Now that the Cold War is over, will the UN break its chains and succeed in implementing the role envisaged for it by the Founding Fathers in 1944–45, namely 'to save succeeding generations from the scourge of war . . .'? At first sight this seems unlikely. The collapse of the last empire, which had masqueraded for seventy years as the Union of Soviet Socialist Republics, has detonated another salvo of post-decolonisation wars to add to the number which are still blazing or smouldering from previous decolonisations. In spite of the greater call on the peacekeeping services of the UN made possible by the emergence of the so-called 'international community' into a virtually veto-free world, the Great Powers and their followers seem as incapable as ever either to prevent or extinguish the flames.

The purpose of this book is not to review the gamut of United Nations activities, the brief description of which occupies over two hundred pages in the handbook produced annually by the New Zealand Ministry of External Relations. It is to examine a representative selection of conflicts which have preoccupied the Security Council from the creation until the present day, with a final look at the new agenda and the future. Certain common factors will emerge which have persisted through the early years when a US-led majority dominated the parliamentary situation in New York, through the years of domination of the 'non-aligned' with the Soviet Union in its baggage train, to the present day with the wheel having turned full circle and the UN dominated by Washington again. These common factors form

the basis for conclusions and predictions which I have assembled in
the final chapter. The overarching conclusion of the reader may well
be, in the words of my former chief in New York, the late Lord
Caradon, that the faults and weaknesses of the UN lie not in the
Charter nor in the Organisation but in the defects of its most powerful
members.

I have brought the Epilogue up to the end of September 1995. I have
had no need to alter the conclusions in Chapter 20: the UN's successes
in El Salvador and Mozambique have been offset by the Somalia fiasco,
the Bosnian quicksand into which the UN sank, and the hostility of the
newly elected Republican Congress in Washington.

PART ONE

The Middle East

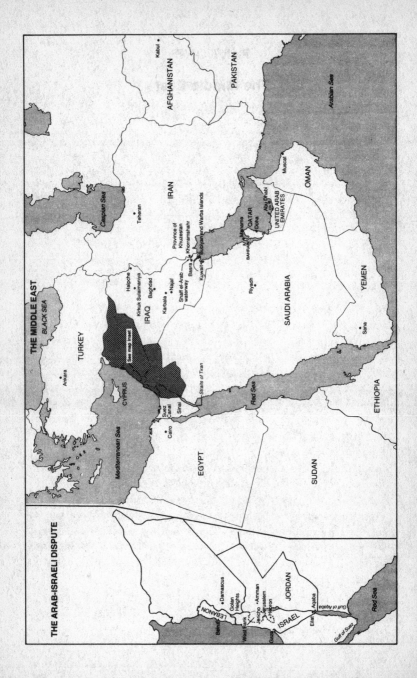

THE MIDDLE EAST

THE ARAB-ISRAELI DISPUTE

CHAPTER ONE

From the Palestine Problem to the Arab/Israeli Dispute

Many of us, including myself, who spent the last years of the British Mandate in Palestine will never recover fully from the shame and humiliation of the dismal retreat in the Spring of 1948. Forty-five years and five major Arab/Israeli wars later, the retrospective scene has lost none of its bleakness. Since 1945, between forty and fifty states have secured their independence from British control of one kind or another. Palestine is the only case where there was no attempt to hand over power to a successor regime, only a unilateral retreat through warring communities.

Perhaps such a denouement was inevitable. During the First World War the recently created Zionist movement actively canvassed their aspiration of a Jewish homeland in Palestine, an entirely understandable objective in the light of the anti-Semitism which had accompanied the growth of European nationalism in the nineteenth century. For a series of different reasons the British government was favourably disposed. Dr Chaim Weizmann, the Zionist leader, was a persuasive man with good connections with the political establishment. In those more biblical days there was a sentimental inclination towards enabling European Jews to return to the Promised Land. In terms of *Realpolitik*, some British leaders saw strategic advantage in establishing a friendly European community close to the vital link of the Suez Canal. Meeting Zionist wishes would also have a positive influence on the important Jewish community in the United States as well as the Jews of Central and Eastern Europe who were being wooed by the Central Powers. These factors converged in 1917 to produce a letter from the Foreign Secretary, Arthur Balfour, to Lord Rothschild, Head of the Zionist Federation. It read as follows:

Foreign Office
November 2nd 1917

Dear Lord Rothschild,
I have much pleasure in conveying to you, on behalf of His Majesty's

Government, the following declaration of sympathy with Jewish Zionist aspirations which has been submitted to, and approved by, the Cabinet.

'His Majesty's Government view with favour the establishment in Palestine of a national home for the Jewish people, and will use their best endeavours to facilitate the achievement of this object, it being clearly understood that nothing shall be done which may prejudice the civil and religious rights of existing non-Jewish communities in Palestine, or the rights and political status enjoyed by Jews in any other country.'

I should be grateful if you would bring this declaration to the knowledge of your Zionist Federation.

Yours faithfully

ARTHUR JAMES BALFOUR

This letter, the Balfour Declaration, celebrated annually in Israel and mourned annually in the Arab world, contained a fatal contradiction. Earlier a Zionist leader had described Palestine as a 'land without a people for a people without a land.' Unfortunately for the future of Middle East peace, this was not the case. 'Existing non-Jewish communities in Palestine', i.e. the Palestinian Arabs, comprised roughly 90 per cent of a total population of 660,000; the Jews, about five thousand of whom were recent immigrants, making up the remaining 10 per cent. The Arab majority did not regard European Jews as long-lost cousins returning to their ancestral home. They were to the Arabs European colonists, as alien as white settlers in sub-Saharan Africa. It would in a relatively densely populated territory be impossible to 'facilitate the achievement' of the Jewish national home without prejudicing the civil rights of the majority. Implementation of the Declaration was certain to lead to conflict.

In the event, after the Allied victory, the Arab provinces of the Ottoman Empire were carved up between Britain and France in a geopolitical pattern that represented the interests of London and Paris: the people in the region were not consulted. In deference to President Woodrow Wilson's espousal of the novel idea of the self-determination of peoples, the provinces were not absorbed into the respective empires. Instead they were established as League of Nations Mandates: Syria and Lebanon went to France; Iraq, Transjordan, and Palestine to Britain. The Balfour Declaration was incorporated in the terms of the British Mandate for Palestine in spite of the virtually universal opposition to it already voiced throughout the Arab world.

For the twenty-five years following the formal award of the Mandate which came into effect in September 1923, successive British governments struggled unavailingly to reconcile the irreconcilable. As early as 1919 the (American) King-Crane Commission had concluded that, in the light of the opposition of nine-tenths of the population of Palestine, only 'a greatly reduced Zionist programme be attempted by the Peace Conference.' In 1922 the Colonial Secretary, Winston Churchill, published an interpretative statement of policy designed to allay fears but which succeeded in antagonising Jews and Arabs. In the period between the wars sporadic clashes erupted between the communities and, with the pressure for increased Jewish immigration following the Hitlerian persecutions of the 1930s, a serious Arab revolt broke out in 1936 and was not put down until 1939. Although the Mandate government achieved a lot functionally in regard to, for example, education, health, agriculture and public administration, the political stalemate persisted: the Jewish leadership wisely accepted whatever was on offer provided that it did not conflict with basic aims; the Arabs remained intransigent. Political initiatives foundered. Partition was rejected after the Peel Commission recommendation of 1937, while the 1939 White Paper, which looked towards a unified independent Palestinian state within ten years and set limits on Jewish immigration, was quickly denounced by the Jewish Agency for Palestine, the representative body of the Jewish community. The Second World War ushered in a lull in local hostilities.

When I arrived in Palestine in 1945 after a brief sojourn there in early 1943, there had been a qualitative change in the situation. The Arab population was quiet, trusting that the British and the newly created, American dominated United Nations would protect their interests. But the Holocaust in Europe had engendered a passionate desire amongst the Jewish community, strongly supported by powerful elements in the United States and elsewhere, for the immediate creation of a Jewish state which could accommodate the survivors and ensure that there was a haven for all Jews for all time. Jewish guerrilla and terrorist activity directed against the British, not the Arabs, rapidly spread and the large British garrison, a hangover from the war, could do little more than contain it. Illegal Jewish immigration was a further thorn in the flesh of the Mandatory government. London adopted the severe expedient of deporting these pathetic boatloads to camps in Cyprus, a measure which aroused bitter emotions.

Britain, weakened and exhausted by war, under domestic pressure to 'bring the boys home', harried by Washington and European governments to meet Zionist aspirations in the face of the appalling horrors of post-Holocaust Europe, unable to find a political solution and confronted by implacable Arab opposition to a Jewish state of any kind in Palestine, threw in the towel. Foreign Secretary Ernest Bevin announced in February 1947 that His Majesty's Government had decided to refer the Palestine problem to the United Nations. To us, young men in the field, this seemed like a clear abdication of responsibility, the only justification being that it would willy-nilly involve the United States, the rising Great Power, in the search for a solution. Looking back forty-five years later, this decision represented the first step down a path which was to be trodden many times, namely the dumping by governments of problems into the lap of the United Nations when national policies had reached impasse. In this particular instance the United Nations had scarcely had time to find its feet, let alone establish a track record in mediation and conflict management. It was a test too far and the result initiated half a century of warfare, guerrilla fighting and terrorism, sporadic threats to world peace and massive displacement of people. At the time of writing, all Palestinians in the world are either living in exile, in refugee camps or under Israeli control, the ultimate proof of the irreconcilable nature of the two halves of the Balfour Declaration.

On 15 May 1947 a special session of the General Assembly decided to establish an eleven-member Special Committee on Palestine (UNSCOP) to study the problem and to report. The endeavour to achieve impartiality resulted in a curious composition – Australia, Canada, Czechoslovakia, Guatemala, the Netherlands, Peru, Sweden, Uruguay, India, Iran and Yugoslavia. This scarcely amounted to a symposium of Middle Eastern expertise and Dr Ralph Bunche, the foremost international civil servant of his generation and father of UN peacekeeping, who acted as Secretary to the Committee, described it in a letter to his wife as 'just about the worst group I have ever had to work with. If they do a good job, it will be a real miracle.'[1]

The Committee visited Palestine in June and July. The Arab leadership, still blind to the fact that their policy of implacable non-cooperation was leading their people to a disaster, boycotted the

[1] *Ralph Bunche: An American Life* by Brian Urquhart, W.W. Norton, 1993

Committee which had wide and detailed discussions with the whole spectrum of Jewish groups. The internal security situation in the Summer of 1947 was unsettled to say the least and I cannot recall the Committee receiving a warm welcome from the Mandatory authorities.

UNSCOP submitted two reports, both drafted by the indefatigable Bunche, at the end of August. The majority report was signed by seven of the participants, the minority report by India, Iran and Yugoslavia. Australia remained neutral. The minority recommended a federal state with Jerusalem as its capital (not entirely unlike the British proposals in the 1939 White Paper), while the majority recommended partition with Jerusalem placed under International Trusteeship. Given the fact that there were still twice as many Arabs as Jews in Palestine in 1946, as well as the density of the population throughout the country, there would have been almost as many Arabs as Jews in the proposed Jewish state, although the Arab state would have contained only about ten thousand Jews.

The majority report was put to the vote in the Special Committee of the General Assembly on 25 November and was approved by twenty-five votes to thirteen with seventeen abstentions, falling one short of the two-thirds majority required for adoption. After frenzied lobbying and amid scenes of wild excitement, the resolution scraped through the Plenary session on 29 November. Arm twisting on an Homeric scale had induced certain states, including Haiti, the Philippines and Liberia, to change their votes. The result was thirty-three in favour, thirteen against with ten abstentions: the two-thirds majority had been narrowly achieved. The Jewish leadership immediately accepted the result, although it fell short of their aspirations. The Arabs rejected it. All Arab and Moslem delegations voted against and walked out. Britain abstained, making clear that it would not assist in the implementation of a plan which could only be put into effect by force.

I have not forgotten the impact of this bombshell on the Palestinian communities in the area in which I was working. They had been attentively following reports of the progress of UNSCOP but few people had anticipated that the United Nations would decide to terminate the British Mandate on the basis of partition, the solution rejected ten years previously. There was stunned shock which quickly translated into a mixture of bravado ('into the sea with the Jews') and fear (rumours proliferated of attacks on villages, massacres of women and children and so on). For a few weeks a semblance of normality persisted; then the superficial veneer of stability began to disintegrate as the two communities engaged in battle. In early 1948 the violence increased and it became clear that the Jewish community was gaining the upper hand. The Arabs were to all intents and purposes leaderless and lacking in arms. Atrocities like the massacre of the villagers of Deir Yassin by Menachem Begin's Irgun Zvei Leumi in April caused panic and the populace began to flee across the nearest borders. Meanwhile the British concentrated on protecting their own withdrawal.

On 14 May the British High Commissioner and his staff left Haifa by warship. The ill-fated Mandate was over. The State of Israel was proclaimed and immediately recognized by the United States and the Soviet Union. UNSCOP was disbanded and, in its place, the General Assembly appointed a Mediator (the Swedish Count Bernadotte) who was commissioned among other things to 'promote a peaceful adjustment of the future situation of Palestine'. This aspiration coincided with the crossing of the frontiers of Palestine by Arab regular armies to add to the confused guerrilla fighting which had been crackling across the country for six months in spite of three calls for a truce by the Security Council. The first round in the Arab/Israeli war had begun.

During the next ten months of intermittent fighting, the United Nations chalked up several notable 'firsts'. UN military observers (unarmed) were deployed for the first time to supervise truces. The Truce Supervision Organisation (UNTSO) is still in place. In July 1948 the Security Council determined for the first time that there had been a threat to the peace within the meaning of Article 39 of the Charter and adopted a mandatory resolution ordering a cease-fire. It was briefly effective. The first appointed UN mediator, Count Bernadotte, was murdered in September by Yitzhak Shamir's Lehi group, which saw Bernadotte's thinking as an obstacle to Lehi's aspirations in Jerusalem. For the first time, the UN, in the person of the Acting Mediator, Ralph Bunche, negotiated armistice agreements between warring armies, which, in March 1949, brought the first round of warfare to a conclusion.

In the period May 1948 to March 1949 the Security Council adopted no less than seventeen resolutions, a foretaste of the future domination of the Council's agenda by the Palestine problem. The General Assembly, on 11 December 1948, adopted an important resolution (No. 194 III) which established a three-nation Conciliation Commission (which achieved nothing), reiterated that Jerusalem be placed under an international regime and, most significantly for the future, resolved that the refugees from the war should be permitted to return to their homes 'and live in peace with their neighbours' or, if they chose not to return, to receive compensation. The Assembly also created a special fund and a special organisation (consolidated a year later as the UN Relief and Works Agency – UNRWA) to look after the seven hundred thousand Palestinian refugees who had been driven from their homes and were living in miserable, tented accommodation. UNRWA is, of course, still in being, caring now for the health, education and welfare of over two million refugees in camps in the Occupied Territories, Jordan, Syria and the Lebanon.

After this initial convulsion the landscape of the Middle East exhibited wholesale changes. Israel was firmly established within the armistice lines on territory which greatly exceeded the extent of the Jewish state as set out in the partition resolution. The mass flight of the Palestinians had reduced the proportion of Arabs to Jews within the boundaries under Israeli control to between 10 per cent and 15 per cent (as opposed to the approximately 40 per cent in the original Jewish state). Large Jewish communities in the Arab world were either expelled or fled, a development which profoundly affected the almost wholly European composition of the Jewish community under the Mandate. The Palestinian 'disaster', as it was called in the Arab world, began to permeate Arab domestic politics, inter-state relations within the Arab League, as well as discrediting the regimes whose armies had performed so lamentably during the war. The military fiasco in Palestine lay behind the rash of military *coups d'état* in Syria from 1949 onwards and the 1952 *coup* in Egypt which overthrew the monarchy and brought Lieutenant-Colonel Gamal Abdel Nasser to power. In this atmosphere of anger and humiliation, no Arab regime dared to contemplate recognition of Israel's existence. The word itself was taboo in Arab public media and maps left a blank space. The expectation among some of the European Israeli leadership that the Arabs, having lost the war, would make peace, was stillborn.

Against this unpromising background, the Palestine Conciliation Commission was in no position to 'promote a peaceful adjustment . . .' Equally Israel was not prepared to allow any of the refugees to return and the Arab world was resolved not to resettle them. For eighteen years after the 1949 Armistice Agreements, the UN tacitly accepted that rough justice had been done and made no sustained attempt to mediate a peaceful settlement. The rump of Palestine (the West Bank) had been absorbed by Jordan; Gaza was under Egyptian administration. The UN succoured the refugees and dealt as best it could with the symptoms of the underlying disease, namely guerrilla pinpricks and disproportionate Israeli retaliations along the armistice lines and, in 1956, another major war – the Suez crisis.

The 1950s were a time of seismic change in the global climate and configuration. This was reflected in the United Nations in which the West had commanded a clear voting majority. Treatment of the Palestine problem in particular and of the Arab Israeli dispute in general mutated accordingly. The Cold War became the fresh threat to world peace: NATO and the Warsaw Pact confronted each other with a burgeoning array of nuclear weapons in Central Europe. The two superpowers patrolled the United Nations recruiting supporters. By the end of the decade, decolonization had almost doubled the membership of the UN from the original fifty-one (now 184). The doctrine of non-alignment between the two power blocs was born at the Bandoeng Conference of 1955 among the newly independent states. This was blended by the founders – Presidents Sukarno of Indonesia, Tito of Yugoslavia, Nasser of Egypt and Prime Minister Nehru of India – with 'positive neutrality', a more dynamic slogan then 'neutralism', the characteristic of states such as Sweden and Switzerland. Above all, the newly formed Non-Aligned Movement sailed under the banner of 'anti-imperialism', a rhetorical firearm more easily levelled against Britain, France, Belgium, Portugal and other Western European colonial powers than the Soviet Union which had skilfully concealed its direct descent from the Tsarist Empire and which, with outrageous but effective cynicism and hypocrisy, was quick to trumpet its championship of national liberation and total independence from the wicked West. Indeed, when I was in Cairo in the early 1960s, many of us concluded that the true meaning of non-alignment was giving the Soviet Union the benefit of all doubts, the West never. I recall an Egyptian cartoonist, with bold disregard for the police state apparatus, depicting one man asking another why he was holding an open umbrella when it was not raining – 'Ah, but it is raining in Moscow.'

In the Middle East, pan-Arab Nasserism, not communism, was the embodiment of this new wave. The magnetic appeal of the young, energetic President swept through the region like a forest fire. His rhetoric carried far and wide by Cairo radio and the Egyptian press, which had no serious competitors anywhere in the Arab world, was heavily charged with anti-Zionism, anti-imperialism (particularly the British variety) and with clarion calls for the destruction of traditional regimes, the 'stooges of imperialism', and for Arab unity under the banner of socialist republicanism (as practised in Cairo). I remember well in the early 1950s in Baghdad sensing the palpable excitement among middle-rank Iraqi officers and their longing to emulate their Egyptian opposite numbers. They were not long in doing so. I recall at the end of the decade the feverish excitement which gripped the Jordanian capital when Nasser, then President of the short-lived United Arab Republic of Egypt and Syria, visited neighbouring Damascus. It was as if he were in the next room. Traditional, pro-Western Arab regimes everywhere trembled in their shoes.

In 1955 the Cold War came to the Arab world. Until then, Britain, France and the United States had monopolized the sale of arms to Arab governments and, since 1950, had operated a tripartite policy of restraint of supplies to Israel and the front-line Arab states in order to reduce the possibility of a further outbreak of fighting. President Nasser chafed at this constraint, seeing it as a manifestation of imperialism. Convinced that Israel was bent on expansion and was acquiring modern weaponry from France in breach of the tripartite agreement, he submitted a substantial shopping list to the United States. The West believed that Nasser, whose fierce anti-Israeli rhetoric was already causing concern, had aggressive intentions rather than defensive as he claimed. His request was refused. In September 1955 Egypt concluded a substantial arms deal with the Soviet Union via Czechoslovakia. Nasser had enabled Moscow to overleap the anti-Soviet ring fence constructed around the Middle East, the strategic importance of which was rapidly increasing as oil replaced coal in the industrialized world.

Suspicion had already been mounting that the Kremlin, following the death of Stalin, was contemplating a more forward policy in the Arab world. In 1954 the first vetoes had been cast (by the Soviet Union) on two draft Palestine resolutions, one mildly critical of Syria over an incident in the northern Demilitarized Zone, and the other of Egypt regarding refusal to permit Israeli shipping to transit the Suez Canal. The Czech arms deal was confirmation of the new, forward Soviet policy and Nasser's stock slumped in Western capitals, particularly in Washington which had originally favoured his revolution as a break with the British-dominated imperial past as manifested by the corrupt and futile monarchy of King Farouk. Needless to say, Nasser's prestige rose in Arab public opinion for his successful defiance of the Western stranglehold on arms supplies.

In 1956 the Arab world steadily polarized between the Western-supported 'traditional' regimes such as monarchical Iraq and Jordan, the Lebanon, Saudi Arabia and the British-protected Gulf states on the one hand and the Soviet-supported 'progressives', Egypt and Syria, on the other. France and the United States championed Israel. In July 1956 the US withdrew an offer of a loan to finance Nasser's dream project, the Aswan High Dam: Britain and the World Bank followed suit. Nasser retaliated by nationalizing the Suez Canal Company: the international roof fell in. (Two years later the Soviet Union agreed to finance and build the Aswan High Dam.)

I was in the Embassy in Ankara at the time. I do not think that any of us believed that the re-internationalization of the Canal was the sole objective of the British and French governments. Toppling Nasser, who had attained demonic status in British eyes, was a more important objective. Hence the consultations and conferences which occupied much of the next three months assumed an unreal air while obvious, indeed undisguised, military preparations went forward. The UN became a forum for consultations rather than collective action. On 13 October the Security Council unanimously adopted a resolution (No. 118) setting out six requirements for a settlement based on conversations between Secretary-General Hammarskjold and the foreign ministers of Egypt, France and Britain. The requirements included free transit, respect for Egyptian sovereignty and the insulation of the Canal from national politics. These were reasonable enough terms but the Soviet Union vetoed a final paragraph critical of the Egyptian government.

For some time Palestinian *fedayeen* (guerrilla) activity had been hotting up from the Egyptian-administered Gaza Strip, although, between 1949 and 1956 the bulk of the Armistice violations had been on the Syria/Israel and Jordan/Israel frontiers. In 1955 Israel had been unanimously condemned for a massive retaliatory raid on Gaza and there had been subsequent calls by the Council for the prevention of violence in the Gaza area.

The *fedayeen* activity, openly sponsored by Nasser, plus the Egyptian military build-up as a consequence of the Czech arms deal, had been worrying the Israelis and it was no secret that there had been discussions between Britain, France and Israel about the Nasserite menace. However, to us in Ankara, it came as a bolt from the blue when, on 29 October, Israeli armour poured across the frontier into Sinai, heading for the Canal with parachute drops in advance of the main columns. It was an even greater shock when the initial British 'police action' to separate the combatants was to conduct an aerial bombing attack on Egyptian airfields. This weird exercise in 'peacekeeping' was followed by the Anglo-French landing in the Canal Zone, by which time the Israelis had secured their objectives with relative immunity from Egyptian air attack. My Turkish friends shared the view of the majority in the Embassy that Britain had taken leave of her senses and that the expedition was immoral, inexpedient and, after the long build-up, militarily incompetent.

At the Security Council Britain and France vetoed two cease-fire resolutions, one tabled by the United States, and the debate was transferred to the General Assembly under the Uniting for Peace procedure (where vetoes were inapplicable), originally devised by the United States when the Council was blocked by Soviet vetos during the Korean War. Britain and France had achieved the apparently impossible: they had united the two confrontational superpowers in the UN at a moment when one of them was hammering a small European country, Hungary. The Soviet veto of a resolution calling for withdrawal of Soviet forces from Hungary passed almost unnoticed.

It quickly became clear that, with the US, the USSR and almost the whole membership of the UN in total and vociferous opposition, not to mention a run on the pound sterling, the British and French had no choice but to withdraw from this sorry adventure. But, to have done so unilaterally and for Egyptian forces to reoccupy the whole Canal Zone would have been impossible without precipitating a major political crisis in both countries.

This was, in my judgement, the finest hour of the UN General Assembly. Resolutions were adopted calling for a cease-fire and Israeli withdrawal (only Australia and New Zealand joined Britain, France and Israel in opposition) and establishing a United Nations Emergency Force (UNEF I) to replace the Anglo/French/Israeli forces in the Canal Zone and Sinai. The idea came from Lester Pearson, the Canadian Minister for External Affairs, the execution of the plan was carried out by Dag Hammarskjold with his admirable staff including the American Ralph Bunche and the British Brian Urquhart. They

performed miracles of improvisation. The General Assembly maintained the momentum until the British and French forces had departed
and American pressure had forced Israel to withdraw behind the
Armistice lines. By March 1957, the situation had returned to what
passed for normal in the Middle East and the Canal had been cleared
under UN auspices: Egypt had not unnaturally refused any help from
Britain and France. UNEF I kept the peace between Israel and
Egypt for ten years with a force which, at peak, comprised about six
thousand troops drawn from ten nations, none of them Permanent
Members of the Security Council. This was the first time ever that an
armed peacekeeping force (as opposed to unarmed observers) had been
deployed; the first time that blue helmets had been used; the first time
that the UN had taken military action with the consent of the parties
to a conflict, an eventuality not envisaged in the Charter. It was the
precedent for what has become the most familiar of all UN activities:
today there are about seventy thousand blue helmets and blue berets
deployed in separate peacekeeping operations across the globe from
Cambodia to El Salvador.

This was also the first occasion on which the UN had acted as a
ladder down which Great Powers could climb when national policies
had stranded them in exposed and untenable positions. Britain and
France could argue, as they did, that this – the UN deployment – was
the consummation that they had intended all along and that, as
members of the UN in good standing, it was natural that they should
accede to the request (not the demand) of the international community.
A shred of dignity in retreat had been retained. Some years would pass
before the UN – East, West and Non-Aligned – would again unite to
take collective action with a common purpose. Suez may have been a
sharp downward turning point in Britain's reputation world-wide and
in the retreat from empire and Great Power status. But the undoubted
gainers were President Nasser, whose prestige soared, and the United
Nations itself.

The next decade was a period of exceptional turbulence even by
Middle Eastern standards. In 1958 the Iraqi monarchy was bloodily
overthrown by a group of 'free officers'. At the beginning of that year
Egypt and Syria had united in the United Arab Republic. The
Hashemite countermove – the creation of a United Arab Kingdom of
Jordan and Iraq – was short lived and the Western security construct,
the Baghdad Pact (Britain, Iraq, Iran, Turkey and Pakistan with the

US as an observer), was diluted to the Central Treaty Organisation (CENTO), following the defection of Iraq after the 1958 coup. Also in 1958, civil war broke out in the Lebanon: American troops eventually stormed the bikini-strewn beaches to assure stability, while British troops briefly arrived in Jordan to shore up King Hussein in the frenzied atmosphere following the Iraqi coup. In the Sudan as well, the military ousted the independence government. Civil war broke out in the Yemen following the death of the old Imam (who had cunningly defused Nasserist pressure by attaching his medieval state to the 'progressive' UAR, which became the United Arab States, UAS). By that time (1962) Nasserism had reached its apogee and was on the decline. In 1961 Syria had seceded from the UAR: a power struggle ensued which would not be resolved until 1970. Egyptian troops became entangled in support of the Yemeni republicans who were being opposed by Saudi-backed royalists.

Meanwhile, neither the UN nor any individual power attempted to promote an Arab/Israeli settlement. Israeli governments would probably have welcomed peace based on the translation of the 1949 Armistice lines into recognized frontiers. But, in the atmosphere of furious competition for public opinion in the Arab world, no Arab regime could contemplate a move towards recognizing that Palestine was anything but sacred Arab soil temporarily ravaged by 'Zionist gangs'. There was no basis here for mediation. In fact President Bourguiba of Tunisia (independent in 1956) was rash enough to suggest in 1965 that it would be sensible to recognize Israel and to revert to the partition proposals of 1947. He was excoriated by his colleagues in the Arab League, particularly Nasser.

With the Egypt/Israel sector quiet thanks to the deployment of UNEF I, the Security Council occupied itself with dealing as best it could with occasional breaches of the Armistices between Jordan/Israel and Syria/Israel with a brief involvement in the Lebanon when the government brought alleged UAR intervention in Lebanese domestic affairs to the UN. Some resolutions were adopted, others vetoed by the Soviet Union when they contained a breath of criticism of the UAR.

The General Assembly concerned itself almost entirely with matters relating to the administration and financing of UNRWA and UNEF I. The latter had generated an important difference of principle which continued to bedevil UN peacekeeping operations until 1987 when

President Gorbachev reversed the historical attitude of the Soviet Union towards the UN and, in particular, pledged unqualified support for peacekeeping. In 1956 the Soviet Union did not vote against the General Assembly resolution establishing UNEF for fear of offending their new friend in Cairo. But the Kremlin took the fundamentalist attitude that any UN military deployments which were not directly under the control of the Security Council in accordance with the 'military articles' in Chapter VII of the Charter were *ultra vires*. Hence, UNEF I, created by the General Assembly with a line of command and control going back to the Secretary General (in Soviet eyes no more than an administrative official), was anathema. France took a similar albeit less purist view. The Soviet Union and its associates voted against all resolutions relating to the financing of UNEF I (France abstained) and refused to contribute its share, insisting that the 'aggressors' should pay for their misdeeds. This developed into a major financial crisis for the UN, which was only eased when a committee was created to examine the whole question of the command and control and financing of UN 'non-threatening' peacekeeping (blue helmets) under Chapter VI (Pacific Settlement of Disputes) of the Charter. Hence the Palestine problem was responsible not only for the first peacekeeping deployment but also for the initiation of a controversy which persisted for thirty years.

The political and military earthquake that erupted in June 1967 made all these considerations seem trifling. In the early months of 1967, tension mounted between Syria and Israel: there were serious clashes on the Armistice lines. In April the Israelis bombed Damascus and six Syrian aircraft were downed. Syria, Egypt and Jordan were on bad terms and the Damascus and Amman radio stations were countering Nasserite propaganda blasts by accusing Egypt of hiding behind the skirts of UNEF I. In mid-May the Soviet Union, either through misinformation or malice, informed Cairo and Damascus that the Israelis were massing on the Syrian frontier. The UNTSO observers saw no evidence of such a build-up. On 16 May, Nasser, stung by the Jordanian and Syrian taunts, started to deploy forces in the Sinai, although large elements of the Egyptian armed forces were still bogged down in the Yemen, and ordered UNEF to withdraw. On 22 May Nasser closed the Straits of Tiran (the opening of the arm of the Red Sea which leads to the Israeli port of Eilat) to Israeli shipping.

I was at the time Political Agent in the Gulf State of Bahrain. When the news of the closure of the Straits came through on the radio, I was entertaining Bahraini friends to dinner. I turned to my guests and said 'This means war'. There was no dissent. Everyone knew beyond shadow of doubt that no Israeli government would tolerate this move even if they were prepared to accept the re-militarization of Sinai and Gaza. Without access through Tiran, Eilat would die.

Controversy still grumbles on about whether the UN Secretary General, U Thant, could have defused the crisis and pre-empted the war. One argument runs that Nasser was bluffing and that he was waiting for U Thant to make vigorous representations for the retention of UNEF so that he, Nasser, could climb down without humiliation, pleading the *force majeure* of the international community. I do not accept this view. It is true that U Thant flew to Cairo to plead with Nasser. But the dates and timings of the various Egyptian moves demonstrate clearly that Nasser had crossed the Rubicon and had no intention of making a return journey. Legally, neither U Thant nor the Security Council could compel Egypt to allow UNEF to stay, quite apart from the fact that Egypt controlled UNEF's logistical lines of communication. The force had been deployed on the basis of an agreement between Nasser and Hammarskjold confirmed by a General Assembly resolution. Assembly resolutions are recommendatory, not mandatory, and the peacekeepers had been deployed with the consent of the host country. Once that consent was withdrawn, the force had no choice but to follow suit. If Israel had at the outset in 1956–57 allowed UNEF forces to be deployed on the Israeli side of the border, there would probably have been no crisis, no June War. But they did not.

Over the next fortnight, the crisis moved quickly to its climax. Frantic consultations were held among the Great Powers and, at U Thant and Ralph Bunche's urging, the Security Council went into session. But all this activity was fruitless: it was evident that the Soviet Union would veto any outcome from the Council which was in any sense critical of Egypt. The United States urged restraint on the parties, but war fever was carrying the situation out of the control of diplomacy. Bahrain was a microcosm of the urban Arab world with a young, educated population long bewitched by the clarion call of Nasser's pan-Arabism. Public excitement reached boiling point. The streets of the capital were a gabble of transistor radios tuned to Cairo. The conviction was absolute that this was it. Egypt and Syria, replete with modern weapons supplied by the friendly superpower, the Soviet Union, and backed by the non-aligned majority, were on the point of redeeming past humiliations and ridding Palestine for ever of the Zionist interlopers. The rhetorical salvos from Cairo, including Nasser's own speeches, left no room for equivocation on this point.

On 5 June, in a devastating pre-emptive strike, the Israeli Air Force destroyed the Egyptian Air Force on the ground. In the next six days Israeli forces conquered the Gaza Strip, swept through the Sinai Peninsula up to the Suez Canal, occupied the West Bank of the Jordan including East Jerusalem and, after hard fighting, forced the Syrians off the Golan Heights. Calls for a cease-fire from the Security Council were ignored until all Israeli objectives had been secured. For all the incandescent rhetoric and the massive acquisitions of Soviet military equipment, the rout of Arab arms was complete and even the credulous Arab public set little store by the propaganda line that British and American aircraft had flown with the Israelis in the first strike – the Big Lie.

CHAPTER TWO

Palestine Redivivus

The Explosion, as the Egyptian writer Mohammed Heikal later described the June War of 1967, created a landscape almost as novel as that of 1949. In my distant Arab outpost of Bahrain, noisy elation gave way to silent despair. The crowds ceased their bellowing outside the Agency compound and, miraculously, the anti-British and anti-regime gush of propaganda from Cairo dried up. The revolutionary Arabs needed friendship and stability in the Arabian peninsula to give them access to the oil money required to rebuild their shattered armies. Overnight the trumpet of Nasserism was stilled, although the President retained his personal popularity until his death three years later. Arab solidarity replaced Arab unity as the slogan of the future. The hectic gust of pan-Arabism had passed, not to return.

The change in the treatment of the Palestine problem in the UN and in the region was equally dramatic. For the first time since 1947 the United Nations addressed the disease rather than confining itself to the symptoms. After a long summer of wrangling in the General Assembly and the Security Council, the now famous Resolution 242 was adopted by the Council on 22 November, the object being to secure a permanent settlement of the Arab/Israeli dispute. This resolution in effect called for a restoration of the status quo before the June War on the basis of a full peace settlement instead of the temporary Armistice Agreements. However, as is the case with so many UN resolutions, it would not have secured the necessary support, let alone unanimity, had it not been for deliberate imprecisions in the wording which enabled states to interpret it in different ways. Specifically:

(1) Israel was to withdraw from 'territories' (not 'the' territories, although the French text carried the definite article) occupied in the recent conflict. The Arabs and their supporters interpreted this as total withdrawal, the Israelis as a basis for negotiation, 'a piece of territory for a piece of peace', as Israeli diplomats used to say. The United States sided with Israel; the USSR and France with the

Arabs. Britain clarified her view in 1970 that withdrawal should be total subject to minor rectifications of the old Armistice Lines.

(2) The Arabs argued that the peaceful settlement provision should be negotiated only after Israeli withdrawal; the Israelis took the view that the whole resolution should be negotiated as an integrated package.

(3) The Palestinians were nowhere mentioned except in the context of a 'just settlement of the refugee problem'. This suited both sides at the time. The Arabs wished to continue to bottle up the genie of Palestinian nationalism, the Israelis had long insisted that the dispute was between Israel and neighbouring states ('Who are these Palestinians?', as a top Israeli minister asked a few years later). This omission proved to be a crucial factor in the future.

(4) The Arabs regarded the appointment of the Secretary-General's Special Representative 'to help achieve a settlement' as formal sanction of their refusal to negotiate directly with Israel. The Israelis were determined to press for direct, face-to-face talks with individual Arab states. This disagreement had been crystallized by the 'Three Noes' of the Khartoum Arab Summit in August – 'No peace, no recognition, no negotiations'. This reaction to humiliation was as crass a diplomatic mistake as was Nasser's military blunder in closing the Straits of Tiran. In the immediate aftermath of the victory, the Israeli government was probably ready, indeed was urged on by the veteran David Ben-Gurion, to withdraw from almost all the conquests in exchange for a full, directly negotiated peace. It was not to be.

Resolution 242 was unquestionably a milestone and it is still, at the time of writing, twenty-seven years later, the only internationally accepted basis for a settlement. At the time the negotiators were perhaps excessively proud that they had closed the chapter of the June War crisis and opened a fresh one which they believed would lead to an early settlement. Many politicians of differing nationalities scrambled to claim exclusive authorship of the text. Nearly three decades later they might be less eager to do so. The ambiguities in 242 enabled the Security Council to close the file on the immediate crisis and to move on to the next item on the agenda. But it is arguable that, by failing to face up to the question of withdrawal and to the need for direct negotiations, the resolution enabled the parties to simulate acquiescence without committing themselves to compromise. Thus the resolution has been an obstacle to genuine progress towards a peaceful settlement.

For the next three years (until early 1971) the Secretary-General's Special Representative, Ambassador Gunnar Jarring of Sweden, shuttled patiently between the parties. Lacking correspondingly vigorous diplomacy from the superpower patrons of the opposing sides, his mission was doomed to failure. In 1969 the Four Powers (US, USSR, Britain and France) held a series of meetings in New York. They, like Jarring, failed and it became clear that Washington and Moscow, so far from continuing the brief cooperation which culminated in Resolution 242, were in no mood to press their protégés to show flexibility. Instead they acted as respective lawyers, the US for Israel, the Soviet Union for Egypt which still led the Arab team.

Meanwhile, the Security Council was busy condemning Israeli activities in the newly Occupied Territories, particularly changes in the status of Jerusalem and Israeli retaliatory attacks on Jordan and Lebanon in response for guerrilla incursions. The heaviest of these was an all-out assault on Beirut airport in December 1968. The Syrian/Israeli front was quiet and neither Egypt nor Israel was disposed to bring to the Council the so-called War of Attrition, the sporadic exchanges of artillery, missile and air attacks across the Suez Canal which caused casualties among the UNTSO observers (who had been moved to the new cease-fire lines) and became so serious that, before a truce was mediated by the US and the UN Secretary-General in 1970, it began to pose a threat to world peace with fifteen to twenty thousand Soviet military advisers in Egypt and Soviet pilots flying combat missions against their Israeli counterparts.

In the Arab world, a fresh consensus was building around a shift of influence towards the traditional, oil-rich states led by Saudi Arabia and around support for a new phenomenon, the rebirth of autonomous Palestinian nationalism. For twenty years the Palestinian leadership, such as it was, had entrusted the destiny of their people to the Arab League, in effect to Egypt. The Palestinian Liberation Organization (PLO), created in 1964 by an Arab summit and led by the noisy buffoon, Ahmad Shukairy, was little more than an adjunct to the Egyptian propaganda machine.

All this changed in 1968 when the new PLO Chairman, Yasser Arafat, disillusioned by the impotence of the Arab League and the fiasco of the June War, decided that the Palestinians must shape their own destiny. It was his PLO which initiated the raids across the Jordan and the Lebanese border and which began the long saga of Arab 'terrorism' with such eye-catching events as the hi-jacking of international civil aircraft on scheduled flights. It was the PLO which challenged King Hussein's authority in Jordan and was bloodily driven out in 1970 (Black September) to establish a state within a state in South Lebanon, exposing that country to fierce Israeli attack and contributing to the civil war which reduced the Lebanon to anarchic chaos from 1975 to 1990. So far as Israel was concerned, autonomous Palestinian nationalism was perceived as a serious threat, the answer being a vigorous campaign of demonization of the PLO as undifferenti-ated terrorists.

Palestinian nationalism found a ready response in the United Na-tions, now dominated by a newly independent majority most of whom were members of the Non-Aligned Movement in which Egypt was an accepted leading player. This parliamentary situation was a far cry from the Western dominated founding membership in which only four African and eight Asian states were represented. That figure had risen to over sixty and is now over ninety. The notions that the Palestinians were a 'people' with a right to self-determination and that Israel was an imperialist implantation in the Arab world were *prima facie* accept-able to the majority. In December 1969, a General Assembly resolu-tion, while criticizing Israeli practices in the Occupied Territories, for the first time affirmed 'the inalienable rights of the people of Palestine', hitherto characterized merely as refugees or referred to as the Arab inhabitants of areas under military occupation. The resolution was adopted with forty-eight votes in favour, twenty-two against (the US, Israel and mainly small Latin American states) with forty-seven absten-tions (including the UK and most of the Western Europeans). By 1974 the Palestinian cause had advanced significantly in UN diplomacy and Yasser Arafat was permitted to address the General Assembly, symbolic gun in one hand, olive branch in the other. Israeli practices in the Occupied Territories were being regularly singled out for detailed criticism. A resolution reaffirming the right of the Palestinian people to self-determination, national independence and sovereignty, emphasizing the indispensability of the realization of these rights for a solution to the question of Palestine, and much more in the same vein, received eighty-nine votes in favour to seven against (including the US and Israel) with thirty abstentions (including the nine members of the European Community). Another resolution, also adopted in November 1974, granted UN observer status to the PLO with ninety-five favourable votes, seventeen against (including the US and the EC) with nineteen abstentions. A major diplomatic watershed had been crossed. In the years to come majority support for the cause of Palestinian self-determination and national sovereignty grew and the number of dissenters diminished. In 1980 the EC, in the Venice Declaration, crossed the Rubicon by recognizing not only the Palestinian right to self-determination but also the necessity of associating the PLO with negotiations.

This transformation of the voting pattern of the UN had a crucial impact, not only positively on the international validation of the Palestine cause, but negatively on Israel's perception of the UN as a mediating instrument, and on the attitude of the United States to the Organization beyond the limits of the Palestine problem. Israel, ironically in view of the origins of the question, came to regard the UN as comprising a built-in majority of hostile or at best less than friendly states, influenced by Arab oil power and Soviet blandishment, totally partial to Arab demands. After the failure of the Jarring Mission, the UN has thus been excluded up to the present day from all negotiating initiatives. It has lost the essential precondition of the mediator, acceptability to both parties. By the same token successive American administrations, even more so Congressional majorities, increasingly perceived themselves as the sole champions of Israel against the hostile hordes; and that, because of this and to a lesser extent other issues such as South Africa on which the US found itself on the receiving end of vituperative rhetoric and unacceptable General Assembly resolutions, the UN was ceasing to be a place in which to conduct serious business. The adoption by the General Assembly in 1975 of a resolution equating Zionism with racism (now repealed) caused the stock of the UN to plummet vertically. In the 1980s animus reached a pitch when there was a real possibility of the United States under the Reagan Administration withdrawing from the Organization. An interesting illustration of the change from the 'good old days' of the UN is the fact that, until 1970, the US had never once vetoed a resolution in the Security Council while the Soviet Union had by that time cast 103 vetoes (many on membership applications), France four, Britain three and (Nationalist) China one (on the membership application of Mongolia). Between 1970 and 1987 the US cast fifty-six vetoes (mainly on

Palestine and Southern Africa), the Soviet Union ten, Britain twenty-four, France twelve and (People's Republic of) China one (on the membership application of Bangladesh).

The second veto cast by the United States, in July 1972, was a contributory cause of the Yom Kippur or Ramadan War of October 1973 which, more than any event since the Cuban missile crisis of 1962, threatened a superpower confrontation which could have escalated into a Third World War. President Sadat of Egypt had decided that the key to a Middle East settlement lay with the United States. In July he expelled the fifteen to twenty thousand Soviet military advisers and, to test the impartiality of Washington, tabled a resolution in the Security Council in moderate language, supporting the mission of Ambassador Jarring, deploring (not the stronger 'condemning') Israel's continuing occupation of the territories seized in 1967 and expressing conviction that a just solution must be based on respect for the rights of 'all states in the area' (by implication including Israel) and the 'rights and legitimate aspirations of the Palestinians'. Thirteen of the fifteen Council members (including Britain) voted for the resolution; China inscrutably did not participate in the vote, while the US, under Israeli pressure, vetoed. This rebuff helped to convince President Sadat that only a military shock would galvanize the negotiating deadlock into movement as well as restoring Arab honour which had been devastated in June 1967.

Sadat had declared 1972 as the 'Year of Decision' and there was general mockery when it passed without incident: Israeli military superiority appeared to be effortless and total. Then, on 6 October 1973, Egyptian forces crossed the Suez Canal and Syria launched a simultaneous armoured assault on the Golan Heights. I was at the time the Under-Secretary responsible for the Middle East and the United Nations in the Foreign and Commonwealth Office and I can testify that the surprise was total and that subsequent claims of foreknowledge have benefited from the genius of hindsight.

The Security Council went into session but, for the first ten days or so, was unable to act. The Arab armies were making substantial progress and Egypt was not prepared to accept a call for a cease-fire. Any such proposition from any quarter would have failed to attract the necessary non-aligned votes, let alone running into the certainty of a Soviet veto. Massive American military aid was flown into the battlefield when there was little to stop the Egyptians advancing on the

Israeli heartland and, by the end of the second week, the tide had turned. The situation on the Syrian front was confused and Jordan had despatched a brigade to buttress the Syrian forces which were by then on the defensive. An Israeli unit had crossed the Suez Canal at the southern end and was bottling up an Egyptian force near the town of Suez. Both sides were ready to stop fighting and, on 22 October, the Security Council adopted resolution 338 calling for a cease-fire and negotiations to implement resolution 242.

High drama followed. The Israeli force took advantage of the cease-fire to tighten its blockade of the Egyptian Third Army. It then emerged that the Soviet Union had alerted airborne forces to fly into the battle zone. The US retaliated by alerting their own airborne forces in Europe. A confrontation between the superpowers became a real possibility. The Security Council on 25 October strengthened its demand for a cease-fire and decided to establish an Emergency Force (UNEF II) to separate the combatants and monitor the cease-fire. The crisis passed. The UN had again done what it had done at the height of the Suez crisis sixteen years previously, namely provided a ladder down which the two superpowers were only too ready to climb when they appreciated the likely consequences of their national policies.

The October War achieved Sadat's objective. Although it ended in an unfavourable draw for the Arabs, the Israelis had received a powerful blow to their belief in their invincibility, as well as substantial casualties. The United States too had been apprized in no uncertain way of the dangers inherent in the Arab/Israeli dispute and of the consequent need for vigorous negotiation to defuse it. The Arabs had recovered their military honour and were thus readier to adopt less intransigent policies.

From the end of 1973 until the Spring of 1978 the Security Council did little except urge the parties to implement resolutions 242 and 338 and renew the mandates of the peacekeeping forces. A conference under UN auspices (boycotted by Syria) convened symbolically on 18 December in Geneva with both superpowers and the parties involved present. It was not to reconvene. Secretary Kissinger had moved to centre stage. His policy was the step by step approach beginning with disengagement agreements between Egypt and Israel and Syria and Israel with no attempt to secure a comprehensive settlement including the Palestine sector. Avoidance of further dangerous conflict rather than solving the underlying problem was his goal. His tactics were to eliminate the Soviet Union and the troublesome UN from the negotiation and to deal bilaterally with the parties. In a paroxysm of shuttle diplomacy he achieved disengagement on both fronts. It was monitored by UNEF II in the case of Egypt/Israel and, from May 1974, by the UN Disengagement and Observer Force (UNDOF) – still in place on the Syrian Golan Heights.

It had been fairly clear since 1971 that President Sadat hankered after extracting Egypt from the Palestine Arab/Israeli imbroglio which had caused his country such heavy losses and economic dislocation. The rapprochement with Washington, enhanced by the personal intimacy which the shuttle diplomacy created between Sadat and Kissinger, was the first step in an evolution which came to fruition with Sadat's flight to Jerusalem in 1977 and the mediation of the Camp David Agreements by President Carter, culminating in the Egypt/Israel Peace Treaty of 1979 under which Egypt recovered the territory occupied by Israel in 1967.

The kaleidoscope had whirled again. The shock of the 1973 war convinced Washington that Israel must be provided with a qualitative military edge over all Arab states in combination – no more last-minute battlefield rescues. The political nexus tightened until it became difficult for an outsider to judge whether American policy was formulated in Washington or Tel Aviv, particularly in regard to the refusal to accept the principle of Palestinian self-determination and the demonization of the PLO. In a nutshell the Palestine question had become a function of American domestic politics to a greater extent than at any previous time. For example, the American Ambassador to the UN, Andy Young, was sacked in 1979 for having an unauthorized meeting with the PLO representative in New York.

Egypt paid the price of peace with Israel by losing, for the first time in modern history, the leadership of the Arab world. Cairo's ostracism from Arab counsels was almost complete and lasted for a decade: the Arab League headquarters was moved to Tunis. Competition for Arab leadership developed between Iraq and Syria, with Saudi finance an important ingredient. The PLO dominated the Arab group agenda in New York, deciding when to call Security Council meetings and drafting resolutions in all UN organs.

In Israel the war shook public confidence in the Labour Party which had ruled since independence: in 1977 the Likud Party led by

Menachem Begin came to power. Begin's policy was to eliminate Egypt from the military equation (Sadat's initiative was launched on the heels of the Israeli elections) by making peace, even though this entailed giving up Sinai, to accelerate the pace of settlement in the Occupied Territories so that the notion of withdrawing from an inch of Eretz Israel would become irrelevant, and to deal militarily with the PLO state within a state in South Lebanon, the whole of that country having been in the grip of civil war since 1975. He regarded the UN with even more contempt and hostility than had his predecessor.

However, the next major UN engagement was to be in Prime Minister Begin's target area, South Lebanon. In March 1978, in retaliation for a rash of damaging cross-border PLO raids, the Israeli Defence Forces (IDF) carried out a major ground invasion of South Lebanon, penetrating several miles into the country. President Carter, anxious that nothing should derail the Camp David negotiations, immediately convened the Security Council, which called for Israeli withdrawal and established an Interim Force (UNIFIL) – still in place – to confirm this withdrawal, restore peace and assist the Lebanese government to resume effective authority in the area. The Israelis ceased fire on the day that Mr Begin's talks in Washington were due to begin, but they did not withdraw fully. Instead they left a strip, now known as the 'security zone', in the hands of a renegade Lebanese officer, Major Saad Haddad. These 'de facto forces' were effectively under Israeli control. Equally, the Lebanese government, because of the civil war, was in no position to resume control in the South. Hence UNIFIL, which built up to over seven thousand personnel, found itself sandwiched between roughly eleven thousand PLO fighters in the north and Major Haddad's militia and the Israelis in the south. With no mandate to enforce their task, the force was trapped in an unstable and fragile situation. For external reasons, namely the Camp David talks, UNIFIL's mandate had been too hastily formulated to be realistic.

Prospects for peace in the Lebanon and for a comprehensive settlement of the Palestine problem worsened with the change of Administration in Washington in 1981. President Carter, notwithstanding powerful domestic and Israeli pressures, had maintained a measure of impartiality. Between 1977 and 1981 the US vetoed only one Middle East resolution, a draft put to the vote in 1980 which called for total Israeli withdrawal and affirmed the Palestinian right to

self-determination and an 'independent state in Palestine'. Britain and
France abstained. In the same period the US supported or abstained
on eight resolutions critical of Israeli actions in the Occupied Territories and calling on Israel to desist. The same was the case with five
resolutions on the Lebanon.

The Reagan Administration adopted an unambiguously pro-Israeli
stance, crudely manifested by the US Delegation in New York. In the
first four-year term, the threat or actuality (three times realized) of
American vetoes precluded any Security Council action on Palestine.
The US supported the Security Council demand that Israel rescind its
decision, taken in December 1981, to impose its laws, jurisdiction and
administration on (i.e. effectively to annex) the Syrian Golan Heights
but vetoed a further draft (Britain and France abstaining) which would
have envisaged mandatory measures if Israel failed to comply.

Reaganite exasperation with the United Nations was not allayed by
the resulting invocation by the Security Council of the Uniting for
Peace procedure (invented by the US over Korea, used by the US
over Suez and by the West over the Soviet invasion of Afghanistan) to
transfer the debate on the Occupied Territories (specifically in this
instance the Golan 'annexation') to the General Assembly on the
grounds that the Security Council had been blocked by the United
States. There followed an emotional Emergency Session, with the
Assembly majority at its most raucous and vitriolically anti-American
and anti-Zionist, culminating in an extreme anti-Israeli and pro-Pales-
tinian resolution which was adopted by a majority of eighty-six to
twenty-one (including the European Community nine) with thirty-
four abstentions (mainly from Latin America and the Caribbean). This
episode was scarcely calculated to encourage Israel and the US to
involve the UN in any way in a negotiating role!

The Likud government in Israel, emboldened by unwavering
American support and the elimination of Egypt from the military
equation, was adopting more forward policies. The Golan episode was
one example. In June 1981, Israeli aircraft attacked and destroyed
Iraqi nuclear installations outside Baghdad. This act attracted the
unanimous (including the US) condemnation of the Security Council,
although I was not aware of any delegation which believed Iraqi
protests of injured innocence. The general view was that the act,
however justifiable against a regime such as Saddam Hussein's, was a
breach of the Charter and that paper condemnation would provide the

Iraqis with a face-saving victory which would avert a foolish military reaction dictated by wounded pride.

From the beginning of 1982 it was clear to us in the corridors of the UN that the Israelis were planning to destroy the PLO power in the Lebanon, even though a UN-mediated cease-fire had been holding for several months. It was not a question of whether but when. It was equally clear that no preventive action could be taken by the Security Council because of United States support for Israel. Washington might not give the green light to Prime Minister Begin to invade the Lebanon but it would not associate itself with a red light flashed from New York. At most, a bilateral amber light might be turned on.

On 5 June (the same day of the same month as the Israeli pre-emptive strike in 1967), on the pretext of a response to the attempted assassination of the Israeli Ambassador in London by an Arab from the Abu Nidal terrorist group, the IDF broke the by now year-long cease-fire and launched a massive invasion of South Lebanon, swept past UNIFIL, overwhelmed the PLO front line and within days was besieging Beirut. Operation 'Peace for Galilee' was under way.

The Security Council, which had been preoccupied with the Falklands crisis since the end of March, reacted quickly but ineffectively. Bad-tempered, sometimes all-night meetings, spawned a crop of resolutions, American vetoes and discarded propositions which would have been vetoed if put to the vote. It was, it seemed, acceptable to 'censure' Israel's action, but not to 'condemn' it. A demand for Israeli withdrawal could pass but not for 'immediate' withdrawal. Resolutions relating to humanitarian concerns – by the time Israel eventually withdrew to the Southern 'security zone' about a year later between ten and twenty thousand civilians had been killed – were in order. To redeploy UNIFIL to separate the combatants – Israel, the PLO fighters and elements of the Syrian 'Arab Defence Force' – on the outskirts of Beirut was unacceptable to Israel, a refusal which was to have serious consequences for the United States.

The attitude of the Arab Group in New York was intriguing. For over a decade the PLO had insensitively bossed about the Arab League and dictated the diplomatic programme. My distinguished Arab colleagues took little trouble to conceal their glee at the sight of the PLO receiving its comeuppance. Only my admirable Lebanese colleague worked himself to distraction to try to save something from the wreck of his country and the ruin of the Arab consensus.

By August all that the Security Council had achieved on the ground was authority to redeploy a limited number of UNTSO observers to the Beirut area where they formed the Observer Beirut Group (OBG). UNIFIL remained in its original zone, although it had been bypassed by the fighting. It is still in place on the fringes of the Israeli security zone, providing some protection for the local villagers from the clashes which regularly take place between Israeli forces and the Israeli sponsored so-called South Lebanon Army on the one hand and the Shi'a Moslem Hizbollah militia on the other. Some people believe that UNIFIL has been too long humiliated and should be withdrawn. They should ask the local inhabitants whether they would feel safer without the UN presence.

In September 1982, the Lebanon plunged into full horror. Throughout August the Israelis had been mercilessly bombing and shelling West Beirut, causing major civilian casualties, in order to avoid house-to-house fighting with the Palestinians. The bombardment was suspended only after maximal pressure from Washington. On 1 September President Reagan was able to announce that US diplomacy had negotiated the withdrawal of the PLO fighters from Beirut. Ambassador Philip Habib had indeed done a first class job with vital assistance from a group of Arab League states. The Israelis had accepted, outside the UN, the deployment of a Multinational Force (MNF), comprising units from the US, France and Italy, to guarantee the safety of the withdrawing PLO units and of their families who would be left behind. Around 10 September the MNF, task accomplished, re-embarked. On 14 September the newly elected President, the Maronite Christian Bashir Gemayel, a close ally of the Israelis, was assassinated. The following day Israeli troops occupied West Beirut to pre-empt revengeful anarchy. On 17 September, local Christian militiamen entered the now unguarded (but Israeli monitored) Palestinian refugee camps of Sabra and Chatila and gruesomely massacred hundreds of old people, women and children. The results of this atrocity were carried by television into the living rooms of the world, attracting unprecedented sympathy in the United States for the Palestinians and creating revulsion in Israeli public opinion. The MNF returned, to be augmented in February 1983 by a token British contingent. Its new task was to help restore the authority of the Lebanese government in and around Beirut.

By the end of 1983 the catastrophic consequences of the Israeli

Operation 'Peace for Galilee' were plain. The PLO presence in Lebanon had been dispersed and Israel's northern border towns were at least temporarily immune from attack. But the gratuitous nature of the invasion plus the continuing Israeli casualties as the IDF became embroiled in the civil war, as well as the perception that Israel had been at least partially responsible for the Sabra and Chatila massacres, divided the Israeli public as never before. In August 1983, Prime Minister Begin suddenly resigned and went into seclusion. The original Israeli plan of making peace with a Maronite-dominated Lebanon foundered after the assassination of Bashir Gemayel. Secretary of State George Shultz negotiated a fresh, detailed agreement with Gemayel's successor in May 1983 but it was stillborn because of Syrian opposition. By the end of the year the Israelis had withdrawn again to the south, having suffered six hundred fatal casualties and alienated virtually all sections of Lebanese society.

For the United States, the outcome was almost as bad. They had failed to prevent the Israelis from invading, although a firm line would have done so. They had blocked effective action in the Security Council. Their diplomacy had defused the worst of the crisis in the late summer of 1982, but they had re-embarked the first wave of the MNF prematurely, thus incurring some responsibility of omission for the massacres. By mid-1983, the MNF was seen by the Druze and Shi'a militias as a partisan force in the civil war in which, to them, the Christian-dominated government and its army were just another faction. The MNF had lost its impartiality. In April, a truck bomb against the US Embassy killed sixty-nine people. Two more in October killed 241 US Marines and fifty-nine French soldiers. The Americans started to shell Druze villages in the Chouf mountains where the Druze and the Maronites were at each others' throats. The Second World War battleship New Jersey was de-mothballed, brought to the Mediterranean and started firing one-ton shells into the Chouf. 'Like the French battleship firing into the continent of Africa in Conrad's *Heart of Darkness*', as an American naval officer was reported as saying. In early 1984 the MNF withdrew in disarray, mission unaccomplished. There is little doubt that this chastening experience has influenced American recalcitrance to engage in military enforcement in today's civil wars in Europe and Africa.

The Lebanon (and the Palestinian refugees) suffered most, descending into chaos and mayhem with scarcely a vestige of government until the end of the decade. Only Syria was a gainer, increasing its political influence in Lebanon, gaining respect from the Israelis for its military performance in battles east of Beirut, and demonstrating to the United States that there could be no peace without Syrian approval.

Focus on the Lebanese disaster had distracted attention from the central issue of Arab/Israeli peace. By 1982 all interested parties had formulated policies and expressed them outside the UN. In May 1980 the European Community had issued the Venice Declaration which called for the right to existence and security of all states including Israel, an end to Israel's territorial occupation of 1967, Palestinian self-determination and association of the PLO with negotiations to secure a peaceful settlement. This policy received a grudging welcome from the Arabs and excited Israeli displeasure. On 1 September 1982, in the statement to which I have referred, President Reagan set out his views in a call for a fresh start. He called for negotiations based on the Camp David Agreements, full Arab recognition of Israel's right to exist behind secure and recognized borders, the recognition of Palestinian 'legitimate rights', a transitional period of autonomy as envisaged at Camp David, and a freeze on Israeli settlement building. The President opposed the creation of an independent Palestinian state, as well as permanent Israeli control over the West Bank and Gaza. 'Self-government by the Palestinians of the West Bank and Gaza in association with Jordan offers the best chance for a durable, just and lasting peace.' The conflict should be solved through negotiations involving an exchange of territory for peace. UN Resolution 242 was the foundation stone of America's Middle East peace effort. The withdrawal provision applied to all fronts, including the West Bank and Gaza.

This declaration of policy, although it fell short of acceptance of Palestinian self-determination and ignored the existence of the PLO, was not far removed from the thinking behind the Venice Declaration. But it failed to attract the Arabs to whom Camp David was heresy and it was dismissed angrily by the Israeli government. It sank without trace in the Lebanese welter but, to this day, with the exception of the dramatic introduction of the PLO into the act on the White House lawn on 13 September 1993, it has constituted the basis of American policy.

By the time that President Reagan made his statement, the general attitude of the Likud government was clear. The PLO was an undifferentiated terrorist organization. The Palestinians were the 'Arab inhabitants of Judaea, Samaria and the Gaza District', or refugees. The withdrawal provision in Resolution 242 had been fulfilled by the withdrawal from Sinai, completed in early 1982. Not an inch of 'Eretz Israel' would be surrendered and a vigorous programme of Israeli settlement had been initiated to render such a proposition unthinkable. No outside government, even the US, would change this. The Arabs in Judaea, Samaria and the Gaza District could have local autonomy over their lives, not over land or natural resources. The problem was between Israel and its neighbours to whom Israel was ready to offer 'peace for peace'. The refugees must be resettled in the Arab world which was big enough and rich enough to accommodate them. If the Arabs in Eretz Israel were discontented, the 'Palestine Arab Kingdom of Jordan', as the Israeli representative in the UN used to refer to the Hashemite Kingdom, was available to them.

Although the Arab League position, under Saudi and Jordanian influence, was slowly softening, Syria was resolved to achieve 'strategic parity' with Israel and all outside efforts failed to persuade the PLO leadership to recognize Israel on condition that Israel reciprocated. The Iran/Iraq war ground on with appalling casualties on both sides. Islamic revivalism, fanned by Iran, flourished in the atmosphere of despair and frustration and made compromise on Palestine more difficult. In the Lebanon, Iranian-backed Shi'a militias started a long night of Western hostage taking. American peace initiatives on Palestine plus the tireless efforts of King Hussein of Jordan bounced off the various rocks. The mid-1980s were a bad time.

In 1987 the first hints appeared of the international sea-change which was to lead the Middle East to the situation of today. The superpowers jointly drafted the resolution (see Chapter 3) which was to help bring the Iran/Iraq war to a close. This unprecedented development heralded the end of the Cold War and the parties to the Palestine problem began to realize that the days of unambiguous superpower championship of opposing sides were ending. President Gorbachev sent such a message to liberation movements world-wide, just as, in September 1987, he announced a fresh policy of cooperation with the United Nations.

In December, frustration exploded in the Gaza Strip. The spontaneous Palestinian uprising, the *intifada*, boiled up throughout the Occupied Territories with stone-throwings, mass demonstrations and other forms of unarmed resistance. The violent Israeli response fuelled the flames and, in the years to come, successive Israeli governments came to realize that there was no hope of a restoration of the relative quiescence of the previous twenty years. The *intifada* might change shape, from stone-throwing to gun battles, from concentration on Israeli targets to killing of 'collaborators'. But, as the Palestinian casualties mounted and world opinion reacted strongly against the sight of Israeli soldiers shooting and clubbing Palestinian children, a public mood grew in Israel that something radical must be done, other than force, to advance the cause of peace.

These factors continued their convergence in 1988. The Iran/Iraq cease-fire in July released Saddam Hussein to resume his pursuit of domination of the Arab world, in particular the oil-rich Arabian peninsula. Four weeks later King Hussein, effectively acknowledging the weight of the *intifada*, publicly severed Jordan's legal and administrative links with the West Bank, thus confronting the PLO, the 'sole legitimate and authentic representative' of the people of Palestine in Arab League eyes since 1974, with the responsibility for delivering the Palestinian goods. In November, the Palestine National Council, meeting in Algiers, called for an international peace conference 'based on Security Council Resolutions 242 and 338', and a confederation between the 'states of Palestine' and Jordan. The Council renounced terrorism. These concessions emerged from a dense fog of heroic and clouded rhetoric. In December, Arafat spoke at the annual General Assembly debate on Palestine (which had throughout been churning out resolutions routinely opposed by Israel, the US and a diminishing minority). The Assembly had moved the venue from New York to Geneva to accommodate Arafat, who had been refused a visa to enter the United States in the last days of the Reagan administration – indeed the refusal constituted Secretary Shultz's curtain call. Arafat, in his Assembly statement and in a subsequent clarifying television interview, unequivocally committed the PLO to recognition of Israel's right to exist, to the renunciation of terrorism, and to the peaceful negotiation of a two-state solution based on Resolution 242. This declaration, for which the European Community had pressed so hard for so long, was dismissed by Israel as a fraud and earned the PLO a low-level dialogue with Washington which was broken off in the summer of 1990 following an asinine and abortive raid by a PLO faction on an Israeli beach. But Arafat had crossed a Rubicon at which all Palestinian leaders had balked since 1917: change was bound to come, although, with the acceleration of the settlement programme on the West Bank, time was running out.

For nearly two years momentum failed to gather. Israel was only prepared to talk to Palestinians of Israeli choosing, certainly not the demon PLO. To Prime Minister Shamir the notion of an international conference, enthusiastically espoused by the General Assembly, was almost as bad. Under the auspices of the dreaded UN, Israel rightly viewed such a conference as an instrument of 100 per cent pressure on Israel, zero on the Arabs. Bilateral, direct negotiations with each of the front-line states separately was the preferred option. Israeli proposals in 1989 were so wide of the international consensus as to attract little interest. The settlement programme accelerated.

By 1990, even the Bush administration was becoming exasperated by Prime Minister Shamir's adamantine policy, slightly less so with the refusal of the Arab states to engage in face-to-face negotiations with Israel. No other Arab government had followed the Egyptian example. In May alarm bells began to sound from another quarter. Although the Soviet Union had to all intents and purposes relinquished its role as Arab champion and was demonstrably close to collapse, an Arab summit held in Baghdad chose to hurl defiance at the remaining superpower, the United States. Saddam Hussein dominated the conference and his bellicose braying included a threat to burn half of Israel with fire, or words to that effect, were there to be an attack on Iraq. He was making his leadership bid in a way which rocked the marriage of convenience between him and the Western powers which had so staunchly supported and armed him against the new enemy, Islamic Iran.

On 2 August, Iraq invaded Kuwait (see Chapter 4). The Security Council acted quickly and decisively, condemning the action and demanding its reversal, imposing mandatory sanctions and a blockade and, in November, authorizing the use of force ('all necessary means') by an American-led coalition to free Kuwait and restore the status quo ante. The Arab League split, with Egypt, Syria, Morocco, Saudi Arabia and the Gulf states joining the anti-Saddam coalition. In January 1991, air bombardment of Iraq began: by the beginning of March Operation Desert Storm had cleared Iraqi forces from Kuwait.

From the outset Saddam Hussein had tried to play the Palestine card, offering discussions on the future of Kuwait in the framework of an overall Middle East peace conference. He was ignored, but it was clear that the US would have to make an early move on Palestine in response for Arab support of and participation in the anti-Saddam coalition. It was also clear to Washington, which had with difficulty restrained Israel from retaliating directly against Iraq when Scud missiles were indiscriminately launched at Tel Aviv, that, the Soviet threat having vanished, Israel was not a 'strategic asset' in regional Middle Eastern conflicts. Between October 1990 and January 1991 the United States supported three resolutions and two presidential statements of the Security Council severely critical of Israeli actions in the Occupied Territories, in particular the killing of twenty Palestinians and wounding of 150 by Israeli police in a riot on the Dome of the Rock in Jerusalem, the deportation of Palestinians and 'scores of casualties' caused by the Israeli security forces in Gaza. The wording of all these documents would in normal times have attracted automatic American vetoes. A new writing was on the wall.

After the victory of Desert Storm, Secretary of State James Baker deployed all his energies to persuade the parties to enter negotiations. After strenuous shuttle diplomacy, the Arabs agreed to direct negotiations provided that the conference was at its inception international. The Israelis agreed, provided that the opening session led directly to bilateral negotiations with Syria, Lebanon and Jordan, with Palestinians from the Occupied Territories as members of the Jordanian delegation. No PLO members and no residents of East Jerusalem were to be included. The European Community and the UN Secretary-General were granted observer status only.

The Madrid Conference opened on 30 October 1991 and adjourned on 2 November after a round of speeches from the Co-Chairmen (President Bush and, very much the junior partner, Gorbachev) and the delegations from Jordan-Palestine, Syria, Lebanon, Egypt and Israel. Nearly all the speeches were predictable, except for that of the leader of the Palestinian delegation, Dr Haydar Abdel Shafi, who spoke movingly and with deep emotion about the opportunity for peace. The proceedings then broke up into bilateral negotiations in Washington, and multilateral talks on functional problems such as refugees, economic development and water supplies which have been held in different capitals. An enormous hurdle had been crossed: the Arab front-line states and the Palestinians had for the first time engaged in direct negotiations with Israel. It only remained for Israel to agree to negotiate with Palestinians freely chosen by Palestinians to square the full circle.

This consummation took nearly two years to materialize. Not surprisingly the bilateral discussions made little progress except on minor procedural matters while the Likud government remained in power in Israel. The positions of the parties on questions of substance, in particular Israeli withdrawal and the nature of autonomy in the Occupied Territories, were too far apart. In June 1992, the Labour party under Yitzhak Rabin defeated the Likud in a general election on a platform of an exchange of land for peace and a rapid move towards a settlement even in the thorny Palestinian dimension. However, for many months, progress was minimal and it seemed that Israel was hoping for breakthroughs with Syria and Jordan before tackling the problem of the Occupied Territories. It was equally clear that, although these two states (the Lebanon depended on Syria) could negotiate agreements in principle, there could be no implementation without parallel progress on Palestine. The situation on the ground deteriorated. The *intifada* ground on and Islamic activists began to benefit from the frustration of the people, especially in Gaza. Violence persisted in South Lebanon with the Hizbollah militia attacking Israeli and South Lebanon army forces. The settlement programme in the Occupied Territories continued at a reduced rate.

In December 1992, the Security Council returned to the charge. The Israeli government, in retaliation for the murder of a policeman, had summarily deported over four hundred so-called Islamic militants across the Lebanese border. The Lebanese refused to accept them and they were forced to camp in the freezing mountains in 'no-man's land'. Their attempts to return were greeted with gunfire. On 18 December the Security Council *unanimously* adopted a resolution *strongly condemning* the Israeli action and *demanding* that Israel ensure the safe and immediate return of the deportees. This forceful language, supported by the US, presaged a move to mandatory measures. In January/ February the UN Secretary-General sent two envoys to Israel to negotiate implementation of the resolution, and himself visited Jerusalem in February. The US was also active and, in the event, Israel agreed to shorten the two years of the expulsion to one and to allow the return of the deportees in batches (the last batch returned in December 1993).

Although the negotiations continued, by the summer of 1993 the outlook was bleak and it looked as though further delay would enable the Islamic militants and the radical opposition within the PLO to gain the upper hand and wreck the process. Then, to the amazement of the whole world, including the United States and the front-line Arab states, it emerged that Israel and the PLO had been holding secret talks under Norwegian auspices for some time, that they had agreed on mutual recognition and to implement as a first step a plan involving Israeli withdrawal from the Gaza Strip and Jericho. This genuinely historic accord was publicly endorsed by Prime Minister Rabin and Yasser Arafat on the White House lawn in the presence of President Clinton on 13 September. For the first time since the publication of the Balfour Declaration in 1917 the two sides had simultaneously recognized each other. As a friend of mine said the following day: 'We can die now. We have seen everything – a man landing on the moon and the Israeli Prime Minister and Arafat shaking hands on the White House lawn.' The stage was set as never before for progress to peace on all fronts, Palestine first.

Seven months later this pristine gleam of optimism was flickering low. Negotiations on Gaza/Jericho have been reminiscent of the fog-bound immobility of the Chancery Court in Dickens' novel *Bleak House*. Pettifogging detail about the extent of the Jericho enclave, border controls, security for the Israeli settlers, jurisdiction, water rights, joint policing and much more has been chewed over to the extent that the questions arise whether the Israelis are procrastinating out of fear of a leap into the unknown, however small, or whether they feel obliged to win every point in the match in order to demonstrate the absolute nature of their control. There has been no relaxation in the activities of the occupying army: it even seems as though patrolling has been deliberately more active and provocative. Nothing has improved for the Palestinians in the Occupied Territories. The Israeli preoccupation with security and with the fragility of the governmental coalition is understandable but time has been given for extremists on both sides to build up their strength and for support for the 'peace process' to decline correspondingly. In this atmosphere terrorism has flourished. Nearly two hundred people, three quarters of them Palestinians, have been killed in political violence, the most horrific episode being the Hebron massacre of 25 February when a Jewish terrorist from the settlement of Kiryat Arba shot down about thirty worshippers in the mosque of Abraham in Hebron. There were further casualties inflicted by the Israeli army in subsequent rioting and the Islamic movement Hamas has perpetrated two acts of terror – suicide bombers killing twelve Israelis in attacks on buses. The Hebron massacre brought the Security Council back into the act, the Palestinians having refused to continue negotiations until the international community had condemned the outrage and some protection from the settlers had been afforded the Palestinians. After *Bleak House*-style negotiations to keep the Americans on board, the Council (the US abstaining on two preambular paragraphs) adopted resolution 904 on 18 March without a vote, strongly condemning the massacre and calling for measures to guarantee the safety of Palestinian civilians, 'including a temporary international or foreign presence' (in practice 160 unarmed Scandinavian and Italian observers outside the UN framework). This microscopic concession represents the only Israeli acceptance of an outside presence in the Occupied Territories apart from the long-established UN agencies. In the event this resolution was just enough to enable the Palestinians to return to the table.

An impatient reader who has glanced through the rest of this book, may have wondered whether the Palestine/Arab-Israel chapters would ever, like Swinburne's weariest river, 'wind somewhere safe to sea'. Length is unavoidable. The Palestine problem spans almost the full lifetime of the UN; it has been the cause of more Security Council resolutions, more vetoed drafts, and more resolutions in the Assembly and other UN organs than any other item on the agenda. A Martian visitor at any time since 1967 could have been forgiven for assuming that the UN existed almost entirely to wrestle with the Arab/Israeli dispute, with occasional incursions into Central and Southern African affairs. The conflict permeated the Middle East and much of the world beyond, and the discourse in the UN could not be explained without amplification relating to developments in the world outside. Moreover Palestine has evoked just about every manifestation of the United Nations, both positive and negative – as a negotiating body, as an instrument of persuasion, as a forum for the mobilization of support or rejection, as a fountain of rhetoric, as a peacekeeper, as a peacemaker, as everything except the function for which it was primarily created, namely as an enforcer.

There was perhaps never a chance that the Security Council, still less the General Assembly, would command the confidence of both sides as an impartial mediator. The UN is a place of votes and, as in all parliamentary institutions, votes are cast for a multitude of reasons, some less edifying than others. Looking back from the vantage point of the 1990s, it is astonishing that a world organization should have decreed – albeit by a slender majority achieved by Homeric lobbying – the partition of a territory, a solution which was implacably opposed by two thirds of the population. To the Arabs at the time, this was evidence that there was still life in the old imperial notion, so powerfully projected into sub-Saharan Africa, that the human value and rights of 'natives' were of little account compared to those of Europeans. Twenty years later, when decolonization and Arab oil power had reversed the parliamentary pendulum, it seemed outrageous to the Israelis that the majority in the UN, while adopting without equivocation Arab views on Israeli withdrawal and the establishment of an independent Palestinian state and many other propositions unwelcome to Israel, should have given no weight to the reasonable Israeli desire for face-to-face negotiation with their adversaries, let alone exerted pressure in speeches and resolutions for Arab recognition of Israel's existence, or condemned acts of Arab international terrorism—the aircraft hi-jackings of the 1970s, the massacre at the Munich Olympics in 1972 (an oblique reference to which in a Security Council resolution was vetoed by the Soviet Union) and the hi-jacking of and murder on the liner *Achille Lauro* in 1985 being only a few examples. All that the minority could do, whether the Arabs in the early years or the United States and Israel in the later decades, was to respond in kind to the volcanic rhetoric of their critics.

But it is a mistake to regard the paper resolutions and the rhetorical flood as meaningless, the empty outpourings of a 'talking shop'. Prime Minister Shamir, in his speech at Madrid in 1991, stated that the UN did not create Israel. Maybe, but it was the vote of the General Assembly which gave international legitimacy to partition and to the admission of the new state to membership. The clamour of the General Assembly since 1967 has inculcated certain principles in the international Middle East agenda which might otherwise have been blurred or diluted or lost through default, for example that the Palestinians are a people with a right to self-determination, that the territories conquered in 1967 are 'Occupied Territories' in the technical sense of the word, that the Fourth Geneva Convention, which sets rules for the conduct of a military occupation, applies to them (hence that any changes to the status quo ante, be it the construction of settlements, deportation of citizens, alleged annexation of Jerusalem, effective annexation of the Golan Heights, are illegal), and that the withdrawal provisions of Resolution 242 apply to all sectors and much more. Even the US and Israel have now come close to accepting this corpus of beliefs which could not have been assembled and emphasized so effectively without the incessant drumbeat of the Assembly. Equally, as I mentioned earlier, there have been times when rhetoric and unimplemented resolutions have acted as a safety valve, an alternative to dangerous military action. To paraphrase Winston Churchill 'Roar, roar is preferable to war war'.

The Security Council has functioned as a narrower but more intensified focal point for many of the above purposes. It has also, in Resolution 242, formulated the only generally accepted framework for a peaceful solution. Operationally it has deployed peacekeeping forces (UNTSO, UNEF II, UNDOF, UNIFIL) which have provided breathing spaces for peaceful negotiations as well as defusing dangerous crises, although the General Assembly has the credit for the first major endeavour in this field, UNEF I. The Council has also served as a barometer or testing ground for the policies of major powers, particularly the United States. Since the 1970s the Arabs and non-aligned states have played a game of grandmother's footsteps, drafting resolutions in progressively more demanding language to test whether policies on, for example, total withdrawal, Palestinian self-determination, condemnation of Israeli actions, even mandatory sanctions, etc. have evolved. This activity has precipitated vetoes and has complicated the work of the Council but it has from time to time sent a clear signal to one side or the other – no, that is a phrase too far to the Arabs, or, as with the deportation by the Israelis of the four hundred Islamists in 1992, that is a breach of the Fourth Geneva Convention too far: watch it.

To someone not conversant with the inwardness behind the apparent absurdities of international diplomacy, it may seem weird that, in spite of five major wars, innumerable guerrilla encounters, and a blizzard of international terrorism, the Security Council has only once, and then briefly and temporarily in 1948, 'determined' that the Palestine problem constitutes a threat to peace. This omission is another instance in which Palestine has demonstrated the political reality behind the UN Charter. The Council can move to mandatory measures, i.e. economic sanctions or military enforcement (as opposed to 'non-threatening' peacekeeping), under Chapter VII of the Charter only after such a 'determination' has been made, as was the case in the Korean War in 1950 and the Iraqi invasion of Kuwait in 1990. But such a decision can only be taken, like all Security Council resolutions on matters of substance rather than procedure, if the necessary majority votes are available with no veto from any one or more of the five Permanent Members. At the beginning, in 1947, Britain was so deeply engaged in the region militarily and diplomatically that it would not have contemplated enforcement action against the Arab armies which entered Palestine in May 1948. Only if Israel had been in danger of total defeat would the Permanent Members have authorized mandatory action to save the situation. The mandatory resolution demanding a cease-fire was not followed by any measures when fighting resumed. From the mid-1950s the Soviet Union used its veto to shield the 'progressive' Arab states and the PLO from censure on seven occasions while, since the early 1970s when the necessary majority could on many occasions have been mobilized to impose sanctions on Israel for failure to withdraw and for breaches of the Fourth Geneva Convention, the US has cast over twenty vetoes, many to deflect even relatively mild criticism of Israel. Palestine has, in a nutshell, provided, for better or for worse, a prime example of how Great Power championship of opposing sides in 'regional' disputes has inhibited UN action and of how the veto power has been used, not as originally intended to prevent Permanent Members from ganging up on each other, but as a protective device for the interests of local so-called 'client states'.

All in all, the only organ of the United Nations which emerges with considerable credit and little blame from nearly half a century of the Palestine problem is the Secretariat. It was Dr Ralph Bunche's skilful diplomacy as Acting Mediator after the murder of Count Bernadotte which brought about the Armistice Agreements, in particular between Egypt and Israel, in 1949. It has been UNRWA (financed by the voluntary contributions of the member states, principally the US and Britain) which has attended to the health, education and welfare of hundreds of thousands, by now millions, of Palestinian refugees. Without the energies and improvisatory skills of the remarkable team of Hammarskjold, Bunche and Urquhart, the deployment of UNEF I could have proved impracticable at the end of the Suez crisis. Urquhart must take the principal credit (he succeeded Bunche as the doyen of UN peacekeeping after the former's death in 1971) for the almost instantaneous mobilization and deployment of UNEF II in an hour of world crisis. He too negotiated the year-long PLO cease-fire in Lebanon in 1981 which was broken by the Israeli invasion in June 1982. On the political front, the failure of Ambassador Jarring's mission to help with the implementation of Resolution 242 lay not with Jarring, but with the parties and their Great Power backers.

This brief catalogue demonstrates that, for all the bias of the members, the horse-trading, log-rolling, domestic and bilateral pressures which contributed to the majority conjunctures and the rejection of the main organs of the UN as valid instruments of mediation, the Secretariat retained the trust and confidence of both sides from the beginning, when Ralph Bunche drafted both the majority and the minority reports of UNSCOP to the present day. The same cannot be said of the membership, individually or in groups.

CHAPTER THREE

The Iran-Iraq War: 1980–88

If the General Assembly's finest hour was the creation of UNEF I in 1956, thus forging an escape hatch for Britain and France to retreat from their aberrant Suez adventure, the same cannot be said of the Security Council, indeed of the UN as a whole, for its handling of the longest and bloodiest inter-state war since 1945. Given that the Iran-Iraq war was precisely the kind of conflict which the United Nations was created to deter or, failing that, to bring to a conclusion, and that the deliberations of the Security Council were not vitiated by superpower rivalry, the Council's performance was, not to mince words, contemptible.

The border between Iran and modern Iraq was for centuries an area of hostility and intermittent warfare, the frontier between expansionist Sunni Islam under the Ottoman Empire and the Shi'a Islam of Iran. In the post-First World War period this rivalry persisted and sporadically exploded into local exchanges of blows. The Shatt el-Arab waterway was a permanent focus of tension while, further north, the two states nearly plunged into open war with each other in the early 1970s as Iran supported a Kurdish rebellion against Baathist Baghdad. The combined *Realpolitik* of the Shah and Saddam Hussein contrived in 1975 an Agreement which settled outstanding problems between the two governments at the expense of the Iraqi Kurds who, not for the first or last time, were exposed unprotected to the ferocities of their own government.

The Iranian revolution of 1978–79 boosted Islamic revivalism throughout the region and disturbed the status quo from Turkey to the Persian Gulf. It was no surprise that the historical animus between Iran and Iraq should have revived. Over half the population of Iraq are Shi'a Moslems and the holiest Shi'a cities of Najaf and Kerbela are located in southern Iraq. The Shi'a community had already suffered from Baathist oppression and Ayatollah Khomeini, not a man to forgive an injury, was implacably hostile to Saddam Hussein both because he regarded him as the leader of an atheist regime and because, at the Shah's request, he had forced Khomeini to abandon his haven in Najaf where he was directing his campaign of subversion of the Iranian regime in 1978.

Animated by the ardour generated by the successful revolution which had, through unarmed action, brought down a powerful, militarily based regime supported by both superpowers, the Tehran mullahs vigorously set about exporting their ideas to their Arab neighbours, focusing in particular on the Shi'a Moslem majority in Iraq. A campaign of subversion was openly launched and the Baghdad government became anxious. In 1980 tension between the two countries mounted. By the summer it became clear to anyone who could read a newspaper that Iraq was planning a punitive attack on Iran, the objective being to 'teach Khomeini a lesson' with the possible additional bonus of toppling the Tehran troublemakers who were confronting more than one civil rebellion simultaneously with armed forces weakened by post-revolutionary anarchy. Baghdad may even have hoped that the ethnic Arab majority in the south-west Iranian oil province of Khuzestan (Arabistan to the Arab world) might be disposed to secede and join its brothers to the West.

This drift towards war did not escape the attention of those of us who were serving in our national delegations to the Security Council, nor of our governments. But no one lifted a finger to mobilize the Council to take preventive action with either of the parties, although it was plain that neither was planning to seek conciliation through the organizations of which they were both members, such as the Non-Aligned Movement (NAM) or the Islamic Conference (OIC), even in OPEC, still less through recourse to the United Nations. No government was disposed to be seen to be pointing a finger at Iraq, an important oil producer and dispenser of lucrative contracts, as a potential aggressor; Iran's militant foreign policies had antagonized Arab governments and, most important, Tehran's first major act of international brigandage – the holding hostage of the staff of the American Embassy in Tehran – had consigned the regime to the nethermost regions of the international doghouse, where there is no sympathy. Even the most anti-American governments were appalled by this outrage.

In September 1980 there were minor frontier scuffles. On 22 September, Saddam Hussein abrogated the 1975 Agreement and Iraqi armoured units crossed into south west Iran in the area of

Khorramshahr. The war had begun. Amazingly the Security Council did not meet for some days. New York was swarming with Foreign Ministers gathered for the opening of the annual session of the General Assembly. But embarrassment at the failure of the Council even to sit round the table was overridden by the insistence of a senior Iraqi official, sent from Baghdad for the purpose, that nothing should be done to inhibit what Iraq believed would be a *blitzkrieg* of a few days' duration. The seven non-aligned members of the Council bowed to this pressure and refused to meet. There was no disposition on the part of the Permanent Members to persuade them otherwise. Saddam had calculated accurately: Iran was already paying for its gratuitous antagonization of the international community, particularly the United States.

After a few days of humiliating stasis and an appeal by the Secretary-General, Mexico and Norway, both non-permanent members, had the temerity to defy the Iraqis and the Council met at their formal request. An Iranian delegation headed by the Prime Minister arrived and blasted the membership for their inaction and pro-Iraqi bias. The first resolution of the Council failed to characterize the outbreak of a major war even as a 'threat to peace', was careful not to allocate blame, called upon both sides to stop using force and did not call for the withdrawal of Iraqi forces which were driving deep into Iranian territory. The Secretary-General's offer of 'good offices' was accepted by the Council. The effect of this feeble bleat on the Iranian delegation can be imagined. Prime Minister Rajaie (later murdered in a bomb attack) outlined Iranian war aims, namely the liberation of Iranian territory and the 'identification (presumably by the UN) and punishment of the aggressor'. We sat round the famous horseshoe table in uneasy silence.

In November the Secretary-General appointed the past and future Prime Minister of Sweden, Olaf Palme (murdered in 1984), as his Special Representative in order to promote peace negotiations. Palme shuttled between the parties for a year-and-a-half until his reappointment as Prime Minister diminished the time he could devote to his mission. He got nowhere, principally because he was diplomatically obliged to address the justificatory pretexts for the Iraqi invasion (to recover a tiny strip of disputed territory and to resume sovereignty over the Shatt el-Arab) and the symptoms of the war (merchant shipping trapped in Basra and the Shatt el-Arab) rather than the real cause, Iraqi aggression in retaliation for Iranian subversion.

Although some of the fiercest fighting was taking place, the Council was content to leave matters in the hands of the Secretary-General for nearly two years. In July 1982 the Council reconvened and adopted a resolution calling for a cease-fire and withdrawal to internationally recognized boundaries. This appeal was repeated in October with an additional paragraph welcoming the readiness of one of the parties (Iraq) to cooperate and calling on the other to do likewise. In February 1983 the President of the Security Council issued a statement rehearsing these two resolutions.

This little flurry of Council activity had the effect of further infuriating the Iranians. The tide of war had turned and the Iraqis were on the defensive, close to losing. Iranian forces were in occupation of Iraqi territory and almost all Iranian soil had been liberated. It did not escape Iranian attention that the Security Council was ready to call for Iranian withdrawal from Iraq but not for Iraqi withdrawal from Iran, and that there was still no question of addressing the origins of the war ('the identification of the aggressor').

The strategies of the contestants had evolved. Following the defeats of 1982, Iraqi policy was to extend the scope of and internationalize the war in the hope of pressurizing Iran to the negotiating table. Iranian policy was the opposite: to limit the fighting to ground warfare and to wear down Iraqi resistance by means of hideously expensive 'human wave' assaults of First World War intensity. The Iranian air force, equipped with American aircraft bought by the monarchy, was close to being grounded for lack of spare parts due to the American boycott. This had originated in the hostage crisis and, as the fortune of war turned in Iran's favour, had expanded into 'Operation Staunch', a worldwide campaign by Washington to deny arms supplies of all kinds to Iran, from all sources. The credibility of Operation Staunch was not enhanced by the revelation in 1986 of the fact that the US had for some time been supplying Iran with much needed anti-tank and anti-aircraft missiles in exchange for the release of American hostages held by pro-Iranian militias in Beirut – the Irangate affair. (Furthermore it also emerged that the Americans had known all along of Israeli military exports to Iran and had done nothing to stop them.) On the other side, Iraq had no difficulty in openly fulfilling its military requirements, mainly from the Soviet Union and France, not to mention other, less overt supplies from different Western countries.

In 1983, Iraq initiated the Tanker War by means of attacks carried out by their newly acquired French aircraft on Iranian oil terminals and tankers in the Persian Gulf. This had the dual purpose of damaging the Iranian economy and of internationalizing the war by provoking the Iranians into retaliation against neutral shipping on the Arab shore. There were no specifically Iraqi targets available for attack: Iraq's access to the Gulf had been blocked since the outset and the Iraqi navy was negligible. All Iraqi oil exports were directed across country to the Mediterranean and the Red Sea. As the war dragged on this Iraqi tactic became increasingly effective.

In 1983 the Security Council even-handedly called for a cessation of attacks on civilian targets (initiated by Iraq), and on both sides to stop hostilities in the Gulf. This resolution was buttressed in 1984 by a further resolution condemning attacks on shipping *en route* for Kuwait and Saudi Arabia, no specific mention being made of Iraqi attacks on the Iranian shore. The first of these resolutions, in its preamble, contained a tiny sop to Iranian sensitivities, insufficient to have any effect, by 'affirming the desirability of an effective examination of the causes of the war.'

Although the Iranians remained hostile to and suspicious of the Security Council because of its pro-Iraqi bias and, as Tehran saw it, subservience to the superpowers, they continued throughout to work with the Secretary-General and his representatives. In 1983 the charge of use of poison gas was first aired and, in 1984, the Secretary-General reported that chemical weapons had been used in aerial bombardment in the area of Iran inspected by his mission. This evoked a statement by the President of the Security Council (the weakest form of Council action) strongly condemning the use of chemical weapons and 'calling on states' (unnamed) to adhere to the 1925 Geneva Protocol banning their use.

In 1984 and 1985 the Secretary-General returned to the charge on two issues, the 'war of the cities' (indiscriminate air and missile bombardment carried out by both sides), and the use of chemical weapons. He was only intermittently successful on the former while, on the latter, Iran (but not Iraq) immediately responded positively to his appeal to both sides not to use poison gas.

By the beginning of 1986, the Security Council showed signs of greater concern. The overall policy of the Great Powers of on the one hand doing little to prevent the armed forces of two almost equally disagreeable regimes from slaughtering each other and, on the other hand, doing nothing to promote the regionally destabilizing catastrophe of an outright Iranian victory, showed no sign of advancing a cessation of hostilities. The war had spread to the Persian Gulf and 125 ships had been attacked. (By the end of the war about half the tonnage sunk during the Second World War had been sunk or written off in the Tanker War.) Iranian ground attacks were coming closer to breaking Iraqi resistance. Iraq had for four years been openly ready to make peace at any price except for the delivery of Saddam Hussein's head to Khomeini (the 'punishment of the aggressor'): only the Ayatollah's implacable will and the fighting spirit of the Iranian infantry were prolonging the war.

In February 1986 the Council unanimously adopted a comprehensive resolution which broke little new ground but brought together the contents of previous resolutions and Presidential statements, i.e. calls for a cease-fire, withdrawal (still Iranian) to international boundaries and an exchange of prisoners of war (mainly Iraqi). One paragraph deplored the 'initial acts which gave rise to the conflict' without specifying whose acts were meant. On 21 March 1986, following another investigative mission by the Secretary-General, a Presidential statement was issued which, for the first time, specifically blamed Iraq for the use of chemical weapons and 'strongly condemned' their continued use.

A year later the Iraqi tactic of internationalizing the conflict approached the peak of success. The Iranians were still battering away at the gates of Basra and, in January 1987, the Kuwaiti government invited the United States and the Soviet Union to re-flag and escort tankers plying to and from Kuwaiti oil terminals. In order not to be upstaged by the Soviet Union, the US responded with alacrity and there were soon about seventy warships of different nations, mainly American, deployed on the Arab side of the Gulf. Inevitably clashes occurred between these warships and the Iranian navy. The Iraqis intensified their air attacks on Iranian terminals and on the unprotected tankers on the Iranian side of the Gulf.

By this time President Gorbachev was in power, the Cold War was ending and Soviet policy in the United Nations was changing from cynical exploitation of non-aligned hostility towards the West to genuine cooperation in the Security Council. This sea change manifested itself for the first time in the context of the Iran-Iraq war. From January to July the Five Permanent Members, for the first time in

history, collectively drafted a mandatory resolution under Chapter VII
of the Charter, adopted as resolution 598 of 20 July 1987. This marked
the first serious attempt in seven years to bring the conflict to a close.
Ludicrously to an outsider aware that the war had cost hundreds of
thousands of lives and extensive damage to property and to Iran's
economic base, the Security Council 'determined' for the first time
that a breach of the peace existed between Iran and Iraq! Apart from
demanding a cease-fire, a prisoner exchange and withdrawal (still
Iranian), the resolution requested the Secretary-General to explore
with the parties the formation of an impartial body to inquire into
responsibility for the conflict and another to 'study the question of
reconstruction', a synonym for reparations for war damage.

Iraq, unsurprisingly, accepted the resolution without delay, provided
that Iran did the same. Iran equivocated and the war ground on with
greater intensity. The 'war of the cities' resumed in 1988 as did the
use of poison gas. In April 1988 Iraqi forces killed at least five
thousand civilians in the Iraqi Kurdish town of Halapche in a poison
gas attack. Even so, the subsequent Security Council resolution addressed its strictures impartially to both sides. Clashes proliferated
between Iranian naval units and American warships in the Gulf. The
Secretary-General's efforts to negotiate the implementation of resolution 598 foundered, and there were consultations but no action within
the Security Council about imposing a unilateral arms embargo on
Iran (although Operation Staunch had long reduced Iran to recourse
to the international black market).

Suddenly, in mid-July 1988, the end came. For the first time since
the revolution in 1979, the Iranians took the initiative in calling the
Security Council. The trigger was the accidental shooting down with
the loss of 290 passengers and crew of an Iranian civil airline by the
USS *Vincennes*. On 18 July the Iranian government formally accepted
Resolution 598. On 20 July the Council adopted a resolution expressing
regret and condolences over the *Vincennes* tragedy and stressing the
need for implementation of 598. A month later, after some Iraqi
probing attacks into Iranian territory and Iranian counter-punches
against Iraqi opposition elements who had been fighting on the Iraqi
side, plus victorious trumpet blasts from Saddam's propaganda
machine, a cease-fire came into effect. Both sides had lost a generation
of young men (the Iranian casualties were probably comparable to
British losses between 1914 and 1918) and were roughly back where

they started. Two years of fruitless negotiation by the Secretary-General followed to implement the terms of 598 beyond the cease-fire and the deployment of a small UN observer force (UNIIMOG) along the land frontier. A handful of prisoners were exchanged but no agreement was reached on the reopening of the Shatt el-Arab, or on the questions of responsibility for the war and reparations. Saddam Hussein, able at last to rest his exhausted armed forces, preoccupied himself with raucous declarations of victory; he saw no reason to make further concessions which would reveal that the Iraqi 'triumph' was in fact no more than a draw and that, without external financial help from the Arab world and military help from the Great Powers, it would have ended in total defeat.

Why did the Iranians suddenly decide to call it a day, to drink the draught of poison, as Ayatollah Khomeini graphically described acceptance of 598, with the aggressor unidentified and unpunished? There were many reasons. Civilian morale was suffering from Iraqi bombing of major cities which the depleted Iranian Air Force was unable to protect. Military morale was under strain from the First World War scale of the casualties and the poison gas attacks. Finance was running low because of reduction in oil exports resulting from Iraqi attacks on terminals and tankers. The foreign armada deployed on the Arab side in the Gulf gave Iran the impression, not entirely unjustified, that they were facing the whole world in arms. Iran was undefeated but exhausted, the prospect of victory no longer in sight. The country could do no more.

The Security Council had one more scene to play in this gruesome drama. As Saddam took his merciless revenge on the Iraqi Kurds for collaborating with Iran, the Council adopted another resolution (in August 1988, after the cease-fire) condemning the use of chemical weapons and calling on all states to exercise firmer controls over relevant exports. 'Appropriate and effective measures' were to 'be considered' should any future use of poison gas take place in violation of international law. However, yet again the text was carefully unbiased, although there was no doubt that Iraq had throughout been the offender, and was now engaged in gassing its own citizens on a grand scale. Parliamentary pressure developed in September in Europe and America to arraign Iraq. The Security Council did not reconvene.

The languid attitude of the Security Council towards the Iran-Iraq

war provided a vivid contrast to the frantic international activity which
had characterized the Arab-Israeli collisions over the previous three to
four decades. In many ways the omissions were more striking than the
commissions. The total failure to take preventive action in the summer
of 1980 – when a firm warning from all five Permanent Members
would almost certainly have stopped Saddam in his track – derived
from the zero rating of Iran on the international league table, scarcely
concealed indifference to the prospect of the mullahs receiving a kick
in the teeth, and assumption that Saddam was probably sabre-rattling.
The failure of the Great Powers to condemn the Iraqi invasion and
demand withdrawal and a cease-fire, both of which would probably
have been complied with by Saddam, still on the lower rungs of the
ladder of megalomania, sprang from the same cause. By the end of
September 1980, the world had been instructed once again in an
important gloss on the definition of aggression, a subject on which the
Legal Committee of the UN had laboured for many years, namely
that the international reaction to an armed attack by one state on
another is conditioned not so much by the gravity of the act itself but
by the international standing and alliances of the victim, and of the
aggressor, respectively. In 1950 South Korea was under American
protection: Kim Il Sung's invasion precipitated a trenchant response.
In 1975 East Timor, newly decolonized by Portugal and yet to secure
UN membership, had no such protector: Indonesia gobbled it up and
received light slaps on the wrist in response. In 1980 Iran was a
troublesome and friendless pariah: this made it open season for Saddam
Hussein.

The international configuration from start to finish was also relevant.
At the outset the superpowers were on the worst terms. In December
1979 the Soviet Union had invaded Afghanistan, thus terminating a
long period of detente. The strong Western reaction had irritated
Moscow and, in January 1980, the Soviet Union had vetoed a Security
Council resolution which would have imposed sanctions on Iran for
refusing to release the American hostages. Although the superpowers
did not differ fundamentally in their attitude towards the war –
neither was prepared to contemplate an Iranian victory – their mutual
antagonism precluded vigorous cooperative action.

The Third World majority found themselves in an embarrassing
quandary which led them to adopt an ostrich-like posture under the
searchlight of the UN. The NAM did not welcome the thought of

public scrutiny of an all-out war between two leading members which they were incapable of influencing; nor did the Organization of the Islamic Conference for the same reason. OPEC too tried to insulate its deliberations on oil prices and quotas from the politics of the war. Astonishingly Iran and Iraq maintained diplomatic missions in their respective capitals until 1987. The Arab world split, with Syria and, intermittently, Libya backing Iran (for anti-Iraqi reasons in the case of Syria; Qaddafi-ite eccentricity in Libya's case), while the remainder swallowed the successive Baghdad myths, first that the war was a repeat of the conquest of the Persian infidels by Arab armies in the seventh century AD ('Saddam's Qadisiyyah') and, after Iraq was forced onto the defensive, that Saddam was the valiant defender of the Eastern gate of the Arab world against the expansionist, imperial Persian hordes. Tens of billions of dollars flowed from Saudi Arabia and the Gulf states to finance the Iraqi war machine, while Egypt and Jordan provided military and logistical support.

For all these reasons there was little enthusiasm for gratuitously initiating public debate at the UN. One of the most consistently violated Charter provisions is Article 12 (1) which in effect precludes the General Assembly from pronouncing on matters under consideration by the Security Council. But this, the longest war in the history of the Organization, never made it to the General Assembly agenda.

Hence, as the two sides battered away, there were always reasons for avoiding decisive action. For the Security Council to have determined that the war was technically a threat to peace would have pointed to the logical next step, non-military measures such as mandatory sanctions. But since sanctions, in particular an arms embargo, would have benefited Iran whose war effort depended on manpower rather than weaponry, and put Iraq at a disadvantage, no major power contemplated such action. It might have helped Iran to victory and, short of that, would have offended rich and influential Arab friends. Economic sanctions would have been ignored by Iraq's regional supporters and any suggestion that they might be imposed would have caused damage to the national (commercial) interests in the Arab world of the proposer. It would have been intolerably cynical (perhaps also unacceptable to the Soviet Union which, if and when chips fell, regarded Iran with its two thousand-kilometre common border, as more important than Iraq) to impose arms embargoes or sanctions on the victim alone: better to do this informally through, for example, Operation Staunch, away from the United Nations.

It is not surprising that it became known as the forgotten war. As the death toll and destruction mounted, the world changed. Argentina invaded the Falklands and was driven out. Israel invaded Lebanon, condemning that country to a dark night of eight years of anarchy, hostage-taking and misery. The Cold War reached its nadir with 'evil empire' rhetoric and a build-up of medium-range ballistic missiles in Europe. Brezhnev died, as did Andropov and Chernenko, giving way to Gorbachev with his self-imposed mission to reinvigorate the weary Titan through the novel concepts of *glasnost* and *perestroika*. The Cold War moved to a close.

All this time the Great Powers continued to ignore the war except to take bilateral steps to discourage an Iranian victory which would have undoubtedly dynamited the regional status quo. A kind of tacit, unstructured policy evolved among all concerned that, so long as the war did not spread (it did not except sporadically to Kuwaiti and Saudi airspace and waters), so long as it did not affect oil supplies and prices (it did not: an oil glut in the 1980s led to a precipitous fall in prices), so long as the Tanker War was damaging only to marine insurers, the two enemies could be left to get on with it. It was only when the improvement in superpower relations coincided with the emergence of a real danger of escalation due to Iranian retaliatory attacks on shipping in the Gulf in late 1986 and early 1987 that the international community came to life and negotiated Resolution 598. That resolution, notwithstanding the vigorous efforts by the Secretary-General to promote its implementation, neither coerced nor persuaded the combatants to cease firing. But it did act, as so many UN resolutions had done in other contexts, particularly in the Arab Israeli dispute, as an internationally validated beacon on which both parties, once exhausted, could converge when it was politically impossible for either bilaterally to hoist the white flag to the other. It thus played an important role in ending the war, and in closing the file on nearly a decade of inglorious, supine international diplomacy.

CHAPTER FOUR

The Gulf Crisis: 1990–

Saddam Hussein emerged from the Iran-Iraq war in triumphalist mood. The staunch support of the Great Powers over the previous eight years had elevated his self-confidence to a dangerous level. With Egypt on the sidelines for having made peace with Israel, and Syria tainted by its support for the Iranian enemy, his leadership of the Arab world must have seemed to him unchallengeable. At home his population was either respectful of his power or cowed by his brutality.

The only fly in his ointment was money. The slump in oil prices had diminished Iraq's income: the country owed large sums abroad, especially to France to pay for high-technology weaponry; Baghdad owed the best part of 100 billion dollars to the oil-rich Arab states which had financed his war effort. Something had to be done to enable him to resume the upward path of civil and military development.

Iraq's oil reserves were second only to those of Saudi Arabia and its credit was good. There was no shortage of Western cabinet ministers and businessmen on the Baghdad trail. As regards his rich, thinly populated and militarily weak neighbours, his line of argument ran that they owed their thrones if not their lives to his heroic defence against the Persian imperialists, and that it would be intolerable to seek repayment of money which was in effect their contribution to a pan-Arab war effort. This view was not received with enthusiasm in the capitals of the Gulf Co-operation Council (Saudi Arabia, Kuwait, Bahrain, Qatar, the United Arab Emirates and Oman). All of them were suffering from the combination of declining oil prices and Saddam's exactions. They must have recalled that, in 1979, they had privately been more anxious about the threat of hegemonic Iraqi expansionism than about Khomeinist subversion, and that they had not been too distressed at the sight of their two large and dangerous neighbours weakening each other in the bloody attrition of war.

It was not surprising that, against this uneasy background, the twin searchlight of Saddam's wrath and ambition should have swivelled onto Kuwait. The Emirate, which had in the nineteenth century been a semi-autonomous tributary of the Ottoman province of Basra, had owed its independent status from 1899 to the British overlordship of the Gulf, and its continued existence to British protection. When Britain created the modern state of Iraq out of the ruins of the Ottoman Empire in the early 1920s, the frontier between the two states had been drawn by a British official and London had brushed aside the Iraqi claim that Kuwait was theirs as the successor state to the Ottoman Empire in the region. Even under the British installed monarchy between 1920 and 1958, successive Iraqi governments sporadically raised the claim to Kuwait. When Kuwait decided in 1961 to dispense with British protection, Abdel Karim Qasim, the Iraqi military dictator who had overthrown the monarchy in 1958, massed forces on the Kuwaiti border, and Iraq's new friends in Moscow twice vetoed the Kuwaiti application for United Nations membership. At the request of the Emir and with the remarkable approval of the arch-anti-imperialist President Nasser, Britain moved naval, air and ground forces to protect Kuwait. They were later replaced by Arab League units and the crisis passed. In 1963 Iraq, then under another military dictator, accepted Kuwait's independence. Although Iraq and Kuwait coexisted in the Arab League and the UN for the next twenty-five years, the relationship was always neurotic. From 1969 until late in the 1970s Iraqi troops occupied a strip of land on the Kuwaiti side of the border. No Iraqi government had accepted with equanimity the British-drawn frontier which blocked Iraqi direct access to the Gulf: demands for the cession or leasing of the Kuwaiti islands of Bubiyan and Warba, which would rectify this situation, were a constant feature of Iraqi diplomacy, and minor frontier scuffles were not uncommon. By 1990 Saddam was airing further grievances, namely that Kuwait was exceeding its OPEC production quota and thus depressing the market price of oil, that Kuwait was draining off crude oil from the Iraqi side of the shared South Rumaila field, and that the Emir was not prepared to forgo repayment of the wartime loan. As the summer progressed public exchanges of rhetoric between the two sides escalated in anger, threat and resentment.

However, even with the experience of 1980 to draw on, the Security Council made no move to defuse the mounting crisis. This was only partly due to diplomatic inertia. The Arab League was complacently convinced that Arab brothers did not fight each other, in spite of centuries of evidence to the contrary, and would have opposed any move by non-regional governments to internationalize the row. To an outside observer, even one living on the edge of Dartmoor, it was clear by July that Saddam was planning to do something unpleasant to Kuwait, even though this might be limited to seizing Bubiyan and Warba islands plus the Kuwaiti share of South Rumaila. The historical evidence suggested that Saddam, for all his bombast, was not an empty sabre rattler, and that his kid-glove treatment at the hands of the international community over Iran would convince him that Great Power reaction to his 'teaching the Kuwaitis a lesson' would not be all that serious.

On 2 August, in the middle of inconclusive negotiations with Kuwait and following an assurance to President Mubarak of Egypt that he would not resort to force, Saddam Hussein struck, taking the diplomatic world as much by surprise as he had in September 1980. Indeed the Emir of Kuwait was reluctant to credit the accuracy of the news that Iraqi forces were advancing unchecked on his capital. At this point any resemblance in the United Nations to the events of 1980 disappeared. Kuwait was a small, defenceless, innocuous state in good standing in the Arab League and the United Nations. It had close ties with the West. Moreover, by invading Kuwait Saddam threatened to dominate Saudi Arabia, the centre of Middle East oil power: it looked as though 60 per cent of the world's known reserves of oil were about to fall to the control of the Iraqi dictator. Combined with the bellicose anti-Israel rhetoric of the early summer, his move had in effect imperilled the only two United States interests in the Middle East, the security of Israel and the status quo in Saudi Arabia, which demanded more than a diplomatic response from Washington. President Bush, a former American Ambassador to the UN, was wisely disposed to fashion the response through the United Nations which, the Cold War over, was in a cooperative rather than a contumacious mood.

Against this propitious background, the Security Council acted decisively and quickly. On the day of the invasion, the Council almost unanimously (the Yemen not participating in the vote) adopted Resolution 660 in the enforcement Chapter VII of the Charter, condemning the Iraqi invasion ('a breach of international peace and security') and demanding immediate and unconditional withdrawal. After a few days of Arab failure to mediate a solution and a ludicrous, quick-to-be-discarded Iraqi fiction that the invasion was a response to a popular

Kuwaiti uprising against the ruling family, the Council met again and, on 6 August, adopted Resolution 661, imposing a wide range of mandatory sanctions on Iraq (excluding humanitarian supplies). Cuba and the Yemen, the awkward squad on the Council, abstained.

Saddam's response was to annex Kuwait as the nineteenth province of Iraq in a 'comprehensive and eternal merger'. This finally cooked his international goose. In spite of the artificiality of the statehood of the majority of the decolonized membership, and the plethora of disputed frontiers, territorial claims and counter-claims across the globe, this was the first time in UN history that one member state had forcibly annexed another. The Council met on 9 August and unanimously (this time including Cuba and the Yemen) adopted Resolution 662 deciding that the annexation was null and void and demanding that Iraq rescind its action. By 18 August the Council was in action again in response to Saddam's forcible closure of diplomatic missions in Kuwait and seizure of large numbers of Western hostages, many of whom were used as human shields at sensitive military installations. Resolution 664 demanded the rescinding of these actions – the vote was again unanimous.

The stream of mandatory resolutions continued until late September – No. 665 effectively imposed a maritime blockade of Iraq, subsequently buttressed by air sanctions (No. 670). No. 666 authorized the Security Council to decide on the dispatch of humanitarian aid to Iraq and Kuwait, No. 667 reverted to Iraqi aggressive acts against diplomatic personnel and premises in Kuwait and the abduction of foreign nationals. In mid-September the Secretary-General, who had no role allocated in any of the resolutions, made personal contact with the Iraqis: nothing came of it.

By the end of the month the outlines of the crisis had become clear. The GCC states had thrown off their historical inhibitions about seeking overt protection from Western 'imperialists': the immediate threat of being incorporated into the brotherly paradise of Iraq was too dire to quibble about such niceties. Beginning in early August at Saudi invitation, a two hundred thousand-strong American-led force plus a multinational naval armada had built up in Saudi Arabia and some of the smaller states to defend against a further Iraqi thrust. Syrian, Egyptian and Moroccan units had joined the Americans and Western Europeans in this coalition, named appropriately enough Desert Shield.

The composition of the Arab participation reflected the chasm which had opened within the Arab League. The participants in Desert Shield were unambiguously committed to the unilateral, unconditional withdrawal of Iraq from Kuwait and the full implementation of all the UN resolutions. Jordan, the Yemen and the PLO, while not condoning the seizure of Kuwait, were advocating an 'Arab solution' under which a settlement would be devised which would save Iraqi face, involving withdrawal of all forces from the area and, in the case of the PLO, linkage with an overall Middle East settlement including the Palestine problem. This rift caused serious damage to inter-Arab relations: hundreds of thousands of Yemeni workers were expelled from Saudi Arabia, relations between Riyadh and Amman plummeted and GCC funds to the PLO dried up.

Saddam played for time in the hope that international stamina would dissipate. He worked on the Arab divisions, suggesting portmanteau conferences which could include discussion of the question of Kuwait, playing the Palestine and Islamic cards, presenting Iraq as a victim of American/Zionist imperialism, and generally appealing to Arab peoples over the heads of their governments. Outside the GCC states, these tactics had some effect. Especially in the Occupied Territories and Jordan, Saddam became a hero to the masses for his defiance of America and Israel.

On the ground, Saddam wisely eased pressure on his eastern flank by accepting all the Iranian war aims as set out in Resolution 598, namely withdrawal from the slivers of Iranian territory occupied in the weeks before the 1988 cease-fire; full exchange of prisoners; reinstatement of the 1975 Agreement, including the division of the Shatt el-Arab; and acceptance in principle of the investigation into the origins of the war and reparations. Elsewhere his actions seemed designed to extinguish any flicker of sympathy for Iraq. The abduction and use of Western hostages as human shields excited disgust world-wide, as did the flight and appalling hardships suffered by the hundreds of thousands of South and East Asians, Egyptians, Sudanese and others who had been working in Iraq. The brutal looting, ransacking and re-population of Kuwait guaranteed 100 per cent rejection of Iraq at all levels of society throughout the Arabian peninsula.

On 8 October Israel gave a temporary boost to Saddam's linkage of the Gulf crisis with the Palestine problem, and succeeded in widening the gap between Arab governments who were committed to the

American-led coalition and their peoples. In suppressing a riot on the Dome of the Rock in Jerusalem, Israeli security forces killed twenty-one Arab civilians and wounded 150, thus marking the bloodiest day of the three-year-old *intifada*. With the Arab coalition in danger, the US voted in favour of a Security Council resolution condemning the acts of Israeli violence and another resolution twelve days later deploring the Israeli refusal to receive an investigative mission by the Secretary-General mandated by the first resolution. This was the first time for many years that Washington had supported such strong criticism of Israeli actions in the Occupied Territories. The tumult eventually died down, but Washington must have realized first that Israel was by no means a 'strategic asset' in the post-Cold War Middle East and that, if the Arab anti-Saddam coalition was to hold, the governments concerned must have some assurance that, after Iraq had been ejected from Kuwait, a vigorous attempt would be made by Washington to revive serious peace negotiations on the core issue of Palestine (see Chapter 2).

On 29 October, the Security Council adopted another resolution by thirteen votes with the usual two abstentions (Cuba and the Yemen). No. 674 concerned Iraq's 'mistreatment and oppression' of Kuwaitis and invited other nations to collate information on grave Iraqi human rights breaches, including hostage taking and the oppression of third-world nationals; and to make such information available to the Security Council. This was the first formal hint that public pressure in the West for war crimes trials was proving effective, although it never came to anything. A further resolution a month later (No. 677 of 28 November) condemned Iraqi attempts to alter the demographic composition of the population of Kuwait.

As the diplomatic manoeuvering continued and the Security Council exhausted all non-military means of coercion of Iraq without effect, it became increasingly clear that the Security Council was advancing on a watershed which it had not crossed since Kim Il Sung invaded South Korea in 1950, namely the formal authorization of the use of force. Because of the Cold War, the 'military articles' of the Charter had remained a dead letter. In theory, under Chapter VII, if non-military measures (sanctions) failed, the Council itself.

> may take ... action by air, sea, or land forces to maintain or restore international peace and security. Such actions may include demonstrations,

blockade, and other operations by air, sea, or land forces of Members of
the United Nations (Article 42).

The forces to carry out such operations were to be made available
through special agreements between members and the Council (Article
43). 'Plans for the application of armed force shall be made by the
Security Council' (Article 46) (including, in this instance, Cuba and
the Yemen!), while the Military Staff Committee (China, France, US,
UK, USSR) 'shall be responsible under the Security Council for the
strategic direction of any armed forces . . .' (Article 47). This structure
lay at the heart of the Charter as originally drafted, comprising the
'teeth' which the League of Nations had lacked.

Even as early as 1950, there had been no question of activating this
machinery in the Korean War. In the temporary absence of the Soviet
Union, the Council had adopted a mandatory resolution delegating the
military response to the invasion to a unified command under the
United States which was authorized to designate the commander.
Hence, although the force in Korea flew the UN flag as well as the
flags of national participants, it was in all but name an American
operation and, as such, does not figure as a separate case study in this
book.

In 1987, President Gorbachev had proposed the resurrection of the
military articles when he reordered Soviet policy towards the UN. In
his statement to the General Assembly on 25 September 1990 the
Soviet Foreign Minister, Edward Shevardnadze, strongly supported
UN action against Iraq, emphasized that all non-military means must
be used to implement the resolutions, and explicitly proposed that the
Military Staff Committee (MSC) be activated and Article 43 agreements to provide forces be concluded so that 'there would be no need
now for individual states to act unilaterally.'

This clear statement of policy followed informal initiatives in New
York by the Soviet Union to convene the MSC. The foothills of the
watershed had been reached in late August over the question of
buttressing the economic sanctions with an economic blockade. Technically this should have involved a move to Article 42 of the Charter in
which blockade is specifically mentioned. But the US and the other
maritime nations were clearly not prepared to go down this road: they
were resolved to keep control of their own forces if shots were fired,
and not to submit them to the uncertainties of unpredictable multi-

national committees such as the Council and the MSC. Hence Resolution 665 avoided the word 'blockade', using instead the clumsy periphrasis 'measures commensurate to the specific circumstances'. As a sop to the Soviet Union and other purists, 'states concerned' were requested to coordinate their actions 'using as appropriate mechanisms of the Military Staff Committees'. To the best of my knowledge this request was ignored, hence the remarks by Shevardnadze a month later, which were also ignored.

By November the crest of the watershed was drawing near. It was obvious that sanctions were not going to budge Saddam in the short time scale required by the American-led coalition. This urgency was not dictated solely by domestic political considerations, the difficulty involved in holding the Arab coalition together over a long period, and military reluctance to keep large numbers of troops hanging about doing nothing in the Gulf for months on end into the intolerable summer heat. The fact of the matter was that Saddam's continued ransacking of Kuwait, a small city state, would by, say, mid-1991 have left nothing to be liberated. This argument counted strongly with those, like myself, who would have preferred to see sanctions given a full opportunity to work in what were ideal circumstances, namely against a country dependent on a single source of income, oil, with no significant sanctions busters and a virtually unanimous international determination to maintain them. Looking back four years later, we were wrong. Saddam's grip on his country and his merciless disregard for the suffering of his own people would have enabled him to outlast the will-power of the United Nations had force not been used.

By November it was evident that not even the shuttle diplomacy of Ba'athist Iraq's superpower ally of eighteen years, the Soviet Union, would persuade Saddam to cut his losses, although he tried to defuse some pressure by releasing the Western hostages in dribs and drabs – they were all home by Christmas. The military build-up in Saudi Arabia and the Gulf transcended the needs of a defensive shield: the outside world sensed that preparations were in hand to move to the offensive. This prospect raised interesting questions. Would the Americans and their partners simply go ahead on the basis of Article 51 of the Charter (the right of individual or collective self-defence) in response to an existing Kuwaiti invitation? If they did so, would the Arab coalition hold and would wider international support crumble? It was obvious that the coalition would not subject itself to the constraints of the military articles of the Charter. Apart from anything else, the notion of military security in a Council comprising Cuba and the Yemen was laughable. But it seemed unlikely that, with memories of Korea and the Cold War still alive, the Soviet Union and China would be prepared to allow the adoption of a resolution which gave the United States and its Western allies *carte blanche* to wage war on behalf of the whole Organization.

To general amazement among UN mavens, the Security Council adopted Resolution 678 on 30 November, with the Soviet Union among the twelve positive voters, China the sole abstainer and the two in the awkward squad voting against. The resolution gave Iraq one last chance to comply with the previous resolutions, setting a deadline of 15 January 1991, after which 'member states cooperating with the government of Kuwait' were authorized to 'use all necessary means' to implement the previous resolutions and to 'restore international peace and security in the area'. All that was asked of the 'states concerned' was to keep the Council informed of progress. There was no mention of the self-defence Article 51 nor of any of the military articles. This was, to borrow a Saddamian phrase, the 'mother of *carte blanche*'. The Council had forfeited control of events until 'international peace and security' had been restored, a phrase which could have embraced the total conquest of Iraq and the removal from office of the originator of the 'breach of international peace and security'. The watershed had been crossed: we veterans of the UN in earlier decades were dumb-founded by the convincing evidence that the Soviet Union had become little more than a junior partner in an American World Enterprise. The Security Council did not meet again in public until the completion of Operation Desert Storm over three months later.

The weeks before the 15 January deadline were filled with hectic but fruitless diplomacy. President Bush offered to 'go the last mile' for peace immediately after the adoption of No. 678. But argument about who should meet whom where delayed a meeting between the Iraqi Foreign Minister and Secretary Baker until early January. It achieved nothing. Efforts by the Soviet Union were equally unavailing. Saddam improved the time with boasts about the Mother of Battles which his forces would inflict on their adversaries: the Western media comple-mented this braggadocio with blood-curdling accounts of the size (the fourth largest army in the world), weight of equipment and battle experience of the Iraqis. Even at the time, my considerable knowledge from years before of the Iraqi military, as well as observation from a distance of their indifferent performance against Iran, made me wonder how long they would last against the First World juggernaut arrayed against them, especially as the Iraqi conscripts would not see themselves as fighting for their homes and families, as they had on the defensive against Iran. My greater concern was that, as soon as Americans and Europeans started killing Arabs in large numbers, there would be popular uproar in the Arab world on a scale which would make it difficult if not impossible for regimes to continue to support the coalition and survive. I was wrong. There were demonstrations and the internal situation in Jordan became volatile, calling forth all King Hussein's skills to control it: Israel clamped down ruthlessly in the Occupied Territories. But it never looked as though general Arab emotion would pass out of control. The GCC states never wavered. Saddam was no Nasser and no single Arab government had a monopoly of propaganda outlets as Cairo had possessed in the 1950s and 1960s. Public opinion had a greater variety of views to consider, and the slavishly controlled Baghdad media had little external appeal.

I must not digress too far from the UN involvement. On 13 January the Secretary-General made a last personal attempt to persuade Saddam to avoid the inevitable. He failed and, on 16 January, the coalition launched a systematic, comprehensive and awe-inspiring aerial assault on Iraqi infrastructure – power stations, bridges, oil refineries, etc. – as well as on communications and command and control centres. Washington was bent on a quick, decisive victory with a minimum of casualties, the strategy being to isolate and weaken the Iraqi forces in Kuwait before launching the ground offensive. The air campaign continued unabated for nearly six weeks with no movement on the ground except for the repulse of a small Iraqi probing attack across the Saudi frontier at the end of January.

There was little the Iraqis could do to counter this devastating bombardment. Some coalition aircraft were brought down and Saddam shot himself once more in the foot by parading British and American air crews in front of Iraqi television. The Iraqi Air Force was quickly removed from the skies or destroyed on the ground, except for about 100 aircraft which fled to Iran, where they were impounded and later confiscated as part of the reparations for the Iran-Iraq war. The most serious Iraqi retaliation was the indiscriminate launching of Scud missiles against Israel and, to a lesser extent, Saudi Arabia. This boosted Saddam's stock with the Palestinians but caused little damage and few casualties. His principal objective was to provoke the Israelis into a direct response, thus placing the Arab governments in the coalition in military alliance with the arch-enemy. Thanks to strenuous efforts by the United States, Israel was persuaded to exercise reluctant restraint. The air campaign against Iraq was to a limited extent distracted from its priority targets by the need to concentrate on the Scuds, although their threat was more political than military.

In the second half of February, as the time for the ground offensive drew near, the Soviet Union returned to the charge with Iraq and made strenuous efforts to mediate a much softened Iraqi position (which for the first time included the word 'withdrawal') with Washington and in private meetings of the Security Council. But the offer still contained qualifications and military momentum had become unstoppable. On 23 February the coalition opened an all-out ground attack. The Mother of Battles turned into a rout. Iraqi prisoners poured in by the tens of thousands. Three days later, with minimal casualties, Kuwait had been cleared of Iraqi occupation, and coalition forces (not including the Arabs) were some way inside Iraq. On 28 February, President Bush ordered a cease-fire. The Iraqi Foreign Minister told the Secretary General that Iraq was ready to comply with all the resolutions. Desert Storm was over but the fleeing Iraqis, in a last gesture of revenge, had fired over 100 Kuwaiti oil fields. When I visited the area ten months later, the fires were out but the desert was still gleaming with black lakes of oil alongside the debris of Saddam's shattered army.

On 2 March, the Council adopted the first cease-fire resolution No. 686 by a curiously low vote – eleven in favour, one against (Cuba), with three abstentions (China, India and the Yemen); perhaps it rubbed Iraq's nose too hard in the defeat for these governments. The resolution demanded Iraqi implementation of the previous twelve resolutions, in particular rescinding the annexation of Kuwait, accepting liability for loss, damage etc. to Kuwait and third parties, release of all Kuwaiti and third-party nationals detained by Iraq and immediate return of Kuwaiti property. Iraq was also to cease hostile or provocative acts against all member states, including missile attacks, release prisoners of war and help to identify mines, booby traps etc. planted in Kuwait. The resolution made clear that, pending Iraqi implementation of all its provisions, Resolution 678 (authorizing the use of force until the restoration of international peace and security) remained valid.

Desert Storm was over but there were more horrors to come. Saddam had survived. Contrary to Western hopes, his generals were either unwilling or unable to get rid of him, in spite of the humiliation of the military debacle. Instead, encouraged by an incautious comment by President Bush to the effect that it was up to the Iraqi people to oblige Saddam to step aside, the long-oppressed Shi'a community in the south and the northern Kurds mounted an uncoordinated but initially effective uprising. The coalition, set on declaring victory and going home, had no intention of being drawn into Iraqi domestic politics. Unwilling to support Shi'a Moslems with their links to the Iranian demons, and reluctant to incur casualties, the conquering armies did nothing to help these rebellions even when the tide turned. By the end of March, the Iraqi armed forces, forbidden to use fixed-wing aircraft under the cease-fire agreement between the field commanders but specifically allowed to use helicopters, were pounding the rebels with gunships and blasting them with tanks, artillery and infantry of the surprisingly intact Republican Guard divisions. Iraqi military might was back to doing what it had always excelled at, the repression of its own people. The massacre of the Shi'ites went on within earshot of the coalition forces on the Iraqi border: they did nothing except to provide sanctuary for refugees. By the end of March, the rebellions had been crushed and hundreds of thousands of Iraqis, both in the south and in the north, were in flight from the ferocious revenge of their government.

Public outrage in the West (the Arab members of the coalition were conspicuously silent) and in Iran forced the Security Council to take action in spite of the hallowed doctrine (sanctified by Article 2 (7) of the Charter) of non-interference in the domestic affairs of states. The result was Resolution 688 of 5 April, a landmark in that it was the first time that the Council had taken action on an internal matter in a sovereign state against the wishes of that state's authorities. The wording reflected the tortuous nature of the passage through the diplomatic mine field. There was no reference to any of the previous Gulf crisis resolutions. The preamble 'recalled' Article 2 (7), expressed concern at the 'threat to *international* (my italics) peace and security' caused by the trans-frontier flight of the refugees, a point reiterated in the first operative paragraph. The preamble 'reaffirmed' the commitment of all Member States to the sovereignty, territorial integrity and political independence of Iraq and of all states in the area. After these sops to the non-interference purists on the Council, the resolution, in its operative section, took a strong line, condemning the repression of the civilian population, demanding its cessation, insisting that Iraq allow access by humanitarian organizations and requesting the Secretary-General to pursue his humanitarian efforts.

In spite of these elaborate verbal precautions, the resolution only just scraped through. The voting provided interesting evidence of which countries themselves had grisly skeletons in their domestic cupboards and thus set greater store on protecting the principle of domestic sovereignty than on the relief of atrocious human suffering. China abstained and came within a whisker of casting a veto (Tiananmen Square and Tibet struggling with the need to accommodate the United States); India (with several civil uprisings in her border provinces) followed suit; Cuba, the Yemen and Zimbabwe voted against. The final vote of ten-three-two was the lowest of any of the Gulf crisis resolutions, a portent for the future.

The resolution was not mandatory in the eyes of the UN lawyers and the Secretary-General felt obliged to negotiate his humanitarian objectives with the Baghdad government rather than order them to comply with his demands. His representatives managed in the end to establish a channel of a kind for humanitarian aid and the deployment of a small number of unarmed UN 'security guards' in the Kurdish towns and cities. By early April the flight of probably more than a million Kurds into Iran and Turkey as well as tens of thousands of Shi'ites into Iran from the south had assumed crisis proportions for the host countries and, more important from the Kurdish point of view, had attracted the attention of the Western media (the Shi'ites were less fortunate in this regard). The harrowing television pictures of Kurdish women and children dying in the freezing mountains created public pressure in the West which overcame the passive attitude of governments. Iraq was ordered by Washington to stop military operations north of the 36th parallel and a 'no-fly zone' was created. 'Safe havens' were established in northern Iraq to persuade the Kurds to return and were protected by ground and air forces of the US, Britain and France. Saddam's troops were forced to retreat southwards. By the end of May the situation had stabilized and 'Free Kurdistan' has maintained itself with difficulty to this day, in spite of

Saddam's economic blockade and sporadic military threats. In UN terms these actions by the coalition, and others which I will touch on regarding southern Iraq, had no direct mandate. They were said to be 'consistent with' or 'in the spirit of' Resolution 688: the numerically increasing awkward squad on the Council looked the other way.

Meanwhile the Security Council had moved from the temporary cease-fire Resolution 686 to what the Soviet Ambassador to the United Nations characterized as the 'mother of all resolutions', No. 687 of 3 April, the document which still governs Iraq's relationship with the United Nations. The original resolution, No. 660, adopted on the day of the invasion of Kuwait, simply demanded Iraqi withdrawal and immediate negotiations between Kuwait and Iraq for the resolution of their differences. Iraqi behaviour over the next eight months and the revelations about the Iraqi military arsenal uncovered during Desert Storm had rendered these simple demands inadequate as a basis for peace. Resolution 687 occupies over nine closely printed pages of UN documentation. The twenty-six preambular paragraphs, apart from covering all the bilateral Kuwait/Iraq issues, foreshadow action on the questions of chemical, bacteriological and nuclear weapons, ballistic missiles, regional arms control, hostage taking, terrorism and humanitarian matters.

The thirty-four operative paragraphs, divided into nine sections, cover the inviolability, demarcation and guarantee of the frontier, the deployment of a UN observer force (UNIKOM) in a demilitarized zone straddling the border, the return of looted Kuwaiti property and abducted Kuwaiti nationals, the supervised destruction of Iraqi weapons of mass destruction and ballistic missiles, the supervised removal of military nuclear material, long-term monitoring to ensure that Iraq does not resume these programmes, compensation and reparations financed by the income from supervised oil exports, the linking of economic sanctions to Iraqi compliance with the resolution, maintenance of the arms embargo and renunciation of terrorism – all to come into effect on Iraqi acceptance. This acceptance was received on 11 April.

Resolution 687 is unquestionably the most intrusive and wide-ranging array of demands made on a sovereign state since the creation of the UN in October 1945. Iraq, defeated, had no choice but to comply, especially since coalition forces, still in place, might lose patience with delay and use the oppression of the Kurds and Shi'ites as a pretext to finish the job by conquering Iraq in the interest of 'restoring international peace and security'. In effect 'the mother of all resolutions' has turned Iraq into a kind of delinquent ward of the Security Council.

Until that time, the Council as a body had played two roles – declaratory (condemning and demanding), and legislative (authorizing member states to take action, e.g. sanctions, blockade and ultimately the use of force). Now it was the turn of the Organization itself to act in an executive capacity. The Secretary-General created an Interdepartmental Coordinating Group to oversee the functioning of UNIKOM; of the Boundary Commissions (which contained three experts appointed by the Secretary-General plus Kuwaiti and Iraqi representatives); the Special Commission of fifteen members to oversee the Compensation Fund set up by Resolution 692 in May 1991; another Special Commission (approved by Resolution 699 in June) to identify and destroy the weapons of mass destruction; and a large team from the International Atomic Energy Agency to look after nuclear material. There were other innovations – the Secretary-General's Representative for the UN Humanitarian Programme and a Gulf oil pollution Disaster Fund under the International Maritime Organization being just two of numerous examples. In addition the Sanctions Committee originally created under resolution 661 in August 1990 was mandated by resolution 700 in June to monitor compliance with the arms embargo.

If the Iraqi government had consulted its long-term interests and the well-being of its people, it would have complied quickly and unreservedly with all the provisions of No. 687 in order to free the country from the self-imposed burdens of war. But this was not Saddam Hussein's way. Boastful declarations of victory, including the striking of medals, and public defiance accompanied a campaign of evasion, procrastination, cheating, concealment, obstruction and threats. The various UN teams had a difficult and sometimes dangerous time of it. Occasionally violence exploded, for example when the UN Special Commission on the weapons issue was denied access to buildings and documents and was harassed by 'patriotic' crowds, when 'spontaneous indignation' triggered demonstrations objecting to the frontier demarcation; most spectacularly when the US, in the last days of President Bush's time in office, fired cruise missiles at a building in the outskirts of Baghdad allegedly containing machine tools relating to the nuclear programme.

In the context of Resolution 688, there have been sporadic clashes between US aircraft and Iraqi ground defences over the northern no-fly zone, and over its southern equivalent, imposed a year later because of Saddam's continuing assaults in the area of the southern marshes. Saddam has not dared to invade the protected area of Iraqi Kurdistan but he has systematically shelled, burnt and assaulted the villages and crops of the Marsh Arabs and other Shi'a communities in the south, as well as draining the marshes in order to flush out the inhabitants. The no-fly zone has had scant effect on these outrages, and reports by the representative of the UN Human Rights Commission to the Security Council have become increasingly heart-rending. It hardly needs saying that, when Mr van der Stoel's first report was submitted to the Security Council in August 1992, a number of delegations felt obliged to make pompous and, to an outsider, sickening reservations about the inappropriateness of an emissary from a body (the Human Rights Commission) deriving from the Economic and Social Council appearing before the majesty of the Security Council: the wound opened by Resolution 688 through the armour of Article 2 (7) was still hurting.

By the spring of 1994, there had been no change in the unregenerate attitude of the Baghdad regime. The new frontier had been demarcated in Kuwait's favour but had been rejected by Iraq. There was no question of withdrawing UNIKOM, rather of its reinforcement. (It has to be said that, although no doubt historically correct, the new frontier alignment is worse for Iraq in terms of access to the Gulf, and will be a thorn in the flesh even when the Ba'athists are replaced by a genuinely friendly government in Baghdad.) Kuwaiti property has been returned but six hundred Kuwaitis abducted to Iraq are still 'missing'. There has been massive destruction of Iraqi weaponry but Iraqi efforts to circumvent the process have diminished the credibility of their belated acceptance of the principle of long-term monitoring. All attempts to activate the war-compensation mechanisms, even the limited sale of Iraqi oil through a UN account to finance the import of medical and other humanitarian supplies, have foundered on Iraqi refusal to allow further breaches of its sovereignty. To sum up, the UN operation to implement Resolution 687 has only partially succeeded due to Iraqi obstructionism. Iraq has been militarily weakened and, for the moment, offers no threat except to its own people. But there is no sign that Iraq has recognized the independence and

sovereignty of Kuwait or that its return to the international community is imminent.

In the light of this unsatisfactory record, there are many people who
argue, as they did at the time, that the coalition should not have
stopped at the Iraqi border, but should have marched on Baghdad,
thrown out Saddam and his government and installed a friendly and
cooperative successor regime. Apart from the fact that such a regime
would have had no domestic Iraqi support in the central, Sunni Arab
belt of t..e country, thus making it impossible for the Americans and
their allies to withdraw without precipitating its fall, such an action
would have destroyed the international basis for the whole operation.
The Arab partners in the coalition, plus many of the other Moslem
and non-aligned members, would have pulled out. Their participation
was grounded in the terms of the original Security Council resolution,
namely to liberate Kuwait. They would not have gone further on the
basis of the argument that the 'restoration of international peace and
security' required the conquest of Iraq and a change of regime. In the
Security Council, China, possibly the Soviet Union which was already
under internal strain for opposing its old ally, and most of the non-
aligned members would have been strongly opposed. With the collapse
of the international consensus, the United States, Britain and France
would have been dangerously isolated in a hostile environment, dependent only on their military power.

What lessons can be learnt for the UN from this dramatic crisis, the
first major post-Cold War test, which led to the deployment of the
largest single expeditionary force since 1945? Looking back after
nearly four years, the association of the Gulf crisis with the advent of a
New World Order was a product of the euphoria of easy victory rather
than of rational thought. It is true that the Security Council acted with
rare speed and decisiveness, and that it adopted in the first few months
almost as many mandatory resolutions as in all its previous history. It
is true that the Council validated an unprecedented series of actions by
member states up to and including the use of force and that, after the
military victory, it mounted a comprehensive array of operations to
punish the aggressor, restore the victim and neutralize any recurrence
of the threat. Short of assuming command and control of the campaign,
as envisaged in the Charter, the Security Council could scarcely have
done more.

However the handling of the crisis was not a precedent for future UN operations. It had unique features, the recurrence of which is improbable. No future dictator, however arrogant and ambitious, is likely to display such breathtaking ineptness as Saddam Hussein. The aggression was so unambiguous and the purported annexation so crass as to unite every member state in the United Nations in opposition. To compound this foolishness by threatening states in close relations with a superpower and to imperil a strategic interest (oil) of crucial importance to the industrialized and developing world alike was almost beyond belief. In addition the military environment for a counter-offensive was uncomplicated – desert terrain virtually uninhabited except for Kuwait City – the reverse of the South East Asian jungles or Balkan mountains. Last but not least, the rich Arab states, plus the economic superpowers (Japan and Germany) who depend to a great extent on Middle Eastern oil, were able to finance the expensive UN-authorized military operations without great hardship, and Saudi Arabia was in a position to increase production to avert a crisis of oil supply or price. Such a conjuncture is the stuff of war games in think tanks, not of real life!

But there are conclusions to be drawn of significance for the future. The military articles of the Charter proved irrelevant even in the most favourable international atmosphere since the creation. We now know that Great Powers will continue to insist, not unreasonably, on national command of their forces in major dynamic campaigns or, at most, joint command in a coherent like-minded alliance such as NATO, and not in so diffuse a structure as the UN. However, it is unlikely that such unqualified *carte blanche* as for Desert Storm will be given to a coalition leader in the future: in the far smaller enforcement operation in Somalia at the end of 1992, a monitoring link was written into the enabling resolution between the coalition command, the Secretary-General and the Council. This was the result of agitation among the membership that the US had somehow hijacked the Council during the Gulf crisis.

As with the Iraqi attack on Iran in 1980, and the Israeli invasion of Lebanon in 1982, there was plenty of advance evidence of Saddam's move. Again no preventive action was taken but this particular failure has stimulated a bustle of international debate about the creation of pre-emptive machinery.

The fact that it took half the world in arms to face down a small, semi-industrialized state brought home the folly of the Cold War competition and commercial greed which had converted the Middle East into a *place d'armes*. The cries of 'never again' culminated in President Bush mobilizing the Five Permanent Members of the Security Council (responsible for 85 per cent of global arms exports) to formulate guidelines for restraint. Sadly, the decision of France and the US to conclude major arms deals with Taiwan torpedoed this initiative just as it was getting under way: China, now a major arms exporter, refused to participate further. The only positive result so far has been the creation, at British initiative, of a United Nations register of arms transfers. This will do something for 'transparency' but the fact has to be faced that Middle Eastern orders (principally from the GCC states, Iran, Syria and Israel) have multiplied approximately four-fold since 1991.

Perhaps the most depressing lesson relates to sanctions. If sanctions were ever to be effective, they should have been against Iraq. But only the most devoted opponent of the use of American-led military force would now argue that sanctions alone would have forced Saddam to withdraw from his conquest. It is enough to take cognizance of his unabated defiance even after four years of sanctions, regardless of the acute suffering of his people, to conclude that they are more of a punitive than a coercive device. Abyssinia, Rhodesia, South Africa, Iraq, Serbia – the list of failures lengthens.

The breach opened in the wall of Article 2 (7) by Resolution 688 has been widened with subsequent UN involvement in a multitude of civil wars, not always at the invitation of or with the consent of parties. As the UN wrestles with the intractabilities of Serbia, Croatia, Bosnia, Somalia and Angola there must be some nostalgic looks over the shoulder at the simple certainties of the Gulf crisis when, for once, international morality and material interest combined with near-universal consensus and effortless military superiority.

PART TWO

Africa

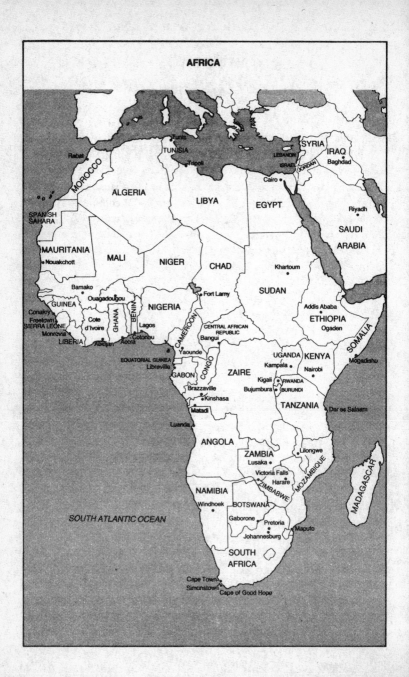

CHAPTER FIVE

The Congo : 1960–64

The European irruption into Africa south of the Sahara in the second half of the nineteenth century, and the almost equally rapid exodus less than 100 years later will seem to African historians of the distant future like other afflictions which have swept the continent, such as drought, locusts, the tsetse fly and, in contemporary times, AIDS. For centuries Africa had accommodated Arab and European slave traders and coastal settlements of earlier, Iberian colonists, as well as the Anglo-Dutch presence in the south. But all that was nothing in comparison with the advent of the British, French, German and Belgian colonists, missionaries, traders, soldiers and administrators who created over thirty new territories with no regard for the wishes or interests of the indigenous inhabitants, separated by frontiers ruled on maps in European capitals, representing neither ethnic nor other natural divisions, only a carve up between competing European governments.

Sub-Saharan Africa in the twentieth century was a late beneficiary of the doctrine of the self-determination of peoples to which lip service was paid in the industrialized world from the end of the First World War. Only white-ruled South Africa and Liberia achieved founding membership of the League of Nations in 1919. The same pair were the sole representatives of sub-Saharan Africa at the creation of the United Nations in 1945 (with Egypt and Ethiopia making up the total African membership). The imperial powers were, it seemed, in no hurry to relinquish control. They adopted a leisurely pace of development of local institutions, imperceptible in some cases, in preparation for eventual independence. The fact that friends of mine, on demobilization in the late 1940s after the Second World War, were being offered full careers in the British Colonial Service in parts of Africa suggested that those whose business it was to plan for the future had their eyes on the perpetuation of the status quo until the end of the century, or even beyond.

Fifteen years later, a flicker of history's eyelid, the tide of decoloniza-

tion was at the flood. By 1960, twenty-two more African states had
secured their independence. By 1970 another fifteen had followed suit.
Today the African group in the United Nations comprises fifty-one
member states, nearly one third of the total membership. European
imperialism is no more. Even apartheid in South Africa, the toughest
nut of all to crack, is finished.

Looking back, it is extraordinary that this virtually instantaneous
transformation took place for the most part quietly. Forty of the forty-
seven newly independent states parted from their colonial overlords
peacefully, after hasty, inadequate preparation but little, in many cases
no, acrimony. 'Armed struggle' was a preliminary to national liberation
in only seven instances; where there had been significant European
settlement – Algeria, Kenya, Namibia and Zimbabwe – or where the
imperial power (in this case Portugal) had refused to accept that its
African possessions were entities separate from the metropolis –
Angola, Mozambique and Guinea Bissau. Furthermore, given the
artificial nature of the great majority of the newly independent states,
it says much for the political wisdom of the members of the Organization of African Unity that the decision to maintain the preposterous
frontiers inherited from the European imperialists has been respected.
What is less surprising is that there have been twenty post-independence civil wars in Africa, only half of which have been brought to the
attention of the Security Council. The first one to do so rocked the
United Nations to its foundations.

With the exception of South Africa, and German South-West
Africa (now Namibia) in which, after the First World War, South
Africa assumed the 'sacred trust of civilization' for the 'well-being and
development' of the people as the League of Nations mandatory power
(phrases which in the circumstances it is difficult to utter with a
straight face), the Belgian Congo was probably the least edifying
example of European colonialism in Africa. Opened up by the
American explorer Henry Stanley, it was ruled from 1878–1908 as the
private estate of King Leopold II of the Belgians. It was during that
period that it featured as the venue of Joseph Conrad's haunting
novella, *Heart of Darkness*, based on his experience as an officer on a
steamer on the Congo river. Conrad has no illusions about imperialism:
'The conquest of the earth, which mostly means the taking it away
from those who have a different complexion or slightly flatter noses
than ourselves, is not a pretty thing when you look into it too much',

his narrator, Marlowe, remarks at the beginning. But Marlowe makes a distinction – Britain comes out of it well – between various brands of imperialism. Belgium is at the bottom of his class. When he reaches the Congo he 'foresaw that in the blinding sunshine of that land I would become acquainted with a flabby, pretending weak-eyed devil of a rapacious and pitiless folly'. Admittedly Conrad was not an historian researching a Ph.D. thesis on the defects of Belgian colonial policy, but he clearly had a point. Protests at the atrocities prevalent in King Leopold's private fiefdom, mainly from British sources, reached such a pitch that, in 1908, the Belgian government was obliged to assume responsibility. Thereafter, for fifty years, Belgium pursued a policy which combined maximal profits from the Congo's lavish natural resources with a degree of benevolent paternalism which, while denying the indigenous inhabitants any serious political and social advancement, provided an adequate standard of living which tempered the exaction of forced labour.

The Belgians succeeded for some years after the Second World War in insulating the Congo from the political currents which were flowing in neighbouring African territories. However, by the late 1950s the game was up. Liberation fever was mounting with the independence of most of Arab North Africa (the Sudan, Libya, Tunisia, Morocco), the inspiration of the independence struggle in Algeria, the emergence of Ghana from the British Gold Coast (1957), President de Gaulle's sweeping decision in 1958 to decolonize the whole of French Africa (over fifteen states), and the anti-imperialist bugle blasts from the non-aligned leadership of Egypt's Nasser, Ghana's Nkrumah and Guinea's Sekou Touré: Cairo radio's African language broadcasts were reaching deep into the continent. Disturbances broke out in the Congo and the Belgian government decided to grant independence on the basis of ludicrously inadequate preparations, in the hope that Belgium would be able to maintain the substance of military and commercial interest while surrendering the simulacrum of sovereignty.

On 30 June 1960 the Congo celebrated independence. Given that the leadership had virtually no experience of government in a modern state; that there were only seventeen Congolese graduates in existence: no doctors, lawyers or engineers; and that there were no Congolese commissioned officers in the armed forces, the prospects for stability in a country the size of Europe with a population of fourteen million divided among hundreds of tribes, were negligible, unless the change were to be in name only. With the strongly pan-African nationalist, volatile and erratic Patrice Lumumba as the first Prime Minister, a continuation of thinly disguised Belgian authority was improbable in spite of the terms of the Congolese-Belgian treaty of June 1960. This provided for the retention on secondment of the great majority of the Belgian administrative and technical personnel and the cession to Belgium of two military bases from which the Congolese government could call on Belgian troops to assist in the maintenance of law and order.

The immediate omens were not promising. At the independence celebrations Lumumba delivered a fiery speech with hostile references to past Belgian misdeeds and humiliations of the people. My personal memory is of a front-page press photograph of King Baudouin reviewing crowds from an open limousine in Leopoldville, the capital. While the king was looking one way, his hand at the salute, an excited Congolese gentleman was running along the other side of the car in the act of drawing the king's sword from its scabbard, a souvenir perhaps, a portent certainly!

The descent to chaos in several parts of the country began less than a week later with the first of a series of mutinies in the *Force Publique*, as the army was known. Officerless groups of soldiers rampaged and Belgian troops, without the invitation of the government, emerged from their bases to protect the terrified European communities. On 11 July, the leader of the mineral-rich Katanga province (the source of 50 per cent of the country's wealth), Moisé Tshombe, declared secession. President Kasavubu and Prime Minister Lumumba, on poor terms since pre-independence times, had lost control, although the latter attempted to recover the loyalty of the soldiers by sacking the Belgian commander and by replacing him with a sergeant-major, Victor Lundula, whom he promoted to major-general, with another non-commissioned officer promoted to colonel as his chief of staff. The name of the latter was Joseph Mobutu. In political terms the Katanga secession was an extreme manifestation of the rift between the political leaders. Lumumba represented a centrist, socialist tendency analogous to Ghana; Kasavubu epoused a federalist approach grounded in traditional tribal loyalties.

It was fortunate that the UN Secretary-General, Dag Hammarskjold, who had taken a close interest in the pell mell process of African decolonization, had despatched his Under Secretary-General, Ralph

Bunche, to attend the independence celebrations on the assumption that the UN would have an important part to play in providing technical assistance to the newly independent state. Bunche was able to keep in touch with the Congolese leaders and with the Secretary-General as the *émeute* flamed across the country. According to Bunche's biographer, Brian Urquhart, himself a Congo veteran, Lumumba and Kasavubu were thinking first in terms of UN assistance in strengthening the army for the maintenance of law and order. But their formal request to the Secretary-General on 12 July was for UN military assistance to repel Belgian 'aggression', i.e. the unauthorized deployment of Belgian troops from the bases, including by 13 July the takeover of Leopoldville airport.

This request laid the foundation of what was to become the largest and most complex combined civil and military operation ever mounted by the United Nations until the Cambodian operation in 1992-93. The military peacekeeping force was not, of course, on the same scale as Korea or the Gulf crisis, even Somalia in 1993. But these were UN-authorized operations controlled by United States-led coalitions. What made the Congo unique was that the operation was conducted from start to finish by the Secretary-General and his staff. It also cost Dag Hammarskjold his life. Furthermore, it was the first time that the UN had been drawn into the morass of a civil war, as opposed to monitoring the separation of combatants along a clearly marked cease-fire line.

Hammarskjold opened the proceedings boldly by calling the Security Council into session, using for the first time Article 99 of the Charter, which authorizes the Secretary-General 'to bring to the attention of the Security Council any matter which in his opinion may threaten the maintenance of international peace and security.' This device is rarely used and is appropriate only when no member state is disposed to call the Council, or when convocation by a member state would itself be controversial. In the case of the Congo the shadow of Cold War involvement was already looming: Hammarskjold's initiative circumvented this for the early, crucial weeks.

The first Council resolution, adopted on 7 July (the day on which the Council also approved Congolese membership of the UN), called upon the Belgian government to withdraw its troops and authorized the Secretary-General to provide the government of the Congo with military assistance. France and Britain, out of European inclination towards Belgium, abstained; more important, the two superpowers supported the resolution. The next resolution, adopted unanimously two weeks later, called for speedy Belgian withdrawal, strengthened Hammarskjold's hand, and, as a warning to those disposed to support the secession of Katanga, requested all states not to 'undermine the territorial integrity and political independence of the Congo'. This move was prompted by a Congolese threat that, if Belgian forces did not withdraw immediately, troops from the USSR would be requested.

Hammarskjold laid down a set of principles for the UN Force in the Congo (ONUC) which still form the bases for UN peacekeeping operations in civil wars. ONUC was a temporary deployment with Congolese consent, in place until national forces could take over. Its command rested with the UN. It could not become a party to any internal conflict. Its operations must be separate and distinct from activities by national authorities. ONUC could not be used to enforce specific political solutions or to influence balances of political power. It would use force only in self-defence. Its composition would take full account of the views of the national government.

Hammarskjold had already been in consultation with the African group in the UN, and ONUC began to deploy on 15 July with a Tunisian advance guard, followed by units from Ethiopia, Ghana, Guinea, and Morocco. At Bunche's suggestion he balanced the exclusively African weight in the scales (designed to allay Congolese fears of re-colonization) with Swedish and Irish contingents (to reassure the European communities). Permanent Member national units were excluded.

On the ground Bunche and his small but experienced multinational staff performed prodigies of improvization and persuasion in the face of obstruction, fear, confusion, opposition from quarters whence support might have been expected, and quicksilver changes from abuse to cooperation from the Congolese leadership. By the beginning of August, with no serious exchanges of fire and no casualties, about ten thousand ONUC troops had been deployed across the country: the Belgians had withdrawn their forces and evacuated their bases, except in Katanga. Bunche described the operation in a letter to his wife as being 'like trying to give first aid to a wounded rattlesnake'.

Cold War shadows were beginning to lengthen but Hammarskjold and Bunche had time for one more achievement. After an abortive visit to Elizabethville, the Katanga capital, by Bunche in an attempt to persuade Tshombe and his Belgian advisers to agree to the withdrawal of Belgian troops, Hammarskjold decided to bring matters to a head. The immediate problem was that Lumumba was demanding a joint military operation by the ANC (the former *Force Publique*) and ONUC to end the Katangese secession or, failing that, a unilateral expedition by the ANC. Hammarskjold, basing himself on the principles he had laid down with the Security Council for ONUC, refused to cooperate, thus souring relations with Lumumba, on the one hand, while on the other he was already coming under fire from Western quarters for refusing to use ONUC forcibly to disarm the ANC. He and Bunche were determined to avoid a situation in which Africans made war on Africans, and the Security Council mandate was clearly limited – force was to be used only in self-defence.

The Security Council acted on 9 August with a resolution (France and Italy abstaining) requesting the withdrawal of Belgian troops from Katanga and reaffirming that ONUC 'will not try to influence the outcome of any internal conflict.' On 12 August Hammarskjold led the first ONUC troops by air into Elizabethville without informing Lumumba. By the time Bunche left for New York at the end of the month, all Belgian regular combat units had left Katanga. But Hammarskjold's refusal to bring an end to the Katangese secession or to enable the Central government to achieve this by force precipitated a final rupture between Lumumba and the Secretariat.

Meanwhile tension had been mounting between the centrist Lumumba and the federalist Kasavubu. On 6 September the Congo slid from a state of sporadic mayhem, restrained only by ONUC, into virtual civil war. Kasavubu dismissed Lumumba; the latter responded in kind. Colonel Mobutu formed a new government by military coup but was only partially successful. The army split and a fresh secessionist movement erupted in the diamond-bearing Kasai province. Any hope of ONUC creating stable government and adequate forces of law and order disappeared. The East/West consensus in the UN evaporated with the West backing Kasavubu/Mobutu, the East Lumumba, leaving no generally accepted government for ONUC to deal with, Hammarskjold still determined not to take sides.

The Congo crisis had brought to fruition an emerging pattern of international attitudes to the 'Third World' and its problems which was to crystallize in the United Nations for the next three decades. Throughout the 1950s, there had been mounting agitation about racial discrimination (apartheid) in South Africa. But this had not seriously affected East/West relations, and the Africans were insufficiently represented in New York to build up a significant head of steam. The events of 1960 wrought profound change. In April, not long after Prime Minister Harold Macmillan had told an unenthusiastic white Parliament in Cape Town that a wind of change was blowing through Africa and that they would be well advised to take note of it, a unit of the South African security forces opened fire on a demonstration in Sharpeville, killing about seventy people. This was a turning point. The world reacted with outrage; the South African government with a policy of ruthless repression which persisted for thirty years. In Cairo, where I was at the time, Nasser, the Middle East being relatively quiescent, was developing the African dimension of 'positive neutrality and non-alignment', the Soviet Ambassador being the most influential diplomat in town. Even so, there was still a South African diplomatic mission in Cairo (in Beirut as well) and an important South African technical assistance programme in Egypt, i.e. something to lose by the adoption of a policy of self-righteous condemnation. It took the regime two or three days to decide how to react to Sharpeville, indeed to let the Egyptian people share in the knowledge of the massacre. Then the heavy progaganda artillery thundered and the South Africans were sent packing: it did not escape attention that the two old imperialists, Britain and France, were the only abstainers on the very mild Security Council resolution (the first time that apartheid had appeared on the Council's agenda), which did no more than 'deplore' the 'recent disturbances and loss of life' as well as the policies and actions of the South African government, which was 'called upon' to abandon apartheid and racial discrimination.

By the summer, the apostles of non-alignment, enthusiastically supported by the Soviet Union and its baggage train, were busy dividing Africa into angels (Nkrumah of Ghana, Sekou Touré of Guinea, Lumumba, The African National Congress and, of course, Nasser himself) and demons (the imperialists, principally Britain and France, and their 'stooges', such as the apartheid regime in South Africa, Tshombe in Katanga and all others who maintained cordial relations with the West). Nasser was in fact laying across the continent of Africa the same template which he had designed for the Arab world. Cairo seethed with African students and exiled political groups from as yet undecolonized territories. A sardonic Egyptian remarked to my wife that the national literacy campaign had been facilitated by the fact that it was necessary only to be able to read the word 'Lumumba' in a banner headline to claim to be literate. I could have added that the Arabic word for 'imperialism' was a close competitor of 'Lumumba' in the headline frequency stakes.

This policy of categorization carried increased conviction because of the magnitude of Western commercial interests in Africa, their support for local politicians who were swimming against the tide of national liberation followed by socialist non-alignment, the stubborn struggle of France against Algerian independence, Western sympathy with the African policy of the Portuguese dictatorship, the fact that the ruling 'white minorities' were mainly of British origin, and other similar factors, all of which played into the hands of the activists in Cairo, Accra, Belgrade, Djakarta, New Delhi and elsewhere.

At the opening of the regular session of the General Assembly in September (after the Kasavubu-Lumumba split) these swirling waters converged into a torrent on the Congo question. The debate was attended by most of the leading actors, including Nasser, Khrushchev, Macmillan, Nkrumah and Eisenhower. Fortunately for the demons, Khrushchev, not for the only time, overplayed his hand. The undignified shoe-banging episode during Macmillan's speech was not an unqualified success in the solemn surroundings of the 'August Body', even with admirers of the Soviet Union, while his intemperate and poisonous attack on Hammarskjold and the Secretariat over their conduct of the Congo operation, and his proposal for replacement of the Secretary-General by a 'troika' of East, West and non-aligned officials, backfired seriously, as evidenced by the ovation given to Hammarskjold's robust response.

Meanwhile, the Security Council had split and, against the opposition of the Soviet Union and Poland, with France abstaining, the debate was transferred on 17 September to the General Assembly under the Uniting for Peace procedure. The Assembly then adopted by seventy votes with no opposition a resolution strongly supporting the Secretary-General and including much of the other language which the Soviet Union had opposed in the Council. This was a clear signal to Moscow that, whatever suspicions there might be and however bitterly loyalties might be strained, the Africans and Asians were still determined to back the UN operation and not allow Cold War rivalries to open up irreparable splits.

There were by now four separate governments in the Congo, namely the secessionists in Katanga and Kasai, Kasavubu and Mobutu in Leopoldville and Gizenga representing Lumumba in his stronghold of Stanleyville (Lumumba himself was under UN protection in Leopold-ville). It was only at the end of the year that the General Assembly, by a narrow margin, recognized Kasavubu and his delegation as the legitimate government, providing the Secretary-General with an inter-locutor without infringing the mandate regarding avoidance of taking sides. On the ground, chaos was recurring, and ONUC suffered casualties in ambushes and other attacks by ANC units.

The UN now found itself mired in the travails of a classic civil war in which each contending party expected international support, where the Great Powers were themselves divided between support for differ-ent contestants, where almost universal obloquy poured onto the Secretariat, and where ONUC could do little more than protect leading Congolese politicians from each other, and try to mediate temporary truces and cease-fires between warring military units. More-over, the loyalty of some of the African contingents in ONUC was being stretched as troop-contributing governments took sides. The downward spiral was given a violent twist in February 1961 when Lumumba and some companions unwisely left their UN-protected base in Leopoldville, and, after being arrested by Mobutu, were handed over to their adversaries in Katanga and murdered.

This outrage had widespread consequences. Inevitably it exacerbated the fighting between pro- and anti-Lumumbist factions. It set off a wave of anti-Belgian sentiment in Africa and several nations withdrew their contingents from ONUC. In Cairo an unedifying drama was enacted. It was clear that there would be a 'spontaneous' expression of indignation outside the Belgian Embassy. The spontaneity was under-lined by the arrival in an empty street of Egyptian press, radio and the newly established television service. I was able to watch this charade from our Embassy windows across the road. A large procession, almost entirely black African, arrived some time later, closely escorted by Egyptian security forces. Fists were shaken at the representatives of British imperialism as the crowd straggled past. Slogans were bellowed, the cameras turned; suddenly it all went wrong. The Africans, men of sterner stuff than docile Egyptian demonstrators, brushed the police aside, stormed the building and set it on fire. This was not in the script. The Belgian staff had an uncomfortable time: I remember seeing them jumping out of windows, some on the first floor, into the back garden as the building burned. Some of the crowd decided to bombard our building and parked cars with stones. Pulling the cars back out of range, with the foreign press representatives urging us on with derisive cheers from the demonstrators' side of the railings, provided a lively distraction from our normal duties.

Lumumba's murder galvanized the Security Council back into a semblance of consensus. After a difficult debate at the end of which the Soviet Union vetoed some of the wording in a draft resolution, the Council adopted a detailed resolution (France and the Soviet Union abstaining) urging the UN to take all appropriate measures to prevent civil war in the Congo, including the use of force if necessary; also urging the evacuation of all Belgian and other foreign military personnel not under UN command, including mercenaries; plus the convening of Parliament and the reorganization of Congolese armed units so that they could not interfere in the political life of the country.

This resolution had no parallel in UN history. The Council had authorized a 'non-threatening' peacekeeping force, neither mandated nor equipped to fight a campaign, to adopt an enforcement role without first determining that a threat to international peace and security existed, i.e. without a formal move to Chapter VII of the Charter, still less the adoption as a first expedient of non-military coercive measures such as economic sanctions. It also left the command and control of such an enforcement operation in the virtually unfettered hands of the Secretary-General, a procedure anathema to Charter purists such as the Soviet Union.

This hybrid was the best the Council could do in the dense labyrinth of the Congo. The Soviet Union had broken off relations with Hammarskjold (as they had done with his predecessor, Trygve Lie, ten years earlier) but were not ready for an all-out confrontation, either with the United States which was backing the Secretary-General and his staff, or with their new Afro-Asian friends who, for all the rhetorical fulminations, still supported the Secretariat operation. Britain and France, sympathetic to Belgium and with important financial interests in breakaway Katanga which was also developing close relations with the (British) Central African Federation of the two Rhodesias and Nyasaland, would have vetoed any enforcement action directed specifically against Belgium. The sum total of this and previous resolutions was that the UN was committed to maintain the integrity of the Congo within its independence borders, and actively to bring the civil war to a conclusion.

An immediate consequence was the assumption by ANC forces loyal to the Leopoldville (Kasavubu-Mobutu) and Stanleyville (Gizenga) factions that the UN was about to crush them. This led to attacks on ONUC units. In March the Sudanese garrison was driven from the Atlantic port of Matadi. In April forty-four Ghanaian troops were killed in an attack on Port-Francqui and, in November, Stanleyville ANC killed thirteen Italian ONUC aircrew. On the other side, in March/April ONUC units intervened in northern Katanga to prevent the Katanga gendarmerie, led by white mercenaries, from crushing anti-Tshombe forces. ONUC established control over the area.

After a series of abortive round-table conferences, ONUC succeeded in persuading all the political leaders, including Kalonji of the Kasai (whose secession had been overwhelmed by Lumumbist forces after a massacre of about a thousand tribesmen) and Tshombe of South Katanga, to agree to the reconvening of the Parliament, a step considered essential by a UN commission temporarily established by the General Assembly resolution of September 1960. In August 1961, a government of national unity under the moderate Cyrille Adoula as Prime Minister was formed with parliamentary approval. The Secretary-General confirmed that the UN would deal with it and provide it with all possible assistance. Gizenga, who served briefly as Deputy Prime Minister, shortly afterwards defected to Stanleyville; but his attempt at secession was defeated by Central Government forces.

However, the Katanga problem was unsolved. Tshombe's assent to the government of national unity was half-hearted and, although the UN succeeded in late August in rounding up and expelling a large number of the mercenaries, Katanga was still financed by the great mining company, Union Minière du Haut-Katanga, armed from European sources and buttressed by hundreds of 'seconded' Belgian officers and mercenaries in the *gendarmerie*. It was also impossible to prevent the expelled mercenaries from re-infiltrating the province. In mid-September, the *gendarmerie* counter-attacked ONUC and, thanks to the use of a jet aircraft piloted by a mercenary, was able to gain a temporary advantage.

On 17 September, Dag Hammarskjold and members of his staff

were killed when their aircraft crashed short of Ndola in Northern Rhodesia, where Hammarskjold was flying to meet Tshombe in an attempt to reconcile him to Prime Minister Adoula in Leopoldville.

This tragedy, like Lumumba's murder, galvanized all parties into action. The UN representative in Leopoldville quickly negotiated a cease-fire between the Katanga *gendarmerie* and ONUC, but this was comprehensively broken by the Katangese who regarded Hammarskjold's death as a major victory. ONUC was reinforced with Ethiopian, Indian and Swedish jet fighters to neutralize the air power of the *gendarmerie*. ANC and Katangese units clashed in northern Katanga.

In November, the Security Council met and adopted a tough resolution (France and Britain abstaining) deprecating Katanga secession and armed action against UN forces, authorizing the Secretary-General to take vigorous action, including the use of force, for the apprehension and deportation of all foreign military and para-military personnel and political advisers not under UN command and mercenaries, requesting states not to supply military equipment or support activities and declaring support for the Central Government of the Congo. The whole thrust of the resolution was directed against the actions of the Katanga leadership and in support of the integrity of the Congo.

This resolution sparked off a violent anti-UN response in Elizabethville, including the severe beating up of my old friend, Brian Urquhart, and two of his companions, by mercenary-inspired 'para-commandos', the murder of an Indian soldier and the abduction of an Indian officer. The *gendarmerie* mounted a campaign of provocative obstruction of ONUC which eventually responded with force. By mid-December ONUC had re-established authority and Tshombe had agreed to respect Central Government authority and the constitution, although he fell short of full abandonment of secession. By June 1962 talks initiated by Prime Minister Adoula in order to persuade Katanga to rejoin the fold had petered out. Tshombe's bobbing and weaving had resumed and, in July, he celebrated Katanga Independence Day with gratuitous fanfare: harassment of ONUC began again. In August the new Secretary-General, U Thant, proposed a Plan of National Reconciliation: again Tshombe equivocated. In December the *gendarmerie* resumed provocative attacks on ONUC. This time the response was decisive. By the end of the year ONUC forces were in full control of Elizabethville and its environs. Ghanaian and Swedish troops had occupied Kamina (one of the original Belgian bases). In the New Year, in spite of threats to dynamite the mining operations, Irish and Indian troops advanced and occupied the remaining towns. Gendarmerie resistance was less than anticipated and the rebellion was over; on 14 January Tshombe ended the secession of Katanga, granted ONUC full freedom of movement and accepted the Plan of National Reconciliation. On 21 January Indian troops entered the last stronghold, Kolwezi. The gendarmerie had ceased to exist as a fighting force.

In February 1963 the Secretary-General was able to report to the Security Council that there was no threat to Congolese independence, that the mandate to prevent civil war had been fulfilled, as well as the removal of foreign military personnel and mercenaries, and that, with the general improvement in law and order, a substantial reduction of ONUC was taking place. In September, the Secretary-General reported his intention to phase out ONUC by the end of the year, with the exception of a small element to remain for six months at the Prime Minister's request. On 30 June 1964, ONUC withdrew in its entirety. In the four-year period the force had lost nearly 250 dead, had experienced five successive commanders (from Sweden, Ireland, Ethiopia, Norway and Nigeria) and had comprised units from thirty countries. Twenty-five years would pass before another UN peacekeeping force would deploy in sub-Saharan Africa.

During and after the events of 1960–64, analysis of the Congo crisis was and still is clouded by the elaboration of conspiracy theories and the search for hidden agendas. Was there a Great Power intelligence agency behind the murder of Lumumba and, if so, which one? What were the inner realities of French and, even more so, British policies, the latter still deeply engaged in the affairs of Central and Southern Africa? Did their reluctant participation in the Security Council consensus cloak machinations such as linking breakaway Katanga with Northern Rhodesia or the whole Central African Federation? Why was the Soviet Union so obsessively anti-Hammarskjold? Was this because the UN had threatened a grand Soviet/African design? At a more practical level, did the Secretariat commit the mistakes so readily laid at its door, for example in failing to disarm the *Force Publique*/ANC from the outset, in maintaining impartiality between the parties when it could have given all-out support to a centralist, a federalist, or even a confederalist solution? Would not the break-up of the Congo have been preferable to the abandonment of the country to the rapacity of the supreme lootocrat, Mobutu, who has succeeded in reducing one of the richest countries in Africa to grinding poverty and economic collapse thanks to his single-minded pursuit of personal wealth?

In my narrative, I have resisted the temptation to explore these intriguing byways and have tried to stick to the main road, namely the evolution of the Security Council mandate and the success or otherwise of the two Secretaries-General, Hammarskjold and U Thant, their staffs and ONUC itself in carrying it out. Looked at from this viewpoint, the operation was a success. Against appalling odds, bombarded by criticism and invective, working in the uncharted territory of domestic conflict in a newly independent state at a time of maximal East/West rivalry, the UN operation maintained the integrity of the state (the principal preoccupation of African governments), helped to restore law and order, mediated the end of the civil war and brought about the removal of disruptive European and other elements from the scene. Had it not been for the UN operation, there can be little doubt that the Congo would have disintegrated, that the infection of fragmentation would have spread throughout the continent, and that the Soviet Union and the United States, with their respective allies, would have entered the fray on behalf of opposing sides in a mounting number of mutually hostile, tribally based territories – in short, a multiplicity of Angolas.

It was fortunate in this regard that the Great Powers were in the last resort prepared to be guided by the desiderata of the African Group. Although the Africans were split between 'radicals' (Nasser's UAR, Ghana, Guinea, etc.) and 'moderates' (the majority of the former French territories), both were united, when the chips were down, on the necessity to maintain Congolese integrity, and thus on support for the UN operation, the only hope. The Soviet Union learnt the lesson (which it was not slow to exploit in the UN over the next quarter century) that, if a Great Power wishes to curry favour with and support from a group of states over which it has neither strategic, economic or historical influence, its best course is to follow not to try to lead, viz. the failure of the assault on Hammarskjold and of the 'troika' proposal.

However, although the operation would probably have foundered without the dynamism, skill and political courage of Dag Hammarskjold over the first fifteen months, his successors absorbed the twice taught lesson that, in the long term, a Secretary-General needs at least minimal support from all the Permanent Members and all the major geographical groups in order to carry out the duties of his office adequately. The chances are that, if Hammarskjold had not died at Ndola, the Soviet boycott would have accomplished his political death as it did with Trygve Lie. His three successors in the Cold War years – U Thant, Waldheim and Perez de Cuellar – went out of their way, too far in my judgement, to avoid giving offence to major UN players, in particular the two superpowers. In Waldheim's last years, I used to wonder whether the rubric about the 'need to protect the Office' had not been so rigorously followed as to render the Office scarcely worth protecting.

As I have suggested, the Congo operation broke new ground in the history of UN military involvement. It bore no relation to the two large-scale military enforcement operations – Korea 1950–54 and the Gulf Crisis 1990–91 – where the Security Council delegated responsibility to American-led military coalitions to fight major campaigns. It bore some resemblance to 'traditional' peacekeeping – the monitoring of truce or cease-fire lines by unarmed observers or lightly armed forces, examples being UNTSO, UNEF 1, UNEF 2 in the Middle East, UNMOGIP and UNIPOM in India-Pakistan. ONUC, as with all other peacekeeping operations, was deployed with the consent of or at the invitation of the party or parties, and command and control of the whole operation was delegated by the Council to the Secretariat, not to a member state or group of states.

There the resemblances end. The Congo was the ancestor of later UN involvement in civil wars – El Salvador and Cambodia being contemporary examples in which the UN operations have been as successful as they were in the Congo – where the military task is more complex and demanding and where it is complemented by a range of civilian activities designed to reconstruct a ruined state. This combination puts a far heavier burden on the Secretary-General and his staff than a straightforward peacekeeping operation. In addition, as I have mentioned earlier, ONUC was mandated in mid-stream to move from its original 'non-threatening' role to enforcement. This is now happening again, with mixed results; Somalia and Bosnia being examples.

Are there lessons to be drawn from the Congo for some of the stickier crises in which the UN is currently mired, such as Bosnia, Somalia and Angola? Probably not. The handling of the Congo crisis reflected the climate of the times in more senses than one. It was not only that Cold War rivalry diluted the Security Council consensus. The United States was a newcomer to African affairs just as the majority of African states were newcomers to independence. Britain and France, although in decline, were still important powers in the African continent. If the worst came to the worst, Belgium could have counted on their veto, and South Africa was still on the early rungs of the ladder to pariah status. There was also a more robust attitude all round to suffering casualties in civil wars. France only gave up in Algeria halfway through the Congo crisis, and the American Calvary in Vietnam lay in the future. The contemporary political judgment in the Western world that public opinion will allow governments to send their soldiers to fight and die only where an emotive national interest – the Falklands – or a crucial strategic commodity – Middle East oil – is in question, was yet to evolve. When the eleven African and three Asian governments, plus Ireland and Sweden, committed infantry units to the Congo, they knew that they might have to fight rather than act only as diplomats in uniform. When the time came, they did not flinch and the bluff of the opposition was successfully called. Today there is a marked reluctance to act similarly in order to prevent Bosnians from tormenting and killing Bosnians, or Somalis Somalis, and so on. The Vietnam syndrome has spread its infection far beyond the frontiers of the United States.

CHAPTER SIX

South Africa – Apartheid

Apartheid in South Africa occupies a unique position in the demonology of the United Nations. Cold War antagonisms, decolonization, and the Palestine problem have generated heavy barrages of rhetorical artillery in the General Assembly, the Security Council and other UN organs about the foreign and domestic policies of member states. Zionism in particular has had a hard time since 1967, and I have heard the rafters of the Security Council ring with denunciations of it on countless occasions. But, even in the context of Palestine, the Council has confined itself in its resolutions to areas within its competence, e.g. withdrawal from occupied territories, observance of the Geneva Conventions, acceptance of Palestinian rights and so forth. Only in the case of South Africa has the Council regarded the internal structure of a member state as relevant to international peace and security, and has applied itself, along with virtually the whole of the UN 'family', to bringing about a fundamental change in the way in which that member orders its domestic affairs.

This long and bitter campaign was not a direct consequence merely of white minority rule over the black majority, which had been going on for three centuries in South Africa and was, from the nineteenth century, a commonplace elsewhere. It is worth recording that South Africa was a well-regarded founder member of both the League of Nations and the United Nations. General (later Field Marshal and Prime Minister) Smuts was the effective creator of the League of Nations mandate system and made a major contribution to the drafting of the Covenant as a whole. He also prepared the first draft of the Preamble of the United Nations Charter with its fine sentiments about faith in fundamental human rights, the dignity and worth of the human person, and the equal rights of men and women. What gave rise to world-wide abhorrence and reduced South Africa to the status of a pariah was the formal, statutory institution by the ruling National Party after 1948 of apartheid, a system which condemned people, regardless of their intellectual, social or economic qualifications, to inferior status in all fields of human activity simply because of the colour of their skin. The repressive and violent methods used to sustain this monstrous structure, including bantustans, pass laws, separate residence, enforced movement of peoples and destruction and seizure of their property, fuelled international condemnation. Agitation mounted in the General Assembly and other UN bodies as the membership increased as a result of decolonization. As early as 1952, the Assembly established a three-nation commission to look into South African racial policies. It was refused entry by the South African government which rejected all attempts to open discussions on the subject. In this regard, South Africa was not alone in invoking Article 2 (7) of the Charter, which precludes UN intervention in the domestic affairs of states. This article was cherished by the majority of members, including the Eastern Europeans, the old Western imperial powers and others who, albeit each for a different reason, had no intention of allowing the UN to pry into their affairs.

As I mentioned in the previous chapter on the Congo crisis, the Sharpeville massacre of March 1960 broke through the barrier of Article 2 (7). For the first time, the Security Council debated a southern African problem. The mildness of the resolution, 'recognizing' that the state of affairs in South Africa 'might' endanger international peace and security, 'deploring' (not condemning) the loss of life, as well as the policies and actions of the South African government and 'calling upon' (not demanding) the government to abandon apartheid, was a measure of the nervousness accompanying this intrusion into domestic affairs. Even so, Britain and France, the former especially with much unfinished decolonization business on its hands, abstained. The rest of the Council voted in favour.

The escalation of the apartheid debate and its progressive permeation of all UN bodies coincided with the onset of decolonization fever in the Organization, a condition which has persisted almost to the present day. Until 1960, the discourse between the handful of African and Asian states on the one hand and the imperial powers on the other had been intermittently touchy but far from rancorous. Britain and France had generally succeeded in warding off, on the grounds of Article 2 (7), over-intrusive probing into constitutional developments in their dependent territories. However, in December 1960, the Assembly, with its new Afro-Asian majority, overwhelmingly adopted the famous Resolution 1514 (originally a Soviet initiative), which blew another gaping

hole in Article 2 (7) and substituted for the previous leisurely dialogue
a harsh, confrontational atmosphere in which it became almost a crime
against humanity to possess dependent territories. Resolution 1514
stated that the subjection of peoples to 'alien subjugation' was a denial
of human rights, was contrary to the Charter and an impediment to
world peace. It called in effect for immediate, unconditional independence for all territories, and its functional committee (the Committee of
Twenty-four), established a year later, developed into an officious
ginger group, harrying all administering powers to complete the cycle
of total decolonization without delay.

Since the major imperial powers, Britain and France, were already
embarked on this road, indeed far down it, except where internal,
strategic or external complications were delaying independence, the
Committee of Twenty-four, its parent the Fourth Committee of the
Assembly and the Assembly itself, focused attention with ever increasing vigour on the most intractable problems of Africa. These consisted
of the Portuguese African territories, which Portugal claimed as overseas provinces, not as non-self-governing territories in the Charter
sense of the phrase; Southern Rhodesia, where Britain had granted
self-government to the tiny white minority in 1923; and Namibia,
which South Africa had been ruling as a part of the Union in all but
name since 1920.

It was against this background that the question of apartheid began
to pepper the Security Council agenda. It was a scenario for an East/
West/Non-Aligned drama which at times rivalled the Middle East
debates in its intensity. Historically it is no longer easy to disentangle
the threads. The genuine decolonization questions – the Portuguese
territories until 1975, Southern Rhodesia from the illegal declaration
of independence in 1965 to the independence of Zimbabwe in 1980,
and Namibia until its independence in 1989 – continually merged with
the issue of apartheid as the non-racist Portuguese were forced into an
alliance of convenience with the Union, as Salisbury and Pretoria
became more difficult to regard as distinct entities, and as South
African-style government was progressively extended to Namibia.
After the Portuguese revolution of 1974, the remaining three issues
increasingly coalesced in the UN glossary as problems of 'illegal,
minority, racist regimes'.

This conjuncture provided the ideal arena for the Soviet Union in
its pursuit of the hearts and minds of the Non-Aligned and of the

discrediting of the West in their eyes. It was easy to line up on the side of the angels by simply following in the tracks of the African Group and occasionally urging them to challenge Western policies more fiercely. The Soviet Union had nothing to lose by posing as the unambiguous champion of national liberation and proffering moral and material aid to African liberation movements. This posturing helped to cloak the fact that the Soviet Union was in practice the old Russian Empire, writ large and undecolonized. Unlike the Middle East, the risk of provoking a military superpower confrontation in Africa was minimal. The Soviet Union had no historical, strategic or material interests in southern Africa, certainly no influence in anti-communist Pretoria. The West on the other hand was wide open to accusations of secret sympathy with and support for the 'racist minority regime' while hypocritically professing rejection of its policy. Strategically the Cape of Good Hope sea lanes were important for the global projection of naval power: Britain had a naval base at Simonstown near Cape Town into the 1970s. Following the closure of the Suez Canal after the June War of 1967, super-tankers were built to carry Middle Eastern crude oil round the Cape to Western refineries. Western commercial and financial interests and investment in South Africa were substantial and southern Africa was an important source of gold, diamonds and strategic metals which were otherwise obtainable mainly from the Soviet Union. Britain's historical and ethnic links in South Africa, fortified by joint military action in two World Wars, were manifested in membership of the Commonwealth (from which South Africa was forced to withdraw in 1961 after Sharpeville). All these considerations inevitably tempered genuine Western antipathy to apartheid while, on the other hand, the former French African states and the new Commonwealth members were urging France and Britain respectively to take a tougher line.

The strategy of the African Group in the Security Council, confident of majority support, including that of two of the Permanent Members (the Soviet Union and China), was to seek the acquiescence of the Western Permanent Members in incrementally stronger language and coercive measures to oblige the South African government to change course. In 1963 the Council adopted a resolution (Britain and France abstaining) imposing a non-mandatory arms embargo. In 1964 the Rivonia trials (as a result of which Nelson Mandela and others were to spend the next quarter of a century in prison) stimulated two further resolutions (on one of which Britain, France and the US abstained) urging the end of the trials, amnesty and the help of all states to induce the South Africans to comply.

In 1970 the Council condemned violation of the arms embargo (Britain, France and the US abstaining) and set out detailed measures to strengthen it. This call was reiterated (France abstaining) two years later along with further condemnation of apartheid, and recognition of the 'legitimacy of the struggle of the oppressed people in South Africa'. In 1974, shortly after the General Assembly had ousted the South African delegation from its seat on a credentials vote, the African Group went for broke by forcing to the vote a draft resolution recommending the expulsion of South Africa from the United Nations. It received ten votes in favour, one above the required minimum, from the USSR, China, Cameroon, Kenya, Mauritania, Byelorussia, Iraq, Indonesia, Peru and Australia. Austria and Costa Rica abstained, and the resolution ran into a triple veto from the US, Britain and France. It was too much for the long-embarrassed West to swallow. They had throughout combined expressions of hatred for and rejection of apartheid with refusal to go along with menacing language – Britain and the US regularly opposed or abstained on almost all the large crop of resolutions in the annual sessions of the Assembly – on the grounds that only persuasion would oblige South Africa to mend its ways. The South African government gave no encouragement to the protagonists of this theory.

As the 1970s progressed, Western exasperation with South Africa and Non-Aligned, including Commonwealth, pressure mounted. In 1976 and 1977 resolutions were unanimously adopted reiterating familiar demands and propositions, such as the legitimacy of the anti-apartheid struggle by the people of South Africa and that apartheid 'seriously disturbed international peace and security', a strong hint that mandatory measures were at last in the offing. In late 1977, the crossing of this Rubicon was accomplished on a narrow front. With President Carter in office in Washington, the Labour party in power in London, the Social Democratic party in Bonn and Canada, with West Germany, the other Western non-permanent member of the Council, the odds were stacked against Pretoria as never before. After a flurry of three vetoed drafts, each of which received ten positive votes, with the Western five voting against notions such as the threat of invocation of the military articles of the Charter, and a ban on investments in and loans to South Africa, agreement was reached on a Chapter VII mandatory arms embargo, including non-cooperation with South Africa in the manufacture and development of nuclear weapons, plus the creation of a Security Council Committee to monitor implementation and to study ways of making the embargo more effective. The two resolutions were unanimous, the result of hard negotiations. Seventeen years after Sharpeville, thirteen years after the incarceration of Mandela and many others, after the bloody suppression of demonstrations, savage restrictions on the human rights of all except the white population, the creation of bantustans, the imposition of pass laws and all the paraphernalia of the apartheid system, the Western powers had at last agreed to a coercive rather than a persuasive approach.

However, the comprehensive mandatory arms embargo, the first of its kind ever imposed by the United Nations, proved worse than useless. South Africa had experienced little difficulty in circumventing the voluntary embargo and it had acquired the technological know-how and industrial base to switch from imports to local manufacture. Thanks to the stimulus of sanctions and the consequent need for self-sufficiency, South Africa quickly became a net exporter of military hardware and is now probably among the top ten in the global league table. Moreover, through technological cooperation with another 'unofficial' nuclear power, South Africa was in a position to test its first nuclear weapon by late 1979. I remember the press report reaching the General Assembly of a mysterious flash in the South Atlantic. Widespread suspicion was aroused, which was only partially allayed by American reassurance that it was not a test. We now know from President de Klerk's revelation of 1993 that it almost certainly was. The President admitted that South Africa possessed nuclear weapons of its own manufacture which were being scrapped (presumably out of fear that they would fall into the hands of an ANC dominated government). Perhaps the greatest irony of all was the unanimous adoption of Resolution 558 in December 1984 requesting all states to stop importing arms, ammunition and military vehicles produced in South Africa!

Throughout the 1980s, the diplomatic battle between the Council and South Africa continued with a slight tilt towards the latter as governments less unsympathetic to South Africa took over in Washington and London. Several calls for commutation of death sentences were unanimously adopted, as were, with occasional American and British abstentions, condemnations of apartheid, of the introduction of the limited 'new constitution' in 1984, of arbitrary arrests, police massacres, the bantustan policy, etc., etc. From 1985 there were specific calls for Nelson Mandela's release. Three attempts, in 1985, 1987, and 1988, to extend mandatory sanctions were vetoed by the US and Britain, France joining the abstainers.

Outside the Council the UN had over the years constructed an elaborate anti-apartheid apparatus. Apart from the hundreds of resolutions adopted in various bodies, a Special Committee on Apartheid was created in 1962 serviced by a Centre against Apartheid. A Trust Fund to help the victims of apartheid was created in 1965, an Education and Training Programme in 1967, and a Commission against apartheid in Sports. In 1973 a Convention was adopted on the Suppression and Punishment of the Crime of Apartheid which characterized it as a crime against humanity. The Assembly also imposed a wide range of voluntary sanctions, including an oil embargo.

All these measures were replicated in regional organizations, in functional bodies such as the Commonwealth and the Non-Aligned Movement and in arrays of non-governmental organizations. By the time President P.W. Botha embarked on his tentative and limited programme of reforms in the 1980s, a kind of global anti-apartheid wall was in place. In these circumstances it was scarcely surprising that, in 1984, the Security Council, against American and British abstentions, declared null and void the 'new constitution' which extended the franchise to peoples of mixed race and Asian descent, but not to black South Africans, and stated that only the establishment of a non-racial, democratic society could improve South Africa's position. Another powerful resolution was adopted later in the year reiterating earlier condemnations, demanding the eradication of apartheid and the dismantling of the bantustan structure. In 1985 the Council unanimously condemned the killing of African protesters and the arrest of United Democratic Front members, and also called for the release of political prisoners, including Nelson Mandela. Similar demands were repeated a few months later, calling also for specific measures (which evoked British and American abstentions).

The South African government showed no sign of acceding to any of these demands, nor to the 'constructive engagement' persuadings of the Reagan Administration (see Chapter 7 on Namibia). The British government too was committed to persuasion rather than coercion. But a Commonwealth 'Group of Eminent Persons', commissioned by a Summit Meeting in 1985, which had extensive discussions in South Africa in 1986, was also rebuffed. The subsequent list of sanctions adopted by the Commonwealth specifically excluded Britain, which adopted a much smaller range. The South African problem was isolating Britain within the Commonwealth just as Southern Rhodesia had done in previous years.

However, change was in the air. Under strong domestic public pressure, the United States adopted certain sanctions bilaterally and the Western private sector began to pull out of the Republic. Investment declined sharply. The European Community and the Commonwealth, with Britain frequently in exasperated isolation, adopted a progressively tough attitude. The international searchlight focused with increased intensity on the release of Nelson Mandela. The Security Council concentrated its fire of condemnation of South African raids on its neighbours and seeking commutation of death sentences passed on political activists.

By the end of the decade the scenery of the international stage was undergoing profound change. As with the unwinding of the Namibian knot, the end of the Cold War exercised a powerful catalytic effect on the forces already undermining the ramshackle structure of apartheid. This global upheaval was more influential than any amount of UN rhetoric, Security Council resolutions, Commonwealth and European Community pressure and Anglo/American cajoling. With the withdrawal of Soviet engagement, the African National Congress and its allies realized that the days of 'moral and material support' had gone. Equally, if not more importantly, the white South African leadership understood that, with the end of the ideological competition between Russian-led communism and American-led capitalism, they were no longer manning a redoubt which the Western powers, however critical of apartheid, would defend in the last ditch, namely the consistent refusal to acquiesce in mandatory action by the Security Council as manifested by forty-five Western vetoes on matters affecting South Africa between 1974 and 1988. Commercial and financial interests in South Africa, a small to medium sized economy in global terms, were not in themselves large enough to warrant the endurance of international opprobrium in their defence.

After President de Klerk succeeded President Botha in 1989, the government and the ANC committed themselves to a negotiated settlement. In December the General Assembly issued a Declaration on Apartheid and its Destructive Consequences. In February 1990 Nelson Mandela and other political prisoners were released, and political organizations were unbanned. In 1990 and 1991, discrimatory acts of legislation, the 'pillars of apartheid', were repealed. By the end of 1991 constitutional discussions began. It was a hard slog, repeatedly interrupted and accompanied by terrible violence in the townships. At last, in November 1993, the Multi-Party Negotiating Council adopted principles and institutions to guide South Africa through a transitional period to the elections of 27 April 1994.

In the new post-Cold War atmosphere of sweetness and light, the UN switched through 180 degrees to match this breath-taking series of developments. Judged from outside, my successors did not have to endure the clouds of surly suspicion and mischief making which I had to work so hard to allay at the equivalent stage in the denouement of the Southern Rhodesian problem. The harsh language of the past disappeared from the reports and resolutions of the Special Committee on Apartheid and the General Assembly. Exhortation replaced condemnation, the principal preoccupations being township violence, as well as social and economic development. For the first time ever, Assembly resolutions on South Africa were adopted by consensus.

In June 1992, the OAU called for a meeting the of Security Council to consider the problem of violence. In contrast to Southern Rhodesian debates, invitations to participate were extended not only to South Africa and the ANC but also to the heads of government of the bantustans and leading members of other 'internal' communities and parties, including the Inkatha leader, Chief Buthelezi. Resolution 765 condemned the escalating violence, urged the South African government to bring it to an end, called upon all the parties to cooperate in combating violence and invited the Secretary-General to appoint a Special Representative for South Africa to recommend measures to create conditions for a peaceful transition to a democratic, non-racial and united South Africa. The Secretary-General appointed Cyrus Vance, formerly American Secretary of State. As a result of his report, the Council met again in August and adopted Resolution 772 which, among other things, authorized the deployment of thirty observers to help with the implementation of the all-party National Peace Accord of 1991 in South Africa. Thirty-two years after the first Council debate on apartheid, the UN had at last established a presence on the ground in South Africa with the agreement of the government. At the end of the year ten more observers were added to the strength of the UN observer mission in South Africa (UNOMSA). By late 1993 the total had risen to one hundred.

In January 1994, in response to one of the Secretary-General's periodic reports to the Security Council, it was agreed in Resolution 894 that the mandate of the UN mission (UNOMSA) (originally to help peace committees in townships) should be expanded to a strength of 2,840 observers (including some from the OAU, the Commonwealth and the European Union). A little earlier, in the autumn of 1993, the General Assembly, the governments of Australia and Canada, the US (including the City of New York and the States of California and Massachusetts), the Commonwealth, the European Union, and the Organization of African Unity lifted all their sanctions against South Africa. Only the Security Council arms embargo remained in force.

The UN took no further initiatives in the run-up to the elections which was characterized by appalling bloodshed, mainly between the Zulu-dominated Inkatha Freedom Party and the ANC, and acts of terrorism by the extreme right. Inkatha agreed to participate at the last moment and the elections took place as planned between 26 and 28 April, one of the most moving events in world history since the end of the Second World War.

It is extremely difficult accurately to evaluate the influence of the pressure of the United Nations anti-apartheid machinery on the evolution of South Africa between 1960 (Sharpeville) and 1990 (the formal abolition of apartheid). The number of speeches and resolutions made and adopted in the General Assembly and other UN bodies must run into several thousands. In the Security Council seven draft resolutions focused specifically on apartheid were vetoed and nearly thirty adopted over the same period. Each of these exercises in the Council involved more than one session and it was the practice of the African Group and its closest supporters to participate *en masse* in the debates, even though there were three African non-permanent Council members. This meant that thousands of speeches were made in the Council: I myself must have listened to several hundred.

However, because of the resolve of the Western Permanent Members to protect South Africa against mandatory action imposed by the Security Council, with the exception of the 1977 arms embargo which acted more as a stimulant than a depressant to South Africa's military capability, all this massed artillery of the international community was firing blank ammunition: certainly the South African government publicly treated it as such and, I imagine, presented it to their own people as the impotent howlings of Afro-Asian busybodies many of whom had cupboards bursting with human rights skeletons more grisly than anything happening in South Africa. Many Western politicians would argue that the public campaign was counter-productive, fortifying the South African backs-to-the-wall laager mentality and that the Western prohibition of stronger action was not only protective of Western strategic and other interests, but also a positive contribution to the eventual moderation of the South African attitude, leading to the abandonment of apartheid.

There is no doubt that the UN anti-apartheid campaign helped to create a major shift in the international climate, which resulted in South Africa's almost total ostracism from participation in international activities in which it would, at the creation of the UN, have expected to play a significant part, for example membership of the relevant geographical group, an appropriate quota of jobs in the Secretariat, and periodic membership of the Security Council, ECOSOC and a multitude of subsidiary bodies. Before the anti-apartheid machine slipped into high gear in 1960, South Africa was far from being a pariah, as witnessed by the fact that Nasserist Egypt remained on diplomatic relations with Pretoria until 1960. Thereafter Pretoria progressively became almost totally isolated from the vast majority of the membership, even before losing its General Assembly seat in 1974.

Did this isolation worry the South Africans? It seemed to. Why otherwise would they have tried so hard to lure West Indian and Sri Lankan cricketers to tour the country, let alone 'rebel' British teams? Why should Pretoria radio have bothered to broadcast statements in the Security Council and the General Assembly made in explanation of negative votes or abstentions on hostile resolutions by Western delegates including myself? Why did South Africa not withdraw totally from the UN after being ousted from its seat in the General Assembly? There are many other similar questions which can be posed, all of which should have seemed marginal to a South African, provided that British and other European, American and Japanese trade, investment and widespread contacts continued. The truth is that, in general terms, the sense of virility deriving from a conviction of being the only person in step is a transient pleasure. Isolation is uncomfortable, particularly when it makes you an embarrassment and a burden to your few remaining friends, more so if you are in any way dependent on their continual goodwill. Political and social isolation may in the long run be as debilitating to national stamina as economic measures. After a time any government, however hard nosed, would consider paying some price to be welcomed back into the international herd. And it must have been clear to all South Africans for most of the thirty years of their international exile that only the abolition of apartheid would achieve this consummation. I would not wish to exaggerate the direct impact on South Africa of the climate which prevailed throughout the UN, or of the tempest of words, most of them uttered to bored junior diplomats manning delegation desks, and the confetti of resolutions, reports, declarations, conventions and the like. But I do not believe that all this activity was as futile as many sceptics would claim. It certainly had an influence on inter-governmental relations within and between regional and functional groupings, some of which rubbed off on relations between South Africa and countries whose views and policies carried weight in Pretoria.

In retrospect, the rhetorical assault, both in words and on paper, the non-binding economic and social measures adopted by the UN at the peak of the pyramid and by bodies such as the Commonwealth, the European Community, and the Nordic countries lower down the slopes, were most influential in areas outside government, both on the morale of the active opposition within South Africa, and on the effectiveness of non-governmental organizations and groups of private individuals in the outside world. In agitating for consumer boycotts, the withdrawal of Western business and financial interests, for maintaining boycotts of sporting contacts and so on and so forth, anti-apartheid groups were strengthened by the knowledge that their actions were being taken in fulfilment of directives overwhelmingly adopted by organs representative of the will of the international community. Activist church groups, black communities in parts of the United States, university campus boycotts of banks which maintained branches in South Africa, and many others probably had more effect on the dwindling of Western private-sector engagement with South Africa, and thus on the progressively demonstrable unworkability of the apartheid system in the eyes of South Africans, than governmental compliance with the non-mandatory measures adopted by multilateral organizations including the UN.

CHAPTER SEVEN

South West Africa to Namibia

South African forces conquered German South West Africa in 1915 and, at the Paris Peace Conference in 1919, South Africa was awarded a Class 'C' mandate over the former German colony. In the division of the spoils of the German Empire, this class of mandate was only one up on outright annexation, the solution which General Smuts unsuccessfully urged on President Woodrow Wilson. A Class 'C' mandate, in accordance with Article 22 (6) of the League of Nations Covenant, could be 'best administered under the laws of the Mandatory as integral portions of its territory', subject to certain safeguards and an annual report to the League Council. This suited South Africa well enough.

At the San Francisco Conference of 1945, which finalized the Charter of the United Nations, the question of the League of Nations Mandates and 'territories which may be detached from enemy states as a result of the Second World War' was dealt with by the creation of the International Trusteeship System. As a trade off for the exclusion of the word 'independence' from Chapter XI of the Charter on non-self-governing territories, it was retained at American insistence in the Trusteeship Chapter XII. The 'freely expressed wishes of the people concerned' were also to be promoted in the same Article 76 of the Charter. Although several trusteeship agreements were concluded with former mandatory powers in Africa, which led to independence, for example British Togoland, Cameroons and Tanganyika, and Belgian Ruanda-Urundi, the South African government was not prepared to do so for South West Africa. After another unsuccessful attempt to secure approval for annexation, the South Africans gave an assurance in 1946 that they would continue to administer South West Africa in accordance with the obligations of the original mandate.

Between 1948, when the new Nationalist Party government in South Africa decided to cease sending reports on South West Africa to the UN, and 1960, a complex triangular contest developed between the General Assembly, the International Court of Justice, and the

Union government. The upshot was that, while the Court and the Assembly ruled in favour of South Africa's continuing international obligations, the Government steadily withdrew all forms of cooperation but stopped short of annexation.

In 1966, the International Court of Justice, by eight votes to seven, rejected on technical grounds the claim advanced in 1960 by Ethiopia and Liberia that South Africa had violated the mandate over South West Africa. The General Assembly reacted quickly by adopting a resolution terminating the mandate and deciding that the territory would come under the direct responsibility of the United Nations. The resolution secured 114 votes in favour, two against (South Africa and Portugal) with three abstentions (Britain, France and Malawi). The following year the Assembly went further by establishing an eleven-nation Council for South West Africa 'to administer South West Africa until independence'. This unrealistic act of creation secured a reduced General Assembly majority of eighty-five in favour, two against with thirty abstentions. In 1960 the Assembly resolved to change the Council's name to the Council for Namibia, the new name for the territory.

The dispute was moving in the direction of the Security Council. In late 1967 the South African government arrested, deported to Pretoria and tried under a retroactive South African terrorism law thirty-seven South West Africans. The General Assembly condemned this act and the Security Council adopted two resolutions calling on South Africa to release and repatriate the prisoners. In the spring of 1968 the South Africans refused permission for a delegation from the Council for Namibia to visit the territory and the Assembly recommended that the Security Council take steps to 'ensure the removal' of the South African presence.

In March 1969, the Security Council for the first time debated the future of Namibia. I was a member of the British delegation and I well recall the occasion. A South African observer might not agree, but I was struck by the absence of the passion which characterized debates on, for example, Palestine and apartheid. Whereas the African members regarded apartheid debates as tests of the sincerity of Western protestations of abhorrence, it was clear that they expected more practical action from the Western powers over Namibia. This in a sense paralleled the Arab attitude to the United States and the Soviet Union respectively over the Arab/Israeli dispute. They expected, and got, obedient 'moral and material' support from the latter: from the former they expected pressure on the party with which the West had influence, leading to progress towards a negotiated solution.

On this occasion the Western delegations warned of the danger of raising false hopes, of the futility of adopting unrealistic resolutions and made clear that they were not prepared to agree to mandatory action to coerce South Africa. In the event the resolution (on which Britain and France abstained) accepted that the South African presence was illegal, 'called on' South Africa to withdraw, declared that a recent South African constitutional bill was a violation of General Assembly resolutions, and urged South Africa to comply with the resolutions calling for the release of the thirty-seven prisoners (they were sentenced to varying terms of imprisonment). This was milder language than that which was being put to the vote on apartheid in the same period.

Needless to say, Pretoria ignored the resolution and the Council met again in August 1969 in a more militant mood. Again, warnings against adopting ineffective resolutions were uttered, and the British delegate made clear that there was no possibility of agreement on Chapter VII mandatory measures, neither sanctions, still less military enforcement. The Council skated close to this thin ice by condemning South Africa's refusal to comply with the earlier resolution, recognizing the 'legitimacy of the Namibian peoples' struggle' (low-level guerrilla activity by the South West Africa Peoples Organization (SWAPO) had begun), calling for independence by 4 October, and describing South Africa's occupation as 'an aggressive encroachment on the authority of the UN' (language close to that of Chapter VII). This was too much for the United States and Finland, which joined the abstention club of Britain and France. Spain, the other Western European non-permanent member, voted enthusiastically for the resolution as a trade-off for African support in Spain's dispute with Britain over Gibraltar in the General Assembly. A few months earlier a similar Spanish tactic over Rhodesia had forced a British and (the first) American veto.

South African contemptuous disregard of the deadline evoked another condemnatory Security Council resolution in January 1970, which again called on all states not to deal with South Africa acting on behalf of Namibia. In addition the Council established a sub-Committee to study means of implementation of the resolutions. Britain and France abstained, as they did on a subsequent, more detailed resolution

adopted in July which called on all states to declare to the South
African government their non-recognition of South African authority
and ensure that their companies and nationals did not deal with
Namibia. The sub-committee was renewed and the Secretary-General
was asked to study what provisions of international law might apply to
Namibia. On the same day (29 July) the Council adopted a second
resolution (Britain abstaining in the curious company of the Soviet
Union and Czechoslovakia, which considered that the General Assem-
bly had already decided the question) deciding to ask the International
Court of Justice (ICJ) for an advisory opinion on the question 'what
are the legal consequences for states of the continued presence of
South Africa in Namibia?'

In 1971 the Court gave its opinion that South Africa was in illegal
occupation and should withdraw; and that UN member states should
refrain from any acts which would imply recognition of the legality of
the South African presence. The Security Council, with the usual two
abstentions, reaffirmed its previous resolutions and agreed with the
Court's opinion. Early in 1972, the Council met again and, by fourteen
votes with no opposition or abstentions (China did not participate in
the vote), invited the Secretary-General, in consultation with a group
of Security Council members (Argentina, Somalia and Yugoslavia), to
contact all the parties concerned to enable the Namibians to exercise
their right to self-determination and called upon the South African
government to cooperate with the Secretary-General. The Secretary-
General, Kurt Waldheim, briefly visited South Africa and Namibia in
March 1972 and his representative, appointed with the approval of the
Security Council, paid a longer visit later in the year. These contacts
had something of a clarifying effect. The South African government
did not deny the Namibian right to self-determination but insisted
that this be accomplished on a 'homelands' (tribal) basis (analogous to
the South African bantustans). The Security Council continued to
insist on self-determination and independence on the basis of national
unity and territorial integrity, and reaffirmed these principles in two
resolutions in 1972. In December 1973 the Council decided to discontinue the Secretary-General's operation and the Assembly recognized
SWAPO as the authentic representative of the Namibian people. In
1974 several factors converged which changed the nature of the
discourse. Since 1961, when the Security Council first addressed the
General Assembly declaration that Angola was a Non-Self-Governing

Territory, Portugal had come under intermittent censure by the Council for operations by its African forces inside neighbouring states, in particular the Congo (Zaire) and Zambia, and for defiance of the mandatory economic sanctions imposed on the illegal regime in Southern Rhodesia in 1966. The Council had also, in 1972, condemned Portugal's colonial policies and reaffirmed the right of the peoples of Angola, Mozambique and Guinea Bissau to self-determination and independence, and had recognized the 'legitimacy of their struggle'. By the early 1970s a large proportion of Portugal's defence budget and military manpower was being spent on fighting the liberation movements in these territories. In April 1974 there was a military coup in Lisbon which was to lead the following year to the decolonization of the Portuguese African Empire and the long-delayed advent of the Cold War into southern Africa.

In the General Assembly, as I have mentioned in the Chapter on apartheid, South Africa was deprived of its seat. This was followed by the triple veto of the attempt in the Council to expel South Africa from the UN and by a toughly worded, albeit unanimously adopted resolution on Namibia demanding South African compliance with UN resolutions, recognition of the Namibian nation, withdrawal and transfer of power to the Namibian people and the abolition of racially discriminatory and politically repressive laws.

In 1975 the Portuguese withdrew from Angola and the tragic future of that country became merged for fifteen years with that of Namibia, with the unedifying accompaniment of covert and overt East/West support for contesting factions including a long drawn out confrontation between Cuban and South African forces. Angola, a large and tribally diverse country, had no less than three mutually hostile liberation movements functioning during the last decade of Portuguese imperialism, namely the European-Marxist style Popular Movement for the Liberation of Angola (MPLA), the northern tribally based National Front for the Liberation of Angola (FNLA) and the southern tribally based National Union for the Total Independence of Angola (UNITA). Each had its overseas sponsors, and in some cases several strange bedfellows: UNITA started out with North Vietnam, China and North Korea and ended up as the favourite of South Africa and the United States. In early 1975 the departing Portuguese reached accord with all three: the United States gave covert assistance to the weakest and least reputable group, the FNLA, which had strong links with Washington's anti-communist bastion, the egregious President Mobutu of Zaire. The FNLA launched a foolish military offensive against the MPLA. The Soviet Union responded by supporting the MPLA, and Cuban troops arrived in Luanda, the capital. The Americans poured more good money after bad via Zaire, the MPLA pushed back the FNLA and UNITA, and South Africa, almost certainly with American encouragement, invaded from Namibia and nearly reached Luanda. The Cuban contingent rose to over fifty thousand at its peak: South Africa and the United States backed Jonas Savimbi of UNITA who, in the 1980s, became a darling of the Western right. South African troops, already in action against SWAPO in Namibia, which used southern Angola as a safe haven, remained in occupation of parts of Angola until 1990.

This imbroglio added a fresh dimension to the Namibian problem. It ceased to be a question of combined South African domestic and foreign policy. It became also a strategic matter. Sam Nujoma, the chairman of SWAPO, was receiving 'moral and material aid' from the Soviet Union, in default of any alternative. SWAPO, the MPLA and the Cubans became in Pretoria's eyes the spearhead of the Moscow drive to raise the red flag in Windhoek, the Namibian capital, then in Pretoria. The South African forces were defending the heartland from the Cunene river on the Angolan frontier. There is no point now in trying to assess blame but it can be said without much fear of contradiction that the brief Kissingerian sortie into the affairs of Southern Africa in 1976 did not represent the Secretary of State's greatest diplomatic triumph. It acted more as a self-fulfilling prophecy of the emergence of a direct Soviet threat.

This harsher atmosphere penetrated to the UN. In June 1975, a draft Security Council resolution was put to the vote which included a determination under Chapter VII of the Charter that the illegal occupation of Namibia constituted a threat to international peace and security. Few Angolans would have contested this proposition, nor for that matter citizens of other states such as Zambia, which had felt the weight of South African military power based in Namibia. The resolution secured ten positive votes and three vetoes (France, Britain and the United States): Italy and Japan abstained. In 1976 the United States improved on its total of four solo vetoes in the Security Council of applications for UN membership by Vietnam (another was cast in 1976 before Vietnam was admitted the following year) by vetoing

Angolan admission, government being in the hands of the Marxist MPLA. Five months later Angola squeaked past an American abstention, the rest of the Council being in favour as they had been on the first occasion. A few weeks earlier another attempt to characterize the South African occupation of Namibia and the 'war being waged there by South Africa' as a threat to international peace and security under Chapter VII was beaten off by the same triple veto as in 1975. In March 1976 the Council had condemned South Africa's 'aggression' against the People's Republic of Angola, demanded respect for Angolan sovereignty, territorial integrity and cessation of the use of Namibia as a base for operations in Angola. The language was tough and its approximation to Chapter VII reduced the positive vote to the minimum of nine, China inscrutably not participating, and France, the US, Britain, Italy and Japan abstaining. Sweden, the other West European non-permanent member, supported the resolution, as it did the vetoed 1976 drafts.

Between 1977 and 1980 it looked as though there might at last be a break in the arid cycle of South African defiance and the adoption or rejection of Security Council resolutions more notable for their revelations of the nuances and limits of policies of Western governments than for any possibility of implementation. President Carter was less obsessed by the Red Peril than his predecessors, more open to the view that 'regional' problems had roots in regional history rather than in Kremlin challenges, and resolved to make a serious attempt to tackle the crises which had for so long been filling the Security Council agenda. I have already mentioned the Western pattern of membership on the Council which was instrumental in securing the mandatory arms embargo against South Africa. In May 1978 the Council adopted unanimously a resolution demanding South African withdrawal from Angola in stronger language (a specific warning of Chapter VII action in the event of non-compliance) than that which had attracted five abstentions in 1976, and which would almost certainly have been vetoed under President Ford.

By that time President Carter was embarked on his peace initiative which culminated in the Camp David Agreements between Israel and Egypt. A comparable initiative on Namibia was launched in the Security Council in the summer of 1978, taking advantage of the strong Western representation. In July, the Council passed a resolution requesting the Secretary-General to nominate a Special Representative

to ensure the independence of Namibia and to submit recommendations to the Council. The Soviet Union and Czechoslovakia abstained
because of hostility to any course other than blunt demands addressed
to Pretoria. In September, the council adopted, with the same two
abstentions, Resolution 435 which approved the Secretary-General's
report, decided to set up a UN Transition Assistance Group
(UNTAG) to help the Special Representative achieve the independence of Namibia through free elections, welcomed SWAPO's readiness
to cooperate, and declared null and void unilateral measures taken by
South Africa in relation to the electoral process. Resolution 435 was to
become for Namibia what Resolution 242 (1967) has been for the
Middle East, i.e. the basic framework for a definitive settlement.

The search for a settlement of the apparently insoluble problem of
Southern Rhodesia was also resumed under the new dispensation
when Britain sought American support for what became the Anglo-
American proposals (see Chapter VIII).

When I parted from direct involvement in UN affairs in 1974 for
the Embassy in Tehran, the three principal problems of Central and
southern Africa seemed doomed to indefinite stalemate. Apartheid was
entrenched by a powerful security and military apparatus which had
all the trappings of invincibility. The South African stranglehold on
Namibia was absolute. Mandatory sanctions against the Smith regime
in Southern Rhodesia had been a fiasco and all political attempts to
end the rebellion had failed. In Tehran I had been marginally involved
with the Anglo-American proposals when leaders of the Rhodesian
Patriotic Front had come to Iran in 1976 to seek support from the
Shah; and with Namibia when the Shah was persuaded to argue in
advance the merits of what became the 1978 proposals with the South
African leadership, with whom he was on friendly terms.

At the beginning of 1979, when I returned to dealing with UN
affairs, the Anglo-American proposals on Rhodesia were close to
extinction and there was no prospect of an end to apartheid in South
Africa. It looked as though Namibia might be the first bastion of white
minority rule to fall. South Africa had not rejected Resolution 435 and
there was evidence of a debate among South African military and
political leaders, with one side favouring a continuation of past inflex-
ibility, the other arguing that South Africa's losses (which were
mounting) in Namibia and Angola should be cut and that the heartland
would be better defended from the Orange River, i.e. accepting the

abandonment of Namibia. Nevertheless there was infinite scope for procrastination in the complex procedures necessary to implement Resolution 435.

In New York I found an atmosphere of some optimism. A contact group of the Western Five of 1978 (United States, Britain, France, West Germany, and Canada) had been formed to help the Secretary-General's representative (Martti Ahtisaari, now President of Finland) in his negotiations with the parties. The Group had survived intact even though Germany and Canada had left the Security Council at the end of 1978. Contingent arrangements were being made for the selection of national military contingents for UNTAG, and appointments were being discussed for the civilian posts.

Setting aside the Angolan complication, the main stumbling block in Namibia appeared to be the South African refusal to accept the prospect of a SWAPO government, and rejection of the characterization of SWAPO as the 'sole, legitimate and authentic' representative of the Namibian people, confirmed by the General Assembly in 1977. The conferral of this title by regional groups such as the Arab League (as regards the PLO), the OAU, the NAM and the General Assembly was a source of bitter controversy. Occupying powers such as Israel and South Africa, as well as minority regimes such as the Smith regime in Southern Rhodesia, wanted to negotiate with indigenous groups of their own choosing, not to be confronted by a single, monolithic movement with massive external support. Western governments argued that the designation pre-judged democratic choices which were precluded by the circumstances of occupation or minority rule. They were not happy at being railroaded by majority voting into accepting as an interlocutor, or as an observer delegation at the UN, or as a participant in Security Council debates, only a single liberation movement favoured by the majority. On the other side of the fence, the example of Angola – three liberation movements leading to civil war on independence – had crystallized the determination of the protagonists of national liberation to reduce this risk by validating only one organization. Hence, in November 1978, the Security Council strongly condemned the internal elections being held in Namibia, declared them in advance null and void, called for their cancellation and warned of Chapter VII action. The Western Five, with the maintenance of South Africa in the Resolution 435 negotiating framework in mind, abstained.

Otherwise, until the end of 1980, the Council concentrated on condemning South African military action in Angola from Namibian bases, demanding its cessation and payment of compensation. Meanwhile the negotiations continued. The independence of Zimbabwe in April, contrary to expectations that Namibia would beat Southern Rhodesia to the post in the independence race, stimulated discussions in the corridors of New York whether this would make South Africa more or less reluctant to settle quickly on Namibia. The consensus was that, having been forced to swallow the unwelcome victory of Robert Mugabe and the virtual extinction of their candidate, Bishop Muzorewa, they would need time before risking another jolt.

However, time was running out for the American-led Namibian initiative in the UN. Ronald Reagan's victory in the Presidential elections in November brought to power a group of people who shared the South African obsession with Soviet imperialism and dislike and contempt for the United Nations with its clamorous Third World majority. We shall never know whether the Pre-Implementation Meeting of the Five and all the parties held in Geneva only a fortnight before President Reagan's inauguration would have gone differently if President Carter had not been on his way out. As it was, the South Africans and the representatives of the internal parties in Namibia showed little or no interest in making progress. A shortly to be familiar new American policy known as 'constructive engagement' with South Africa was already in the wind and Pretoria rightly anticipated that, in a few weeks time, they would be relieved of embarrassing pressure from the Five and UN Secretariat to make concessions to SWAPO and the front-line African states, such as agreeing to a date to begin implementation of Resolution 435.

The new regime got off to a cracking start. Either out of exasperation or as a test of Western policies, or both, the African group in the Security Council insisted against strong advice to bring to the vote on 30 April 1981 four separate resolutions each imposing a different series of mandatory sanctions against South Africa under Chapter VII. It was difficult to keep a straight face as the American, British and French pencils rose and fell at the same time, an aggregate of twelve vetoes, a world record. At the end of August a mention of Chapter VII in the preamble to a resolution condemning another major South African incursion into Angola drew another American veto, this time with Britain abstaining and France voting in favour. The multiple veto exercise had had precisely the effect which many of us feared. It confirmed the conviction of the new Administration that a Soviet-Cuban-radical-African cabal was in the driving seat in New York. In fact the fiasco had been promoted by one African delegate who persuaded his fellows to go along with his initiative: the later condemnation of the South African raid was a routine exercise which did not merit a veto.

The Reagan administration decided on a Namibian policy exactly the reverse of that of their predecessors. The Five and the Secretariat had worked on the assumption that the Cuban military presence in Angola was a response to the South African and South African-backed UNITA threat and that implementation of Resolution 435 would reduce these dangers and lead to Cuban withdrawal. The last thing we had wanted was to link the two issues – Cuban withdrawal and implementation of 435. There was no evidence that the South Africans were making this link. The new American team took the view that the Cubans were the spearhead of a Soviet drive into southern Africa and that Cuban withdrawal from Angola must precede, or at least take place in tandem with South African withdrawal from Namibia. This linkage became the cornerstone of American policy. It was not acceptable to the remainder of the Five and ran counter to majority opinion in the UN, not simply that of the Soviet Union and the African Group. It also enabled the South Africans to appear far more cooperative over implementation of Resolution 435 in the certain knowledge that their protestations would not be put to the test. Indeed the Secretary-General, after a visit to southern Africa in 1983, was able to report to the Security Council that virtually all obstacles had been removed, except for agreement on Cuban withdrawal.

The unity of the Five withered. By the end of 1983 France and Canada had withdrawn and the Contact Group ceased to function as a whole. The American negotiating team was by that time able to rely on Britain alone for support.

For almost the full eight years of the Reagan presidency, Chester Crocker, the American knight errant in Africa, sought to slay the Cuban dragon and free the Namibian princess. His quest, accompanied intermittently by his faithful British squire, followed a zig-zag route through the tangled undergrowth of a forest inhabited by benevolent and malevolent spirits which had to be cajoled, threatened, or bought off. His five hundred-page account,[1] shorn. of modesty in the best tradition of the medieval encomiast, is indispensable reading for the student of this labyrinthine exercise in decolonization. It is admittedly heavy-going. Stylistically Mr Crocker lives in that circle of the semantic inferno where slang and jargon commingle. In substance, it is not so much that he fails to see the wood for the trees, rather that he feels obliged to subject each tree to a microscopic examination before continuing his journey through the forest.

From time to time the United Nations looms across the path of his negotiations with the parties. In 1983, 1985 and 1987 the Security Council adopted resolutions reiterating the validity of Resolution 435 and rejecting South African linkage with 'irrelevant and extraneous issues' (code for the Cubans in Angola). American abstentions constituted a signal to Pretoria that Washington still adhered to Resolution 435 as the road to a settlement, but would not bring pressure to bear through the UN or abandon the policy of linkage. In 1986 the General Assembly sponsored an international conference on Namibia at which the Secretary-General, the first speaker, explained that all outstanding obstacles to implementation had been removed. The UN was ready to begin; only South African insistence on linkage with Cuban withdrawal was holding up progress. All speakers denounced linkage.

A number of Council resolutions were unanimously adopted condemning South African attacks on Angola from Namibian bases and demanding South African withdrawal. However, when measures under Chapter VII of the Charter were either specifically included or threatened in the event of non-compliance, the US and Britain were quick to cast joint vetoes with France abstaining, in occasional company with other Western members. Between 1985 and 1988, they blocked seven resolutions directed at South Africa over apartheid, Namiba, Angola and raids into Botswana, Zambia and Zimbabwe.

The end of the Cold War precipitated the denouement. By 1987 Mikhail Gorbachev had left Soviet-supported liberation movements, governments and others in Asia and Africa in no doubt that confrontation with the United States was over, that Moscow intended to use the UN as a vehicle for genuine cooperation in the interest of international peace and that, although moral support for deserving causes might continue, further material support was out of the question. This left

---

[1] *High Noon in South Africa: Making Peace in a Rough Neighbourhood* by Chester A. Crocker, W. W. Norton, April 1993.

the Cubans with no choice and Crocker was able to conclude what he had been working towards for so long, namely a series of agreements, tied up by the end of the decade, between Angola, Cuba and South Africa for the mutual withdrawal of their forces from Angola and for the implementation of Resolution 435. With Cuban withdrawal, the South Africans, who were becoming increasingly disillusioned as a result of the relatively heavy casualties incurred by their forward policy, had run out of excuses for procrastination.

On 20 December 1988, the Security Council established a small mission (UNAVEM) to verify Cuban withdrawal from Angola and welcomed the agreements reached between the parties. In 1989 the Council adopted a number of resolutions enabling the process set out in Resolution 435 to be activated. There was a brief and bloody setback in April when hundreds of SWAPO fighters poured across the Angolan border to establish bases in Namibia during the transitional period. They were mown down by South African forces. The process was quickly put back on track and the UN Transitional Group (UNTAG), comprising roughly eight thousand peacekeepers and civilians, deployed to organize and supervise elections and to monitor South African withdrawal. Considering that South Africa had been ruling the territory for over seventy years and that it had been a major military operational base since the 1960s, the South African withdrawal was remarkably quick and free of incident. In November, the elections were held and SWAPO won a majority of the seats. On 21 March 1990, Namibia became independent under the presidency of the veteran SWAPO leader, Sam Nujoma. The Red Flag did not fly over Windhoek after all, and the arch-opponent of apartheid, Nelson Mandela, was released from prison just in time to attend the independence celebrations.

The UN played a more significant role in Namibia's long march to independence than it did over Southern Rhodesia. In the latter case, it set the rules and remained on the touchline, urging the administering power, Britain, to do its duty. By the 1966 resolution of the General Assembly the UN assumed direct responsibility for Namibia, although it was unable to make this effective without South African acquiescence. The UN Council for Namibia was an expensive charade and the Security Council would have done as well without it. As with Rhodesia, the Assembly and the Council set the rules, i.e. South African withdrawal and Namibian self-determination leading to

independence. But, because Namibia was an international responsibility, the Security Council not only laid down the procedure for achieving
these goals in Resolution 435 but also created a mechanism, the
Contact Group of Five working with the Secretariat, for implementing
the procedure. None of the parties, including South Africa, rejected
this negotiating structure. It was, however, brushed aside by the
incoming Reagan administration.

I still believe that this was a mistake and that the same result could
have been achieved in a shorter time scale and with less loss of life all
round if Washington had continued vigorously down the path mapped
out by President Carter's negotiators and their colleagues in the Five
and the Secretariat. The Crocker mission was conducted with great
skill and tenacity but the premise – linking a Namibian settlement to
Cuban withdrawal from Angola – put the cart before the horse and
thus inhibited progress until developments in Soviet policy prompted
Cuban withdrawal. The Americans and South Africans exaggerated
Soviet aspirations and capabilities. By the 1980s the Soviet Union had
sacrificed much of the goodwill of the Non-Aligned Movement by
invading a member state, Afghanistan, with 100,000 troops in a cynical
exercise in 'fraternal assistance'. The Soviet Union and Cuba were
helping Angola at the latter's request because of the MPLA's vulner-
ability to South African and UNITA military force, not in order to
'plant the Red Flag in Windhoek'. Sam Nujoma was an old-fashioned
nationalist leader who sought military assistance from the Soviet
Union out of necessity not conviction. The obsession with the global
competition with Russian-led communism distorted American percep-
tions and played into the hands of the procrastinators in the South
African camp. The UN could do nothing to correct this astigmatism
except to hold the United States to Resolution 435 as the basis for a
solution.

It is not as though all is well that ended well. Namibia is now a
peaceful and harmless neighbour of South Africa, but the perceived
necessity as part of the Crocker/Pretoria strategy to build up UNITA
militarily and to inflate Savimbi's ego by public acclaim at the highest
level has extracted a terrible price (discussed in Chapter IX) from the
suffering people of Angola, a price which they are still paying in a
scale of casualties and ruin transcending that of the worst years of the
1970s and 1980s.

CHAPTER EIGHT

Southern Rhodesia to Zimbabwe

If anyone in the 1950s had predicted that this particular exercise in decolonization was destined to saturate British foreign policy worldwide, come close to destroying the Commonwealth and vitiate our relations with partners and allies to the extent that the Foreign Office became sardonically known in European capitals as the Rhodesia Department, he or she would have been consigned to the nearest lunatic asylum.

London's control over Southern Rhodesia had always been tenuous. It had been ruled by the British South Africa Company until 1923 when it was taken over by the British government on the basis of internal autonomy. A local referendum in 1922 had come down in favour of 'responsible government' rather than union with South Africa. Although the *Encyclopedia Britannica* of the time described the franchise as 'most liberal' with persons with 'necessary qualifications' being admitted to the electorate 'without distinction of sex or race', only sixty of the country's nearly one million black citizens were eligible to vote! Power was in the hands of the approximately fifty thousand white settlers. In spite of further white immigration, particularly after the Second World War when Britain encouraged demobilized servicemen to settle in Rhodesia, a proportion of less than 5 per cent white to more than 95 per cent black persisted until Zimbabwean independence in 1980, when there were roughly 250,000 whites to nearly seven million blacks.

In the 1950s, Britain tried to amalgamate the three territories originally created by the British South Africa Company (Southern Rhodesia, Northern Rhodesia and Nyasaland) into the control of the Central African Federation. This experiment, which was finally abandoned in 1963, was conducted without serious interference from the United Nations. Throughout the 1950s, Britain won the argument in New York that Southern Rhodesia, having been granted internal self-government thirty years previously, was not a self-governing territory within the meaning of Chapter XI of the Charter and did not therefore

fall within the competence of the UN. The Assembly was also prepared to wait and see whether the Central African Federation would
take off, and whether majority African rights would be realized
within it.

Events of the early 1960s delineated a new playing field and a new
set of goalposts was erected. The adoption of Resolution 1514 in the
Assembly and the establishment of the Committee of Twenty-four
precipitated a challenge to the British defensive position. The Committee affirmed that Southern Rhodesia was a non-self-governing territory
and the Assembly requested the British government to suspend a
newly adopted constitution (which ensured the indefinite perpetuation
of white rule), to take steps to entrench majority rights, to repeal
discriminatory legislation and to convene a conference of all Rhodesian
parties to draw up a constitution on the basis of one-man-one-vote.
African antipathy to the Southern Rhodesian white leadership had
been further aroused by the contacts between the whites and the
Katanga secessionists during the Congo crisis. After the collapse of the
Federation in 1963, the first shots were fired in the Security Council
against Britain's assertion that neither London nor the UN had a right
to intervene in Rhodesian domestic affairs. A draft resolution was put
to the vote calling on Britain not to transfer any powers or attributes
of sovereignty to Southern Rhodesia before implementing the General
Assembly's resolutions, and not to transfer armed forces or aircraft to
the regime. Britain vetoed the draft: the US and France abstained.

Northern Rhodesia (Zambia) and Nyasaland (Malawi) became independent in 1964 and were admitted to UN membership. The white
leadership in Southern Rhodesia tried unsuccessfully to negotiate
independence with the Conservative government in London, which
insisted on unimpeded progress to majority rule and that any settlement
must be acceptable to all the people of Rhodesia. The Committee of
Twenty-four continued to exert pressure and, in May 1965, the
Security Council adopted a resolution (Britain, the US and France
abstaining) requesting Britain and all member states not to accept a
unilateral declaration of independence and calling on Britain to convene
a constitutional conference. However, momentum had become unstoppable and, in November 1965, in spite of strenuous efforts and dire
warnings of the consequences by the Labour government in London,
the new Prime Minister, Ian Smith, declared independence.

Britain immediately imposed bilaterally a range of economic and financial sanctions and called for a meeting of the Security Council: the General Assembly had already condemned the unilaterial declaration (UDI) at an emergency meeting. This was the first time that the Council had been called by an administering power to debate a situation in a territory under its sovereignty. The Council adopted a short resolution condemning the UDI and calling on all states not to recognize or assist the 'illegal racist minority regime'. This was followed a week later, on 20 November, by a longer resolution calling on Britain to quell the rebellion, condemning the usurpation of power, and again calling on all states not to recognize nor to entertain diplomatic or other relations with the illegal regime. All states were requested to break economic relations with Southern Rhodesia, and to embargo oil and petroleum products. All UN projects and teams in Rhodesia were withdrawn.

Why did Britain lead the way to the Security Council after so many years of maintaining that the internal affairs of Rhodesia were no business of the UN, and after vetoing a resolution only two years previously in defence of this hands-off policy? UDI was, after all, a rebellion against British authority by British people in a British territory.

The answer to this is simple. The government in London was faced with two options, each equally unacceptable. Prime Minister Harold Wilson had made clear in advance of UDI that force would not be used to solve the problem. To have done so would have been militarily difficult and politically catastrophic. British public opinion would have been split from top to bottom, transcending party lines. Most white Rhodesians were of British stock and a high proportion, including Ian Smith himself, had served in the British armed forces during the Second World War. Many Rhodesian officers had stayed on, especially in the Royal Air Force. If I had been asked whether the army, navy and RAF units in Bahrain, where I was at the time, would have obeyed orders to fight their old comrades and kith and kin in Rhodesia, I would have been hard put to it to reply with an unqualified 'yes'. The military option was a non-starter. The alternative was to accept, with a show of reluctance, the new status quo in Salisbury, which would have destroyed the Commonwealth, ruined our relations with most of the rest of the newly decolonized world, and would have separated Britain from the United States and much of Western Europe. That, too, was an option not to be considered seriously. The third course was to do what the government had done over Palestine in

1947, namely take the initiative to dump the problem on the United Nations. As Mr Harold Wilson explained to the General Assembly in December 1965, 'in theory and in constitutional law, this is a bilateral matter between the British Parliament, who alone have the responsibility of decision in Rhodesia'. But Britain, 'having embarked on a series of measures of unprecedented severity', asked for the fullest support of every UN member. Thus the contradiction between maintaining British responsibility and involving the whole international community was neatly resolved. The activity in the UN also had the merit of buying time for the British government to resume negotiations with the Smith regime in an attempt to bring about an end to the rebellion.

These tactics worked with a varying degree of success over the next fifteen years. The African nations accepted that Britain was trying to restore legality and promote majority rule. But, to my certain knowledge, they could never rid themselves of the conviction that the greatest ex-imperial power in the world, which still projected its military strength world-wide and aspired to a place at the top table with the superpowers, could have done its duty and crushed a rebellion by a handful of colonial settlers if it had genuinely resolved to do so. How many times was I faced with the question whether Britain would have used force to free a white majority which was being illegally tyrannised by a black minority? Not an easy one to answer.

In 1966, Britain set another remarkable precedent. The mandatory provisions of the Charter as set out in Chapter VII had been invoked only twice since 1945, first to order a cease-fire in Palestine in July 1947 and secondly to authorize the United States and its allies to use force to reverse the North Korean invasion of South Korea in June 1950. Britain now invented a threat to international peace and security in a rebellious colony in which scarcely a shot had been fired, in order to convert the voluntary economic measures already adopted into mandatory sanctions. In April Britain called an emergency meeting of the Security Council to gain authority for British naval vessels to use force to prevent the arrival of tankers at the port of Beira for transhipment of oil by pipeline to Rhodesia. In December, at British initiative, the Council met again and formally determined under Articles 39 and 41 of the Charter that there was a threat to international peace and security. A range of sanctions were imposed and member states were reminded that failure to comply would constitute a violation of Article 25 of the Charter which states: 'The Members of the UN agree to accept and carry out the decisions of the Security Council in accordance with the present Charter.' This was the first time that the UN had imposed mandatory sanctions, and the membership was clearly taken aback at the bizarre circumstances. The Charter purists, led by the Soviet Union, were in a quandary between pleasing the Africans and adhering to principle. They compromised by abstaining. The first resolution secured only ten positive votes, the second scored eleven.

This initiative was the direct consequence of the failure of the talks between Messrs Smith and Wilson on board HMS *Tiger*, when it seemed as though settlement proposals had been agreed, only to be rejected by Salisbury. In September, Mr Wilson, who was committed to a policy of no independence before majority rule (known as NIBMAR), told Commonwealth prime ministers of his proposals for mandatory sanctions. He had already predicted that sanctions, particularly if oil were added to the list, would work within 'weeks not months'. This remarkable forecast struck many people, including myself, as being the product either of naive wishful thinking or disingenuousness. Although sanctions were bound to have a serious effect in the short term on an economy which was heavily dependent on exports, notably tobacco, and thus on foreign exchange earnings, Rhodesia was almost surrounded by countries (the Union of South Africa and the Portuguese territories) whose governments, regardless of international law, were openly committed to defying the embargo. For example, if oil could not be delivered to Salisbury via the Beira pipeline, it could and would be delivered by road from South Africa. Additionally, Zambia and Botswana (independent in 1966), the only independent members of the African Group contiguous to Rhodesia, were economically too dependent on Rhodesia and South Africa respectively to impose sanctions with any rigour. Sanctions were thus likely to cause discomfort and resentment, but not to bring the regime to its knees. There was of course no question of the Western Permanent Members extending mandatory sanctions to South Africa and Portugal for their defiance of Article 25 of the Charter.

In the Security Council a pattern set in of responses to actions by the Smith regime or to the failure of periodical negotiating initiatives between Britain and Salisbury in the form of tightening and extending sanctions. To start with, Rhodesian exports were embargoed but, except for oil, arms and imports directly from Britain, imports into

Rhodesia continued. In early 1968, following the execution of three Africans who had successfully appealed to the Privy Council in London, Britain returned to the Council to close this and most other gaps. The upshot was the unanimous adoption of Resolution 253 of 29 May 1968 which, along with a routine call on Britain to end the rebellion, imposed a comprehensive range of mandatory sanctions, called for assistance to Zambia, which would be seriously affected by the measures, and established a Committee (of the whole Council membership) to monitor implementation.

In October 1968 a further round of Smith/Wilson negotiations took place on HMS *Fearless*. Smith was offered more favourable terms than on HMS *Tiger* but was not prepared to contemplate majority rule short of the Greek Kalends. The 'weeks not months' had become years but there was no sign of sanctions, albeit now almost total, having the desired effect. Indeed, the following year saw an upturn in almost all sectors of the Rhodesian economy, an increase in GDP of over 10 per cent.

In this more favourable climate, the regime introduced a new constitution designed to block for ever the prospect of majority African rule, and Rhodesia was declared a republic. The Security Council reacted in March 1970. Following repeated recommendations from the General Assembly via the Committee of Twenty-four that Britain should use force to end the rebellion, similar propositions were advanced in the Security Council, but without securing the necessary nine votes to provoke a veto. On 17 March, thanks to the favourable vote of Spain (as with Namibia, a trade off for African support over Gibraltar), a draft resolution secured nine votes. It condemned Britain's refusal to use force and decided that the mandatory sanctions imposed on Rhodesia should be extended to South Africa and Portugal. Finland, France and the two Latin American members abstained and Britain vetoed. I clearly recall the agonies being suffered by the United States delegation. The US had never vetoed a resolution. 'Nyet' was the brush with which the Soviet Union was heavily tarred (103 vetoes up to that date) and the Americans were anxious to maintain their virginity (twenty years and nearly seventy American vetoes later it all seems like a fuss about nothing). The American delegate took a breath and vetoed along with us. If my memory is accurate, he might have abstained and left us in isolation if his request for more time to seek instructions from Washington had not been brushed aside by the African sponsors who were moving in for the kill.

The excellent Ambassador of Finland, Max Jakobsen, who would have made an outstanding Secretary-General if the Soviet Union had not vetoed his candidacy in favour of the pliable Kurt Waldheim some months later, came to the rescue the following day with agreed changes to the vetoed draft. The eventual resolution, unanimous except for a Spanish abstention (I forget the reason why), condemned the proclamation of republican status, reaffirmed British responsibility, and intensified the sanctions by calling for the severance of diplomatic, consular, trade and military relations as well as transportation links to and from Rhodesia. It was around this time that the Rhodesian virus began to infect Britain's international relations beyond the Commonwealth. Britain was the only state which took the Sanctions Committee (created by Resolution 253) seriously and friendly countries such as France, Japan and West Germany became exasperated and embarrassed by British finger-pointing at their firms for sanctions busting. Pressure from African states in and out of the Commonwealth on Britain's allies and partners to oblige London to do its duty and deliver Rhodesian self-determination added to this exasperation, as did lobbying and counter-lobbying over resolutions in the Security Council and the General Assembly. By the same token, cracks were widening in the British public and parliamentary landscape, exacerbated by the demonstrable failure of sanctions and the complaints by people with friends and families in Rhodesia at travel and financial restrictions. The annual passage of the Sanctions Order through Parliament became increasingly bad-tempered and uncertain. The kith and kin argument was not a solely Conservative prerogative.

In June 1970, the Conservatives won the general election. My African colleagues confidently expected a tilt in favour of the Salisbury regime. But the Council was able unanimously to reaffirm all previous decisions, condemnations and responsibilities in November. In 1971 the new Foreign Secretary, Sir Alec Douglas Home, launched another round of negotiations and reached agreement with Ian Smith on a basis more generally favourable to Salisbury than anything which had been previously proposed. The terms of settlement would in theory have led to majority rule but not for a generation at least. The British government stuck to its pre-UDI commitment that any settlement must be acceptable to the Rhodesian people as a whole and sent a delegation (the Pearce Commission) to test public opinion. The African population rejected the proposals as being too slow in terms of majority rule and because they did not trust their white rulers not to renege on their commitments once independence had been granted. The leader of the African National Council which had been formed to coordinate the response to the Pearce Commission was Bishop Abel Muzorewa.

The cycle of General Assembly and Security Council resolutions continued, the latter focusing mainly on condemnation of breaches of sanctions, including the American decision to resume imports of Rhodesian chrome, of the presence of South African security forces in Rhodesia, and 'acts of provocation and harassment against Zambia by the illegal regime in collusion with the racist regime of South Africa.' Zambia was commended for implementing sanctions and Britain was repeatedly urged to carry out its responsibilities. An attempt in 1973 to extend sanctions to South Africa and the Portuguese territories was jointly vetoed by the US and Britain.

Ian Smith and his colleagues may have been heartened by the palpable failure of sanctions, and by the fact that each successive set of British proposals since 1966 was more favourable to their cause than its predecessor. But time was working against the regime. Decolonization and self-determination had secured world-wide currency, not simply in the Third World. Liberation movements and the proponents of armed struggle could count on 'moral and material' support from a wider base than the Soviet Union, its satellites and the People's Republic of China, the last named becoming increasingly involved in Africa. In 1972 serious guerrilla activity broke out in Rhodesia, directed from the Zambian side of the border. In 1974 a heavier blow fell, namely the revolution in Portugal and the imminence of Portuguese withdrawal from Mozambique.

By 1975 Rhodesia had, instead of a friendly opponent of sanctions, the militant left-wing FRELIMO government in power in Maputo, which committed itself to sever all relations with Rhodesia. Pressure to settle came now not only from Britain and the UN but also from South Africa where the government realized that the Rhodesians could not hold out indefinitely. In South African minds the alternative to a peaceful settlement could be the eventual incorporation into the Union of several million more black Africans with a tiny minority of less than 250,000 whites as compensation; moreover whites of predominantly British stock. Rhodesian casualties were mounting in the guerrilla war and, economically, Rhodesia was suffering along with other non-petroleum producers from the recession caused by the dramatic oil-price hikes of 1973–74.

The tempo of peace initiatives quickened. The Labour party returned to power in Britain in 1974. Prime Minister Vorster of South Africa and President Kaunda of Zambia organized a conference at Victoria Falls in August 1975 and the Rhodesians met the nationalist leader Joshua Nkomo the following March. Both failed to pin Ian Smith down to an acceptable formula. Secretary of State Kissinger, in his meteoric descent on Africa in April 1976, primarily to tackle the Angolan problem, had greater success in concert with Prime Minister Vorster. By the end of the year Smith had apparently agreed to a two-year transition to majority rule. But his agreement was hedged around with conditions that the nationalist leadership – which had the same year combined into the Patriotic Front comprising ZAPU (Joshua Nkomo based in Zambia) and ZANU (Robert Mugabe based in Mozambique) – were unable to accept. Real power, i.e. key Cabinet portfolios and command of the security forces, would have remained in white hands or under white control. The Geneva Conference chaired by Britain petered out in failure at the end of the year. The Security Council had played no part in these activities except that the Geneva Conference Chairman, Ivor Richard, was the British Representative at the UN. I had a feeling at the time, born of brief contact with one of the African parties, that there was resentment about what appeared to be the reluctance of the British government to be pitchforked into a negotiation by the transient Kissinger, which they would not, if left to themselves, have initiated; and that the appointment as Chairman of a mere Ambassador to the UN was regarded as something of a slight.

In 1977 the Labour government, in concert with the new US administration, embarked on a tactic which, for the first time, drew the United Nations from the touchline onto the field of play. After an exploratory tour of Africa by the new Foreign Secretary, David Owen, and Anglo-American shuttling at official level between African leaders, what became known as the Anglo-American proposals emerged. These were a blueprint envisaging an independence constitution with a single-chamber National Assembly elected by universal suffrages with a Bill of Rights, all to be implemented in a transitional period of six months, with the government headed by a British Resident Commissioner (Lord Carver, formerly Chief of the Defence Staff) who, with a UN representative, would oversee elections and the transfer of power.

Law and Order would be the responsibility of the existing police force and a 'United Nations Zimbabwe Force'. In September 1977, the Security Council adopted a resolution (the USSR abstaining) requesting the Secretary-General to appoint a representative (General Prem Chand, a veteran UN peacekeeping officer). This approach was a change from the previous pattern of first trying to persuade Mr Smith and his colleagues to modify their position. It was followed by meetings between the Anglo-American team and the Patriotic Front. The blueprint, which was presented in Salisbury in September, was neither wholly rejected nor accepted by the parties. Negotiations continued in an increasingly desultory fashion until the Labour government fell in the spring of 1979. But the proposals were overtaken by two factors – on the one hand the intensification of the war and the fierce incursions by the Rhodesian air force and special forces into Zambia and Mozambique, condemned strongly by the Security Council on several occasions, and, on the other hand, the search by the Smith regime for an 'internal settlement' through persuading African leaders, led by Bishop Muzorewa, the Reverend Ndabaninge Sithole and Chief Chirau, to cooperate in a transfer of authority which would in practice leave real power in white hands. Agreement was reached in March 1978 on a one-year transition to 'Zimbabwe-Rhodesia' on this basis. The Council condemned such moves and declared any internal settlement to be illegal (the Western Five abstained). Four of the Five (minus France) also abstained on a 1978 resolution regretting the decision of the US Government to allow Ian Smith and leaders of the internal settlement to visit the United States. The Security Council had agreed to being addressed by Messrs Nkomo and Mugabe but had refused, on ostensibly legalistic grounds, to give a hearing to Ian Smith and the black leaders in the internal settlement.

The last act in the fifteen-year drama opened with the coming to power of the Conservative government of Margaret Thatcher in May, 1979. By that time an election had been held in Rhodesia (in April) and Bishop Muzorewa had become Prime Minister of Zimbabwe-Rhodesia: the Security Council had immediately adopted a resolution condemning the 'attempts by the illegal regime ... to retain and extend a racist minority rule' and declaring the elections null and void. The resolution also called on all states not to recognize any representatives of, or organ established by, that process. Britain, France and the US abstained. Set against this dismissive view, Lord Boyd, a former Colonial Secretary, who had been sent by Mrs Thatcher as Leader of the Opposition to observe the elections, had reported that they had been free and fair (even though they had excluded any participation by the principal African parties, ZANU and ZAPU). From statements made during the British election campaign it seemed as though the policy of the new government would be to recognize Muzorewa, lift sanctions and hope that the rest of the world would follow suit.

However, the new leadership quickly realized that such a policy would not work. No other country, including the United States, would follow Britain down the road of recognition. No one else would lift sanctions. Britain would be isolated with South Africa in breach of international law. Muzorewa would be no better off and the international consequences for Britain would be serious, to put it mildly. But Britain needed an acceptable solution and needed it quickly. Lord Carrington, the new Foreign Secretary, was determined to shed the albatross of Rhodesia from the neck of British foreign policy. Anti-sanctions feeling was running high in the Conservative party and it looked as though it might be possible to renew the Sanctions Order in Parliament in November only with Labour and Liberal support. This was something which the government was not prepared to contemplate.

Mrs Thatcher and Lord Carrington wisely decided not to try to revive the Anglo-American proposals which were sinking with the weight of their detail. Instead they decided to simplify the situation by calling all parties, including Smith and Muzorewa, ZANU and ZAPU, together in London to draft an independence constitution, the normal procedure for decolonization of a territory where there was no problem. Before issuing invitations, they needed an international imprimatur for this novel approach. I was in no doubt that this was unobtainable from the Security Council, let alone the General Assembly, which was too unambiguously committed to the Patriotic Front and the unadorned demands of the stack of resolutions adopted over the years, too contumacious in regard to the actions of an 'imperial' power and too vulnerable to the trouble-making propensities of the Soviet Union. The Council would never have given Britain the go ahead without interminable negotiation and the attachment of unacceptable constraints.

It was in this dilemma that the Commonwealth, comprising all geographical groups in the international community except for the Eastern Europeans, came into its own. Moreover, Zambia and Nigeria were both non-permanent members of the Security Council and two of the other three African Front Line States, Tanzania and Botswana, were also members of the Commonwealth. Fortuitously a Commonwealth Summit was due to take place in Lusaka in August. Margaret Thatcher with great skill persuaded her Commonwealth colleagues of the merit of the new, simplified, approach. Invitations were issued to the parties and the Lancaster House Conference opened in September.

I arrived in New York shortly after the Lusaka Summit to find an atmosphere heavy with suspicion. Even my American colleagues, who had been working hard with my predecessor on the Anglo-American proposals and in the Contact Group on Namibia, did not seem overjoyed at the new turn of events. It was common knowledge that the first instinct of the Conservative government had been to recognize Muzorewa and lift sanctions. There was a widespread belief, fostered by the Soviet Union and radical Third World delegations – Cuba was in the chair of the Non-Aligned Movement – that Lancaster House was a put up job to legitimize the Bishop and extract Britain from the sanctions hook. Parliamentary and press speculation in London did nothing to allay these fears. I was reasonably confident that the Russians would do what the mainstream Africans wanted, but I realized that I would have to rely heavily on the steadfastness of my Commonwealth colleagues. Without the Lusaka agreement, there would have been little or no hope of keeping the UN on board. Apart from all other considerations, a deep-rooted habit of busybodying – the lifeblood of the Committee of Twenty-four – would have kept the Council and the Committee snapping at the heels of the delegates in London.

In the event, the Commonwealth delegations kept their recalcitrant brothers in order and, during the Lancaster House negotiations, the Council met only once, in order to denounce the Rhodesian regime for attacks on Zambian territory. In December I was able to take to the podium to announce to the General Assembly that agreement had been reached at Lancaster House on an independence constitution to come into effect after a short transitional period, at the end of which free and fair elections would be held. For the first and only time in my experience of the UN a British statement on a decolonization issue was greeted with applause. Farce immediately followed as the General Assembly, ploughing ahead with the ritual Rhodesia debate from which it had been impossible to deflect it, voted on a resolution which took no account of the negotiations or their successful outcome, even that negotiations had been taking place. I made no attempt to restrain my amusement at this demonstration of the detachment from reality of the 'August Body'. The Assembly, not for the first or only time, was like a bobsleigh team doomed to the iron clamp of its piste, even though the games were over and the competitors had dispersed to other pursuits.

The Security Council remained in the real world, taking a step the reverberations of which are still to be felt. With the success of Lancaster House, the return of Rhodesia to legality and the appointment of a British Governor, Lord Soames, to Salisbury, the British government signalled its intention to lift sanctions. This did not go down well in New York where the majority view was that sanctions should remain in place as a coercive threat until Zimbabwe achieved independence. I argued that this was nonsense. Sanctions had been imposed at British initiative because of the rebellion which was now over. British sovereignty had been restored. To keep sanctions on would be for Britain to impose sanctions on itself. My government had no intention of doing this and would lift sanctions, whatever anyone else did. I made no headway with these arguments, even with my American colleagues, and the Council met to debate the question. The argument, vigorously advanced, was that only the Council could undo what it had originally done. My fear was that the Soviet Union would veto the resolution: Britain alone would lift sanctions and there would be a blazing row in New York at the outset of the transitional period in Rhodesia. Fortunately Soviet subservience to African wishes overrode desire to make life difficult for us. Resolution 460 was adopted with thirteen votes in favour, the Soviet Union and Czechoslovakia abstaining. The resolution lifted all the sanctions and dissolved the Sanctions Committee: it closed with a menacing admonition to Britain to ensure that no South African forces remained in Southern Rhodesia.

Resolution 460 established an important precedent. Rhodesian sanctions were, as I noted earlier, the first Chapter VII non-military measures ever imposed and it now appeared that such measures could only be ended by a positive resolution of the Council even though the situation which gave rise to their imposition had objectively changed, i.e. no sanctions could be lifted unless there were at least nine positive votes, and no Permanent Member veto, in favour of doing so. This doctrine has cut in different ways in contemporary terms. For example, the arms embargo on 'Yugoslavia' was imposed in 1991 before that country formally disintegrated. But it is now impossible to lift it from the Bosnian government without a resolution. This would almost certainly be vetoed by the Russian Federation. Mandatory sanctions were imposed on Iraq because of its invasion and occupation of Kuwait. Even though that occupation ended three years ago, the sanctions will remain in place until the Permanent Five are ready to see them lifted.

The transitional period in Rhodesia was only two months long. At the time it seemed interminable. It was clear to all of us in New York that the Governor had inherited responsibility without power and that he was dependent on the fragile goodwill of the contesting parties. It seemed to many of my colleagues that the authorities in Salisbury were tilting violently towards the Smith/Muzorewa combination. The security forces appeared to be roaming at will while the ZANU and ZAPU fighters were corralled in assembly areas by the Commonwealth Monitoring Force. Complaints about intimidation by the Patriotic Front reached gale force while it was well known that South Africa was pouring millions of dollars into Muzorewa's campaign and that the Bishop's henchmen were no novices at intimidation. The most neuralgic issue was the presence of South African security forces in Rhodesia, mentioned at the end of Resolution 460. Over the years the Council had called for their withdrawal and press speculation flourished on the allegations that South African army units, as opposed to police, were deployed in the country.

This volcano erupted in January with the revelation that a company of South African infantry was deployed on the Rhodesian side of the border at Beit Bridge and that other units were in position deeper within the country. The Council went into bad-tempered session and I had a rough time. The eventual draft resolution, although watered down to avoid a British veto, was still unacceptable to London. It called on Britain to ensure the withdrawal of South African forces (something which we were in no position to do), to adopt various measures (beyond our ability in the circumstances) to ensure that all eligible Zimbabweans could participate in the elections, and to free South African political prisoners and freedom fighters (it was not specified how we were to set about these tasks). As the vote drew near, I was encouraged by the African reaction to a vivid exchange of buffets between my Soviet colleague (a veteran UN diplomat who had lost a leg in the war) and myself. In an abusive statement, he had cast doubt on the ability of Britain to organize a free and fair election. This gave me the opportunity, in right of reply, to make a number of uncomplimentary points about the USSR, concluding with the assertion that, if we required advice on how to run free and fair elections, the Soviet Union was probably the last country in the world from which we would seek it. During a short recess my African colleagues asked me to cool it. Why, I enquired? I was enjoying the distraction from the shot and shell they had been directing at me. Their reply was that they did not want the injection of East/West hostility to wreck the independence process. They were having enough difficulty as it was in restraining their more radical colleagues in the NAM. I realized then that the ship was still afloat and that those who mattered on the African side were not going to sink it.

We still had the problem of the resolution. An abstention would have looked weak at home and we had been told that the debate was being closely followed in Salisbury and that a British veto could upset the applecart. We decided to take a leaf out of the Chinese book and not participate in the vote. All my colleagues were watching attentively to see at what point I raised my pencil – yes, no, or abstain. When I failed to raise it at all, there was a buzz of surprise followed by some hilarity and subsequent congratulation on our ingenuity. The crisis passed.

This incident relieved the pressure of suspicion and the Council did not meet again during the transition. There was intense speculation among the membership about the election prospects. The African consensus, shared by all except the ZANU representative, who confidently predicted the result almost as it happened, was similar to that of London, Salisbury and Pretoria, namely that ZAPU (Nkomo) would win all the twenty Ndebele seats and that the remainder would divide between ZANU (Mugabe) and Muzorewa, with the former winning the majority: a plurality leading to a Nkomo/Muzorewa coalition was a likely outcome.

When the final results came in on 5 March, with ZANU having won fifty-seven seats, Nkomo twenty and Muzorewa three, giving Mugabe an overall majority even counting the twenty seats reserved for the whites, African and non-aligned joy was unconfined; still more so when it was realized, after a spurt of suspicion, that the British government had accepted this result, unpalatable though it clearly was in the light of earlier support for Muzorewa and hostility to the Marxist Mugabe. Indeed, one of my African colleagues told me that they would not have given me such a hard time if I had tipped them off confidentially that we were fixing the results for an outright ZANU win! In July the Council signed off at long last on Rhodesia by unanimously recommending Zimbabwe's membership of the UN to the General Assembly.

I have since brooded on two questions. Why did the Lancaster House initiative succeed when all previous efforts had failed, and how much of a part did the UN play from beginning to end in the search for a settlement? My answer to the first question has, I believe, general application to all apparently intractable problems. My theorem is that negotiations for a peaceful settlement of disputes succeed only when all the parties, albeit each for a different reason, need a settlement simultaneously. This conjuncture came about for the first time in Southern Rhodesia in 1979. Smith/Muzorewa needed a settlement because the internal solution was demonstrably not winning support and they realized that, sooner or later, the Patriotic Front would prevail on the battlefield. Zambia and Mozambique, hosts to the Patriotic Front, needed a settlement because of the damage being done to their weak economies and political structures by the Rhodesian military raids. The Patriotic Front needed a settlement to satisfy their hosts and because they foresaw a long and bloody struggle before final victory on the battlefield. South Africa needed a settlement because of reluctance to be forced to absorb a defeated Rhodesian white community or face further militancy, perhaps anarchy, to the north. Most important, Britain for the first time needed a settlement to a tight timescale because of the refusal of the government to rely on opposition votes to renew the Sanctions Order. Never before had all the pieces on the board been in place at the same time.

As regards the part played by the UN, sanctions were a contributory but not a determining factor. Economically they had nuisance value, and damaged certain sectors of the economy. But it can be argued that they also stimulated it by encouraging entrepreneurship and diversification. They would never have succeeded on their own. The psychological sense of isolation induced by the strengthening and tightening of sanctions may well have been more damaging to white morale than the economic effects of the embargos. The most significant impact of sanctions was on international recognition. Governments were ready enough to cheat and to turn a blind eye to sanctions busting. But no government was prepared openly to recognize the Smith regime and end up in the international doghouse along with South Africa and, for the first nine years, Portugal. Had it not been for this factor, there could well have been creeping recognition of the Smith regime. This was perhaps the most telling contribution.

It is also true that the UN – General Assembly and Security Council – provided a focal point for the mobilization of an international consensus, fixing responsibility for a solution squarely on Britain and on what would constitute acceptable terms, namely immediately self-determination for all the people of Southern Rhodesia, leading to sovereign independence on the basis of majority rule. These notions may have been expressed in tiresomely strident and repetitive terms but they had to be taken into account by successive British governments in their negotiations with the parties. This was the price which London had to pay for the tactical advantage of having the UN to refer to when faced with the dilemma created by the original UDI.

On the negative side, the insistent repetition of OAU, Non-Aligned and General Assembly declarations and resolutions hardened the majority view into a wholly one-sided posture, favourable without qualification to the Patriotic Front and correspondingly hostile to African leaders who sought a solution in cooperation with the white regime. This factor eliminated the UN in any of its forms from playing a part in negotiations for a settlement. In footballing terms, the UN constituted a group of clamorous fans on the terraces, urging on one side and barracking all others. It was not a player, certainly not a referee.

The truth is that, once UDI was proclaimed and it was evident that Britain would not use force to reverse it, only regional developments were likely to sap the will of the Smith regime to hold out with, at the most, cosmetic compromise. South African and Portuguese support were crucial strategically as well as economically. The collapse of the Portuguese empire was the beginning of the end. The South Africans saw this immediately and started to bring pressure to bear on the Smith regime to settle. ZANU, the more military effective of the two wings of the Patriotic Front, saw this too, and stepped up the guerrilla campaign from the newly independent and politically radical Mozambique. South African insistence, the intensification of the war and the demonstrable lack of popular support for the 'internal' black leadership were the forces which eventually brought the regime to the table at Lancaster House in an accommodating frame of mind. The words and actions of the United Nations were peripheral in their influence, atmospheric rather than operational.

PART THREE

Lessons and Legacies of History

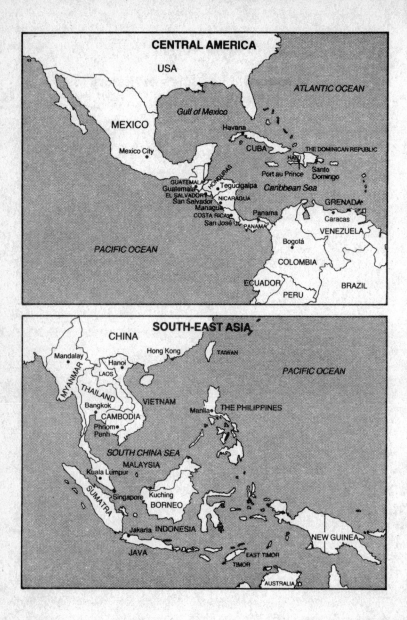

CENTRAL AMERICA

USA

ATLANTIC OCEAN

Gulf of Mexico

MEXICO

Mexico City

Havana

CUBA

THE DOMINICAN REPUBLIC

HAITI

Port au Prince

Santo Domingo

Caribbean Sea

GUATEMALA

Guatemala

HONDURAS

Tegucigalpa

EL SALVADOR

San Salvador

NICARAGUA

Managua

GRENADA

COSTA RICA

San José

Panama

Caracas

PANAMA

VENEZUELA

PACIFIC OCEAN

Bogotá

COLOMBIA

ECUADOR

PERU

BRAZIL

SOUTH-EAST ASIA

CHINA

Mandalay

Hanoi

Hong Kong

TAIWAN

PACIFIC OCEAN

MYANMAR

LAOS

THAILAND

VIETNAM

Bangkok

CAMBODIA

Manila

THE PHILIPPINES

Phnom Penh

SOUTH CHINA SEA

MALAYSIA

Kuala Lumpur

SUMATRA

Singapore

Kuching

BORNEO

Jakarta

INDONESIA

NEW GUINEA

JAVA

EAST TIMOR

TIMOR

AUSTRALIA

CHAPTER NINE

Angola

(How not to do it)

In Chapter 7 I described how Angolan independence merged into civil war between the Soviet and Cuban supported MPLA government and the South African and latterly American supported UNITA movement led by Jonas Savimbi; and how the wretched people of Angola became pawns in the artificial East/West confrontation as orchestrated by the Reagan administration in the 1980s in the search for Namibian independence. With the 1988 agreement on Cuban withdrawal and the beginning of implementation of the Namibian independence process, it looked as though this factitious construct had served its purpose and that Angola might be able to contemplate peace after nearly thirty years of armed struggle against the Portuguese, civil war and savage incursions by the Republic of South Africa. It was not to be.

To begin with, a glow of optimism illuminated the scene. The UN Angola Verification Mission (UNAVEM) established by the Security Council in December 1988 to certify the northward redeployment and withdrawal of the fifty-thousand-strong Cuban contingent with all their arms and equipment, had an easy time. It comprised only seventy unarmed military observers plus twenty civilian support staff. They were stationed mainly at seaports and airports with a handful monitoring withdrawal from the south of the country. The Cubans were highly disciplined, and the political decision to withdraw had been made in Havana. The Secretary-General was able to submit periodic reports to the Council detailing the numbers which had left in relation to the agreed schedule. There was a slight delay when UNITA attacked a water-purification installation and killed four Cuban soldiers, wounding five. However, in June 1991, the Secretary-General reported that all fifty thousand plus all their equipment had left Angola one month ahead of the planned schedule. So far, so good and UNAVEM had been able to reduce its numbers slightly as the Cubans progressively departed.

A month earlier Portugal, the United States and the Soviet Union had succeeded in forging a cease-fire agreement – the Lisbon Peace Accords – between the MPLA government and UNITA. This agreement was predicated on 'free and fair' elections taking place between September and November 1992. In the negotiations, UNITA had wanted elections after a much shorter delay, plus a large UN presence on the ground with far-reaching powers. The MPLA had wanted a three-year delay and a small UN presence which would not intrude on Angolan sovereignty. The compromise on the time-table was matched by a compromise on the UN role, namely that UNAVEM would be mandated to verify the carrying out of the accords, i.e. to verify the arrangements made between the parties for monitoring the cease-fire, to corroborate the reorganization of the Angolan police and military and to observe the elections. The UN was not involved in the negotiations of the accords and was only admitted to the various Joint Commissions by invitation: the peace brokers, Portugal, the US and the USSR (soon to be the Russian Federation), were also involved in an observer role. The role of the UN was confirmed by the Security Council in October 1991.

At the time, the Lisbon Accords were hailed as a diplomatic triumph of superpower cooperation in the wake of the Gulf crisis, the culmination of Chester Crocker's (by then retired from the scene) long negotiation on Namibia. This seemed a fair judgement. In retrospect the seeds of disaster had been sown. First, the accords were a victory for UNITA. Armed to the teeth by South Africa and the United States, cossetted by Washington, including a photo-call reception by President Reagan, Savimbi had succeeded in being accepted not as a rebel making terms with a government but as an equal with the government. This impression was enhanced by the fact that, whereas UNITA had in effect been 'recognized' by the US, the government had not, and indeed was not to be recognized by Washington until May 1993, by which time UNITA alone was responsible for the resumption of the civil war. These accolades meant that Savimbi, no stranger to megalomania, could with justification regard himself and his movement not as aspirants to a share in government but to unfettered power over Angola. Secondly, the UN should have been a full partner in the negotiations, rather than being landed with a peripheral role in a rigid timetable of events, the successful execution of which, to quote Dame Joan Anstee, the Secretary-General's representative in Luanda from 1992–93, rested with the two parties relying on 'a kind of Boy Scouts honour in a situation which had not exactly been conducive to the development of the Boy Scout spirit.'

Miraculously, all went well for several months. The Secretary-General was able to report that the cease-fire was holding with only minor infringements, although the cantonment of MPLA and UNITA forces to assembly areas was painfully slow. In March 1992, the Security Council agreed to the plan whereby UNAVEM would observe and verify the forthcoming elections, with the concurrence of the parties. This extended mandate was another fatal blunder. Joan Anstee was told to conduct a 'small and manageable operation'. This rubric displayed either grotesque frivolity or unforgivable indifference on the part of the Security Council. Perhaps the two mediators, the United States and the Soviet Union, regarded the civil war as having been perpetuated entirely by their own past involvement, and that peace would automatically follow their withdrawal from championship of the opposing combatants. Perhaps they did not care much what happened in a remote part of Africa once it was drained of wider international significance. In next door Namibia in 1989, nearly eight thousand UN personnel had been deployed to organize (not simply to monitor and verify) elections among a tiny population compared to that of Angola. In Cambodia from 1991–93 the UN deployed twenty thousand personnel for a similar purpose. UNAVEM started with less than 450 unarmed observers, with an additional 100 after the decision to monitor the elections was taken in March, and another 400 for the one-month period of the actual elections. Considering that Angola is the size of Germany, France and Spain put together, that it had been a savage battlefield of one kind or another for thirty years and that it had never before experienced a Western-style or any other kind of election, these resources, coupled with the limited nature of the mandate, were laughable. Furthermore, no one seems to have given thought to the near certainty that, in a winner-takes-all type of election, the loser would not meekly move to the opposition benches as a 'loyal opposition' to its bitter erstwhile enemy. No contingency plans appear to have been contemplated to meet such an obvious eventuality.

In June the Secretary-General submitted a report to the Council which, while confirming the maintenance of the cease-fire and progress in electoral preparations, warned of the fragility of the situation, of intimidation and hatreds, of harsh propaganda accusations and of the fact that only 4 per cent of the UNITA forces and 16 per cent of the government forces had demobilized and that only 6 per cent (3,200 personnel) of the new, combined Angolan army was in being. The Security Council continued to keep its fingers crossed that all would be well on the day.

Again it looked as though this optimism was justified. The election date drew near, UNAVEM sent out two hundred observation teams of two persons each and monitored all the stages of the elections as best it could. On 29/30 September, over 90 per cent of registered voters turned out in a peaceful atmosphere.

A few days later, UNITA began to spread accusations of fraud. On 5 October UNITA generals were withdrawn from the embryonic Angolan armed forces. On 17 October the National Electoral Council announced the results of the polling which Joan Anstee certified as having been 'generally free and fair'. The MPLA had won 57 per cent of the vote (129 seats) to UNITA's 31 per cent (seventy seats) in the parliamentary elections. President Dos Santos had won 49.57 per cent of the vote to Savimbi's 40.07 per cent in the presidential race, fractionally short of the required 50 per cent. UNITA cried foul and resumed the war at the end of the month.

Over the past eighteen months the fighting has been probably more intense that it was at any time before the Lisbon Accords of 1991. In the summer of 1993 the UN estimate was that as many as a thousand people (mainly civilians) a day were dying as a result of the fighting. At the end of January 1994, the Secretary-General reported that about 3.3 million people were displaced, drought-affected, or in need of various forms of aid as a consequence of the war. Appalling reports of sieges and massacres have proliferated.

UNAVEM, its mandate in ruins and its numbers reduced, has become the principle mediating agency in concert with several African leaders. Negotiations have taken place in Angola itself, in Abidjan, Addis Ababa and currently in Lusaka. The Security Council has adopted what I think of as the Arab/Israel posture, pumping out forlorn resolutions of which the offending party takes no notice. After every report by the Secretary-General, the Council's language has become harsher, the demands more exclusively directed at UNITA – 'strong' condemnations, demands to cease hostilities, to return to the Lisbon Accords, withdraw from seized territory, etc. In September

1993 an oil and arms embargo was imposed on UNITA, already awash with South African and American military supplies and with free access to more through the porous border with Zaire. An additional embargo on trade and travel has been threatened with a deadline which has moved by the month as UNITA does just enough at each round of negotiations to buy more time without implementing what look superficially like concessions – a wrestle with a ghost. By the spring of 1994, hostilities were continuing. Neither side seems capable of a knock-out blow, only of medieval sieges and the creation of mass suffering and death to the civilian population, while negotiations drag on.

There is no indication that the Security Council will do more than strengthen sanctions and continue the bombardment of words. Unlike Bosnia, there is no disposition to send thousands of blue-helmeted peace-keepers to escort the humanitarian aid which the UN and non-governmental agencies are struggling to supply. Unlike Somalia, there is no inclination to send troops to break the sieges of the towns by force. Unlike the Gulf, there is no intention of fighting UNITA into submission, although the numbers of soldiers involved in the fighting are probably very small. Unlike Kurdistan in 1991, there is insufficient television coverage of the horrors to stimulate public outrage and force governments to change course and adopt any of the above policies.

Angola, in the eyes of the international community, is declining in importance into just another contemporary African tragedy like Liberia, Rwanda, Burundi and the Sudan, civil wars in which the UN has either avoided involvement or is only peripherally engaged with mediation and small, 'non-threatening' peace-keeping deployments. The country was unlucky enough, although its internal conflicts were entirely local in origin, to become a victim of the great clash of ideologies which we call the Cold War, and of the conflict-ridden denouement of white minority rule in southern Africa. By taking sides in the civil war, the Great Powers unwittingly ensured that a heavy price would be paid by the Angolan people themselves; of the outside world, only Fidel Castro put his men where his mouth was. It cannot be much consolation to the spirits of the hundreds of thousands of dead, maimed and displaced Angolans and their families that politicians, thousands of miles away, should have decreed that they would be better off dead than defended by Reds.

For the UN itself the lessons are clear. Insist on being a participant in negotiations for settlements which the Secretariat and member states will be expected to carry out on the ground. Reject any mandate which is unworkable. Insist, before agreeing to put a mandate into practice, that adequate funds and personnel will be available. Make sure that contingency plans are drawn up against the likelihood that things will go wrong. I know as well as the next person that, in multilateral diplomacy, there is a powerful impetus towards settling for any agreement as being better than none so that the file can be closed and the next problem on the agenda addressed. Even so, Angola must stand alone as the quintessence of how not to do it.

CHAPTER TEN

Mozambique

Like her sister ex-Portuguese African colony, Angola, Mozambique has suffered abominably from confused and precipitate decolonization, and from factitious involvement in the death throes of white minority rule in central and southern Africa. On the face of it, Mozambique was the more fortunate in that there was only one liberation movement, FRELIMO, engaged in armed struggle against the Portuguese. However, on departure, the Portuguese exodus of hundreds of thousands of people, taking with them as much of the country's portable infrastructure as they could carry, was probably more drastic than in Angola. Moreover, the Portuguese who left went mainly to South Africa where they formed a dangerous focus for anti-FRELIMO activity. More seriously, the FRELIMO government, after independence in 1975, actively participated in the UN sanctions against Southern Rhodesia at considerable economic cost (in 1976 the Security Council called for international assistance to Mozambique to offset this damage) and provided sanctuary and support for the more militarily effective guerrilla movement operating in Rhodesia, Robert Mugabe's ZANU.

Even in the best of circumstances, the FRELIMO government would have found it hard to run the country efficiently. Ramshackle, left-wing, dependent on the support of the Soviet Union whose inadequacies were becoming manifest by the late 1970s, FRELIMO made heavy weather of the transition from freedom fighting to governing; some of their more doctrinaire economic policies were disastrous. In any case, the ransacking which accompanied the Portuguese departure would have daunted the most competent successor administration. However, these were relatively minor problems compared to the short- and long-term penalties inflicted on Mozambique for helping the opposition to the white regime in Southern Rhodesia. In the final two or three years before the Lancaster House Agreement, Mozambique was subjected to damaging air raids and ground incursions by the Rhodesian armed forces. This was one of the factors which helped to bring ZANU to the conference table in 1979. Furthermore, the

Smith/Muzorewa regime sponsored and supported an anti-FRE-LIMO guerrilla group within Mozambique. This was the movement which became known as RENAMO, comprising ex-FRELIMO malcontents and other disaffected elements. It never seemed to have a political ideology beyond opposition to the government. After the independence of Zimbabwe neutralized its original sponsors, South African intelligence services took over their function. Even when the dynamic and pragmatic President Samora Machel switched from Soviet to Western patronage, charmed Ronald Reagan and Margaret Thatcher and made peace with South Africa (the Nkomati Accords of 1984), this covert support continued. RENAMO established offices in Washington and formed close relations with right-wing organizations. Even so it never achieved the 'freedom fighter' accolade conferred on Savimbi and UNITA. But the Anglo-American policy of 'constructive engagement' failed to convince South African covert intelligence that it would be better to have a stable, pro-Western Mozambique as neighbour than to continue to foment civil war, death, destruction and refugees by the hundreds of thousands. By the end of the 1980s the country was in ruins, possibly even worse off than Angola: Western, Zimbabwean and Malawian military and economic aid was keeping FRELIMO afloat, but it seemed incapable of crushing RENAMO. Both sides were exhausted and tentative contacts began between them.

In the early 1990s, a peace initiative was launched by Italian church organizations long established in Mozambique. This process developed into a full-scale conference in Rome under Italian government chairmanship. On 4 October 1992, a General Peace Agreement was signed by President Chissano of Mozambique (who succeeded Machel in 1986 when the latter was killed in an air crash), President Dhlakama of RENAMO and by the Italian governmental and non-governmental mediators. Also present were presidents and senior ministers from neighbouring African states, including South Africa, and observers from the UN Secretariat, the United States, France, Britain, Portugal, and the OAU. The nearly sixty-page long Agreement was divided into several protocols dealing with basic principles: the formation of political parties and electoral arrangements; refugees and displaced persons; military matters, including a cease-fire and guarantees; and foreign aid. The United Nations was given a central role, unlike in Angola, in all areas of the Agreement, including the following:

1) Chairing the Supervisory and Monitoring Commission (CSC)

formed to guarantee implementation of the whole Agreement and coordinate the other subordinate Commissions.

2) Drawing up and implementing a plan for resettling refugees and displaced persons.

3) Chairing the Cease-Fire Commission (CFC – 'The UN shall assist in the implementation, verification and monitoring of the entire demobilisation process.'

4) Chairing CORE, the commission for the reintegration into society of demobilized soldiers.

5) Chairing the Election Supervisory and Monitoring Commission.

6) Deploying forces in Mozambique from the day of the cease-fire to verify compliance and investigate violations.

7) Supervision of the movement to assembly areas and cantonment of government and RENAMO forces; no force or person to leave such areas without authorization from and supervision of the UN.

8) Collection of inventories of troop and weapons strengths, weapons to be stored under UN control.

9) Coordination and supervision of all humanitarian assistance operations.

On the day of the signature, President Chissano sent a letter to the UN Secretary-General seeking the agreement of the United Nations to carry out these and other related functions. On 13 October, the Security Council adopted a resolution welcoming the Agreement, taking note of the proposed role of the UN and authorizing the Secretary-General to appoint a Special Representative (the Italian politician, Sr. Aldo Ajello), to send a preliminary team of military observers to Mozambique, and to report back. On 15 October (E Day), the General Peace Agreement including the cease-fire came into effect. However, violations of the cease-fire were frequent and, on 27 October, the Council called upon the parties to behave themselves and to cooperate with the Special Representative. Sr. Ajello brought the parties together in early November and appointed the Supervisory and Monitoring Commission (CSC) in which, apart from the parties, the mediators and observers of the Rome Conference were members at the outset. The subsidiary Commissions were then appointed.

In his report to the Council, the Secretary-General frankly set out the difficulties and risks involved in the operation, stressing the size of the country, the devastated infrastructure, disrupted economy and the complexity of the processes in the Agreement. He concluded that the risks were worth taking, but that successful elections would be impossible unless the military situation was first brought under control.

The Council decided to go ahead. On 16 December it adopted Resolution 797 establishing the UN Operation in Mozambique (ONUMOZ) until 31 October 1993, the putative date of the elections. The ONUMOZ mandate included interlocking political, military, electoral and humanitarian tasks. Sr. Ajello would coordinate the overall direction; the military force would monitor and verify the cease-fire, demobilization, and storage of weapons. This range of activity would be closely linked with the humanitarian aspects of reintegrating demobilized soldiers into society. ONUMOZ would also monitor the withdrawal of the Zimbabwean and Malawian forces which had been guarding Mozambique's transportation network. ONUMOZ's Electoral Division would provide technical assistance to and monitor the electoral preparations, and its Humanitarian Division (UNOMAC) would assist the return of people displaced by war and famine.

In spite of delays, and with further urging by the Council, ONUMOZ was fully deployed by May 1993, the Secretary-General having already concluded that the October date for the elections was unrealistic. The UNHCR had made a start in March with repatriating roughly 1.5 million Mozambican refugees (mainly in Malawi), a task estimated to take three years to complete. By June the withdrawal of the foreign troops was accomplished.

Further delays led to the Secretary-General drawing up a revised overall timetable, and the UN assuming the chairmanship of the Joint Commission for the formation of the Mozambican Defence Force. The new date for the elections was set tentatively for October 1994. Until late in the year, progress was patchy and the whole operation hung in the balance. In August direct talks opened between Presidents Chissano and Dhlakama (an encouraging sign) but only thirty-six of the forty-nine assembly areas for demobilization and collection of weapons had been agreed by the CFC. ONUMOZ teams had been deployed in twenty-three of these areas and five battalions of ONUMOZ infantry were patrolling the four transport corridors to these areas. Cease-fire violations were declining although banditry was rife in remote regions. Progress was being made towards formation of the new Defence Force: 100 officers (450 by October) were being trained in Zimbabwe. The humanitarian programme was well under way. But no agreement had been reached on the Electoral Law and the Composition of the Electoral Commission. In September the Security Council issued a hortatory resolution deploring lack of progress in certain areas and urging speedy agreement on outstanding questions.

The Secretary-General visited Mozambique in October and submitted a full report to the Council on 1 November. He was able to report substantial agreement on the problem of the Assembly Areas, on the Election Commission, and on the timing for the preparation of the electoral law. He flatly rejected a RENAMO proposal (shades of UNITA) that elections could take place before the completion of military demobilization. Agreement was formally reached on the new timetable – concentration of troops in assembly areas in November, start of the demobilization process in January 1994, 50 per cent of demobilization completed by March and the rest by May, the new Defence Force to be operational by September, voter registration to take place between April and June, the electoral campaign from 1 September to mid-October with elections by the end of October.

The report contained details of ONUMOZ's strength and deployment, which amounted to six thousand in the military contingent from nine countries, the largest troop contributors being Bangladesh, Italy, Zambia and Uruguay. He noted that one third of the Mozambican refugees had been repatriated and about one fifth of the internally displaced four to five million people had returned to their home areas.

In an addendum, the Secretary-General revealed that the overall cost of ONUMOZ (about seven thousand military and civilian personnel) was budgeted at $20,000,000 a month. The Security Council produced another resolution on 5 November commenting on the report, commending, urging and renewing ONUMOZ's mandate for six months subject to a further report by the end of January.

On 28 January the Secretary-General reported that the new timetable was proceeding on schedule. The Electoral Law had been approved and the National Elections Commission nominated. Chissano and Dhlakama were meeting on a regular basis. The cease-fire was generally holding and almost half the displaced persons and 40 per cent of the external refugees had returned home. By late January over sixteen thousand soldiers (nine thousand government and seven thousand RENAMO) had checked into assembly areas and seventeen thousand weapons had been collected. The disarmament and demobilization of para-military groups had started.

The report qualified these optimistic pronouncements with warnings of the problems lying ahead. Fourteen assembly areas had not been opened: demobilization was slow and complex, and reintegration of soldiers into society was beset with economic difficulties: most of the RENAMO soldiers were in rags and had nothing with which to start a new life; the hardships of army life had discouraged recruitment into the new Defence Force; demobilized soldiers unable to find employment could well become sources of instability; government soldiers in assembly areas had rioted over demands for back pay; and the transformation of RENAMO from guerrilla army into political party was exercizing heavy demands on financial resources.

By the time this book is published the elections should have taken place and Mozambique's future should be clearer, for better or for worse. At the time of writing (spring 1994) the omens are favourable. It is pleasant to think that the central role played by the UN (analogous to Cambodia) derives from the lesson of the Angolan fiasco. The Rome Agreement was concluded days after the Angolan elections took place. The Secretary-General and his representative, under the authority of the Security Council, were put in the driving seat rather than being helpless passengers, as in Angola. They could call a halt when things went wrong, refuse to proceed unless their conditions were met and insist rather than cajole, the underlying threat being that, unless the parties came into line, they would be abandoned to their fate. The UN operation, again in contrast to Angola, was provided with sufficient funds and personnel to persuade the parties that, if they behaved, the UN could deliver on its undertakings.

The political background was also propitious. Great Power interest in Mozambique had evaporated and, with national reconciliation in South Africa, RENAMO must have realized that they were no longer an 'asset' to their covert supporters. Much credit must lie with the Italian Church organization which launched the peace initiative. Without this catalyst the chances are that the Security Council, after the failure in Angola, with increasing entanglement in Bosnia, Croatia and Somalia, would have been glad to look the other way and do nothing. As it was, the involvement of the major Western powers and African leaders in the Rome negotiations gave authority to the proceedings, which passed to the Council and thence to the Secretariat operation on the ground.

CHAPTER ELEVEN

Central America – Nicaragua and El Salvador

Since the end of the Second World War, Central America has been plagued by poverty, social injustice, militarism, civil war, external subversion, monopoly capitalism and occasional inter-state hostilities. Little of this mayhem has reached the agenda of the Security Council. The United States has, since the early nineteenth century – the Monroe Doctrine was proclaimed in 1828 – been allergic to meddling in Latin America by non-hemispheric powers, be it bilaterally or as part of multilateral organizations. With the advent of the capitalism-versus-communism ideological struggle, the Monroe Doctrine trans-muted into a kind of proto-Brezhnev Doctrine. Just as, after the suppression of the Prague Spring in 1968, Leonid Brezhnev enunciated the principle that the sovereign independence of communist states was limited by the obligation to remain within the socialist fold, so the United States has been unwilling to tolerate the Red Flag or any approximation to it being flown alongside national flags between the Rio Grande and the Panama Canal. Doctrinal heresy in this regard has been punished by a number of means: subversion in concert with friendly sub-regional governments (President Arbenz of Guatemala, whose reformist doctrines had imperiled the interests of the United Fruit Company, suffered this fate in 1954); total isolation, including a comprehensive economic embargo, without UN authority (Cuba from the early 1960s, and Nicaragua under the Sandinistas in the 1980s); sponsoring and arming rebel movements (the Contras in Nicaragua between 1980 and 1988); and, in the last resort when the military task was relatively straightforward, full-scale invasion (The Dominican Republic in 1965 and Grenada in 1983).

In spite of Washington's preference to deal with Central America and the Caribbean either bilaterally or through the Organization of American States, some of these issues surfaced briefly in the Security Council. In the pre-1970 days when the United States prided itself on its veto-free virginity, Washington succeeded either in neutralizing action in the Security Council, as with the Guatemalan case in 1954 when judicious procrastination delayed matters until Arbenz had been overthrown, or by throwing a small sop to the Council like the agreement to accept a two-man observer mission (DOMREP) designated by the Secretary-General in the Dominican Republic from 1965 until the American forces withdrew in 1966. The Cuban missile crisis of 1962, so brilliantly handled by President Kennedy and his staff, became a *cause célèbre* of Security Council polemic but, with two Permanent Members at each other's throats, no resolution or other Council action was even contemplated.

In more recent years the United States has been less sensitive to outside opinion in preventing prolonged Security Council involvement in affairs close to home. In 1973, in the Nixon presidency, a resolution urging the conclusion of a new Panama Canal Treaty (Panama was a non-permanent member at the time) received an American veto (and a British abstention for the sake of company). In the 1980s (under the Reagan administration) the United States vetoed eight resolutions relating to Nicaragua – complaints about the mining of Nicaraguan ports, about American disregard for judgements by the International Court of Justice, and American-imposed coercive sanctions. In all cases the faithful British abstained while, on almost all, the remainder of the Council voted in favour. The US (Britain abstained) also vetoed a resolution 'deeply deploring' the Grenada invasion and, this time with France and Britain, another 'strongly deploring' the invasion of Panama to remove the egregious Manuel Noriega in 1989.

The 1980s had ushered in a particularly sanguinary period, even by local standards, in Central American history. Civil war had been smouldering in Guatemala since the 1960s between successive military regimes and left-wing groups whose purpose was to improve the dreadful lot of the Indian majority population. A military coup in 1962 brought an even more than usually ferocious dictator to power. In the next two years ten thousand unarmed civilians are said to have been killed and 100,000 more fled into neighbouring Mexico. A left-wing rebel movement in El Salvador, the FMLN, challenged the right-wing government with varying degrees of success, in spite of American policy of linking military and economic aid with efforts aimed at democratization. As far as Washington was concerned, the rebellion in El Salvador was linked to the Sandinistas in Nicaragua and through them to Cuba and Moscow. From the late 1970s to the late 1980s the Salvadorean civil war is said to have cost up to seventy thousand lives, mainly civilian. And the Contra rebellion, fuelled by Washington from bases in Honduras and to a lesser extent Costa Rica, ground on in Nicaragua. By 1988 it was estimated to have cost twenty thousand mainly civilian lives.

From early in the decade, Latin American governments were coming together to promote peace in Central America. In 1983 the governments of Colombia, Mexico, Panama and Venezuela formed what became known from the venue of the original meeting as the Contadora Group. At the time this coalition was not, according to outside observers, welcome to Washington, which preferred to maintain the lead role in peacemaking and peacekeeping. This United States reluctance was, if it existed, par for the course. Washington was caught in a bind familiar to those of us who played a part in British 'spheres of influence', where local sovereign independence was more apparent than real and where friendly but sometimes disreputable governments were under pressure from internal and external forces which had gained substantial popular support. The Administration was ideologically resolved to purge its hinterland of dangerous notions such as socialism, more so Marxism-Leninism with its connotation of Soviet 'moral and material' support. Pragmatically it was imperative to prevent such dangerous infections from reaching Mexico where a political and economic upheaval would directly threaten the 'shining city on the hill' with additional floods of Hispanic immigrants. However, the majority of Central American governments were corrupt and inefficient; the bulk of their peoples were in dire straits at the hands of a minority of rich landowners; and the representatives of the American free-market economy had much to answer for. No wonder left-wing revolutionaries were prospering. But Washington was not prepared to contemplate another Cuba. This tangled web led to the pursuit of several strands of policy simultaneously, a combination of military and covert aid to rotten regimes which were operating death squads and all other means of repression, with political pressure on the right-wing civilian and military leaders to behave more democratically, to improve human rights observance and to make sacrifices to better the lot of the masses. The intrusion of a group of regional governments, however well meaning, into this high-wire act cannot have been welcome to some of the Washington players, already facing storms of criticism from the American media and elements in the Congress.

But the process begun at Contadora gathered momentum. The five

Central American Heads of State (Costa Rica, El Salvador, Guatemala, Honduras and Nicaragua) joined in. Under the leadership of President Arias of Costa Rica (who was awarded the Nobel Peace Prize in 1987 for his achievement), the five formulated what became known as the Esquipelas Agreements, the final declaration of a summit held in Guatemala in August 1987. These Agreements, addressing Central America as a whole, dealt with national reconciliation, an end to hostilities, democratization, free elections, termination of aid to insurrectionist movements and non-use of the territory of one state to attack other states, control and limitation of weapons, and international verification. The UN and the OAS were invited to verify free elections and the programme in general by participating in an International Verification and Follow-up Commission (CIVS).

This initiative came at a fortunate time internationally. The Cold War was winding down: the Gorbachev policy of withdrawing material support from liberation movements in Asia, Africa and Latin America was under way. The Five Permanent Members of the Security Council were uniquely cooperating over the problem of the Iran/Iraq war. The feral dislike of the UN in Reaganite circles was diminishing. The requirement to support sons-of-bitches provided that they were 'our' sons-of-bitches (the Nicaraguan Contras and the Salvadorean military being prime examples) was becoming irrelevant as the ideological imperative dissolved.

After close consultation between the UN and OAS Secretariats and further ministerial meetings of the Central American Five, the first major step forward was taken. The Nicaraguan government agreed to hold elections in early 1990 and a plan was drawn up for the demobilization, repatriation or relocation of the Contras. The UN agreed to monitor the elections. Around the same time, the Salvadorean government and the FMLN began peace negotiations under the auspices of the UN Secretary-General, and the 'Joint Plan' for the demobilization of the Contras embraced similar action in regard to the FMLN. In July 1989 the Security Council unanimously adopted a resolution commending all these efforts, supporting the involvement of the Secretary-General and noting with appreciation the agreement to deploy a UN mission to observe the Nicaraguan elections. In September, the Secretary-General recommended to the Council the establishment of an Observer Group (ONUCA) to verify the security arrangements in the Esquipelas Agreements, i.e. the cessation of aid to irregular forces and the non-use of the territory of one state to attack another. ONUCA was established for six months in November, comprising 260 unarmed military observers plus an air wing and a naval unit. Patrolling was carried out in small groups, mainly in the border areas between Costa Rica and Nicaragua; Honduras and Nicaragua; Honduras and El Salvador; and Guatemala and El Salvador. In December, the Council enlarged ONUCA's mandate to include verification of the cessation of hostilities and demobilization of irregular forces. In early 1990 an armed Venezuelan battalion was added to the force to oversee the demobilization and destruction of the weapons of the Nicaraguan Resistance (the Contras). In March the Nicaraguan elections had taken place, monitored by the UN, and the Sandinistas had been defeated at the polls.

At the end of April power was handed over; a cease-fire came into effect with a separation of forces. In May the Security Council extended ONUCA's mandate, to expire with the completion of Nicaraguan demobilization. On 29 June the Secretary-General reported that the process was complete: over twenty thousand Contras had been demobilized and over fifteen thousand small arms plus heavier weapons had been handed over.

However, the Council continued to extend ONUCA's mandate until it was subsumed in ONUSAL, created by the Council in May 1991 to monitor agreements reached between the Salvadorean government and the FMLN to resolve the civil war, to promote democratization, guarantee human rights and reunify Salvadorean society. ONUSAL began by monitoring the Agreement on Human Rights, investigating violations and following up action taken by the parties to correct them.

At the end of 1991, after negotiations stage-managed by the Secretary-General in New York, the various agreements reached were consolidated in the Act of New York, which completed negotiations on all aspects of Esquipelas: the final peace accords were signed in Mexico City in January 1992.

ONUSAL's mandate was progressively extended by the Security Council to embrace its expanded responsibilities – verifying the cease-fire and separation of forces, monitoring public order while the new National Civil Police Force was established, and ultimately, on 27 May 1993, observation of the presidential, legislative and municipal elections due in March 1994. At its peak ONUSAL comprised about a thousand military and civilian personnel, roughly the same strength as ONUCA.

The Secretary-General's periodic reports to the Security Council revealed astonishing progress in all fields as well as the inevitable delays, obstacles and violations of the Agreements. In December 1992, the Secretary-General could confirm that the armed conflict was over. In November 1993, he reported favourably on the implementation of the findings of the 'Commission on the Truth', a body established under his aegis to investigate serious acts of violence committed since 1980 (massacres of peasants by the Armed Forces, assassinations by death squads, violence by the FMLN and assassination of judges). In May 1993 there was a serious problem when an explosion in Managua, capital of Nicaragua, led to the revelation of the existence of a number of clandestine FMLN arms caches inside and outside El Salvador. Fortunately the FMLN came clean. The Secretary-General reported in August that the FMLN military structure had been dismantled and the caches destroyed. He had already reported that the armed forces had been purged of undesirable officers, that the agreed reduction in the strength of the armed forces had taken place and that the former 'National Intelligence Department' had been disbanded. At the end of 1993 there was anxiety about a resumption of death-squad murders and about delay in final implementation of the recommendations of the Commission on the Truth. Other delays and hold-ups were mentioned as the electoral campaign got under way in November, the objective being to clear the decks of the litter of the past before the elections took place. In March/April 1994, elections were held without serious incident. There were inevitable irregularities, but none so great as to vitiate the process.

There is a classical quality about the successful engagement of the UN in Central America which would warm the hearts of the Founding Fathers of the Organization, especially those who regarded the UN, like the League of Nations, as primarily intended to protect the rights of small, weak states against more powerful predators. Central America had become involved in the interplay of Great Power politics, whose actions were exacerbating and perpetuating sub-regional disputes and conflicts. The sub-regional powers, in the spirit of Chapter VI of the Charter (the Pacific Settlement of Disputes) and without recourse to mandatory, coercive action, took matters into their own hands and formulated the principles on which comprehensive reconciliation could be achieved. Realizing that, on their own, they commanded insufficient authority to persuade the contesting parties, they simultaneously invoked the support of the regional organization (the OAS) and the world organization (the Secretary-General and the Security Council). The Council, notwithstanding doubts among certain members, had little choice but to respond positively and unanimously, delegating the command and control of its peacekeeping element on the ground to the Secretary-General and his successive (both Latin American) representatives. The United States, whose Central American policies had for over a century been controversial, to put it mildly, wisely stood back and let the parties get on with it. The upshot was that the process worked: perhaps the Esquipelas principles will now be applied to Guatemala, the only Central American state in which civil war still rumbles on.

CHAPTER TWELVE

Cambodia

(How – eventually – to do it)

It may seem strange to outsiders that the Vietnam War, of which Cambodia was a near fatal casualty, never figured on the Security Council agenda except for a single resolution in 1964 deploring the penetration of Vietnamese forces into Cambodia. The fact was that neither of the superpowers wanted the UN to meddle in their separate and opposing adventures in South East Asia. Moreover, until the final years, China was, thanks to United States insistence, represented in the UN by the Nationalist regime in Taiwan, one of the more ludicrous aberrations of the post-Second World War years. Between 1964 and 1968 the Secretary-General, U Thant, himself a Buddhist and Burmese, made a series of offers of 'good offices' to the parties in the Vietnam War. But he was always brushed off by one or another.

Prince Norodom Sihanouk, the seemingly eternal albeit intermittent leader of Cambodia – he was first enthroned by the Vichy authorities in 1941 – had secured his country's independence in 1953. He succeeded in maintaining a fragile neutrality until the late 1960s when the 'secret' American bombing of North Vietnamese 'sanctuaries'in Cambodia helped to precipitate the military coup which temporarily ousted him. This was the first shot in a campaign of brutal air and ground attacks by American and South Vietnamese forces in the early 1970s which destroyed the rickety economic, political and social sub-structure of the country. The way was clear for the radicalized Khmer Rouge to take over. Pol Pot's killing fields began in 1975; four years later one third of the population of Cambodia had been massacred. As in Angola a decade later, a far-off people had paid an horrific price for the privilege of being willy-nilly drawn into the web of perceived American interests, and the self-defeating labyrinth of *Realpolitik* diplomacy.

The Security Council enters the scene only after the Vietnamese, exasperated beyond endurance by Pol Pot's provocations, invaded Cambodia in 1978 and drove out the Khmer Rouge regime, installing a new government responsive to Hanoi. Instead of receiving a public vote of thanks from the UN for ridding Cambodia of a latter-day combination of Hitler and Stalin, and saving the lives of countless Cambodians, the Vietnamese found themselves on the receiving end of draft resolutions in January and March 1979 calling for a cease-fire and the withdrawal of 'foreign forces'. The Soviet Union, Vietnam's patron and supplier of military hardware, cast two vetoes and the Council did not return to the stage until 1991.

The action moved to the General Assembly where, for several years, a distasteful farce was enacted over the representation of Cambodia (or Democratic Kampuchea, as the Khmer Rouge had renamed it). No one seemed to fancy the idea of an empty Cambodian seat: only South Africa was in that position. The Soviet Union and the radical non-aligned states backed the Vietnamese-installed Hun Sen government in Phnom Penh. China, for anti-Soviet and anti-Vietnamese reasons, ardently supported the Khmer Rouge delegation. I remember asking my Chinese colleague how his government could support a monster like Pol Pot. He conceded that the Khmer Rouge had 'made mistakes' but maintained that it was the legitimate government. This struck me as not only worthy of the gold medal for diplomatic understatement but also of dubious validity, since the Khmer Rouge were no longer in control of any territory, except for a small strip of jungle along the Thai border. The United States, for reasons similar to those of the Chinese, took the same view as Peking. The ASEAN states (Malaysia, Singapore, the Philippines, Indonesia and Thailand) were more anxious to placate China than Vietnam and the Soviet Union. The European Community were disposed to please ASEAN.

Hence, I found myself year by year in the unenviable position of voting in favour of representatives of probably the most atrocious regime in the world since 1945 (Stalin's worst massacres being over by then), which did not even control the country and people it purported to represent. It was the custom, adding to the Grand Guignol atmosphere, to follow the voting with a short statement in explanation of the vote, comprising a blistering attack on the Khmer Rouge regime for which we had just voted. It was then politic to leave the Assembly Chamber at speed to avoid the outstretched handshakes of the Pol Pot delegation.

In terms of substance, the General Assembly did rather better. Each year it adopted a resolution calling for the withdrawal of foreign

forces, the provision of humanitarian assistance to the civilian population and self-determination for the Cambodian people. The resolution
invited the Secretary-General to use his good offices to contribute to a
peaceful solution. This placed the UN at the centre of the action
against the time when the words of the resolution could be translated
into deeds. In 1981 an International Conference on Cambodia was
held in New York, in which seventy countries participated with the
Secretary-General in a lead role. The terms of reference were spelt out
in a General Assembly resolution which called for UN-verified withdrawal of foreign forces, UN measures to ensure law and order and
observance of human rights, UN measures to ensure non-interference
by outside powers, and UN-supervised free elections. These principles
figured prominently in the final Conference document.

Through the 1980s the Secretary-General and his representatives
kept in touch with the parties and with interested governments and
put 'sets of ideas' to them for implementation of the resolutions. By
1987–88 the competing Cambodian factions were beginning to meet.
At French initiative, seventeen countries plus the parties attended the
Paris Conference on Cambodia from 30 July to 30 August 1989. The
Secretary-General put a number of proposals to the parties to bridge
differences, outlining the necessary steps for internationally supervised
elections, for the repatriation of refugees and for the reconstruction of
Cambodia. No firm agreement was reached at the Conference but the
ice was breaking. The end of the Cold War had brought all five
Permanent Members to the Conference in a cooperative frame of
mind. As with other apparently intractable disputes which I have
discussed in earlier chapters, the catalyst of withdrawal of superpower
championship of opposing sides in so called 'regional conflicts' was at
work. Vietnam, unable to maintain its presence in Cambodia without
Soviet financial support, announced that its forces would withdraw in
September 1989. This engendered a sense of urgency. If effective
transitional arrangements were not put in hand quickly, the ultimate
catastrophe of a Khmer Rouge renaissance and the resumption of mass
slaughter lay ahead. On the ground the Khmer Rouge in the Thai
border area were still a formidable fighting force and they were known
to have infiltrated many of the refugee camps across the frontier.

In 1990 the Five Permanent Members held a series of discussions in
close contact with the Secretary-General who confirmed that the UN
would assume a role agreed with the parties and approved by the

Security Council provided that the mandate was well defined, realistic and practicable and that the necessary resources for its successful implementation would be forthcoming. The Australian government proposed a lead role for the UN which despatched fact-finding missions to Cambodia to study infrastructural, administrative, repatriation and other problems. A comprehensive settlement programme was taking shape on the administration of Cambodia in a transitional period to elections under UN auspices. This framework was endorsed by the Security Council on 16 October in a resolution which established a United Nations Advanced Mission in Cambodia (UNAMIC) and called upon the newly created all-party (except Khmer Rouge) Supreme National Council of Cambodia to cooperate with it. This Council now occupied the Cambodian seat in the Assembly.

The Paris Conference resumed in October and reached agreement on a 'comprehensive political settlement of the Cambodian conflict'. This agreement was signed by all the Cambodian parties, including the Khmer Rouge. The Security Council authorized the Secretary-General to designate a Special Representative (the experienced Japanese UN diplomat Yasushi Akashi was appointed at the beginning of 1992) and requested him to submit a detailed implementation plan. On 8 January the Council passed another resolution dealing mainly with the acute problem of mine clearance. On 19 February the Secretary-General submitted his report.

This thirty-page document describes in detail how the Secretary General proposed to put into effect the authority delegated by the Supreme National Council to the United Nations to assume 'all powers necessary' to ensure the implementation of the Paris Agreement in the following seven components: human rights; electoral, military, civil administration, police, repatriation of refugees (360,000 in camps in Thailand) and rehabilitation. This amounted to *carte blanche*, in effect, to run the country until the electorate chose a Constituent Assembly of 120 members. The UN Transitional Authority in Cambodia (UNTAC) was to organize and conduct the elections, including writing the electoral law, registering voters and supervising the polls. For those civic tasks UNTAC needed roughly ten thousand personnel. UNTAC's military role was to 'stabilize the security situation and build confidence among the parties to the conflict.' Verification of the withdrawal of foreign forces, supervision of the cease-fire, including regroupment, cantonment, disarming and demobilization, weapon control and mine clearance, were specific military tasks. UNTAC would need about sixteen thousand military personnel of all ranks for these duties, including infantry, engineers, air support, medical units, military police, a logistic battalion and a naval element. Analogous arrangements were set out for civil administration, including finance, public security and foreign affairs, as well as refugee repatriation and economic rehabilitation on 28 February 1992. The Security Council approved the Secretary-General's plan and urged on him the speedy deployment of UNTAC so that elections could be held by May 1993 at the latest.

The next fifteen months were tense, punctuated by violence and intimidation, and obstacles which often seemed insuperable. To outside observers such as myself, the dice were heavily loaded against UNTAC. The operation was conducted entirely within Chapter VI of the Charter, i.e. through persuasion and the consent of the parties, with no coercive or military enforcement measures in the mandate. But the Khmer Rouge (PDK) were not prepared to cooperate and refused to allow UNTAC personnel into the areas under their control. In his periodic reports to the Security Council during 1992, the Secretary-General and Mr Akashi repeatedly reverted to the dilemma: should they press on with the overall UNTAC plan regardless of the non-cooperation of the PDK, or should they suspend operations until diplomatic pressure had brought the recalcitrants on board? All efforts by regional governments failed and the Security Council consistently backed the Secretary-General's judgement that the programme should continue regardless of the non-cooperation of the PDK. This meant that the cantonment and disarmament of forces did not take place except on a small scale. The CPP (Hun Sen) forces, the national army, had no intention of disarming while the Khmer Rouge kept their weapons and remained in their strongholds. The same was true of the forces under the control of FUNCINPEC (Prince Sihanouk and his son Prince Ranarridh) and the smaller Buddhist Liberal Democratic Party. Needless to say, this situation led to breaches of the cease-fire, intimidatory attacks by armed factions (not only the PDK) and the necessity for the electoral personnel (registrars and poll supervisors) to function under the protection of UNTAC military detachments. The urgings and demands of the Security Council had no more effect on the PDK than the efforts of friendly regional governments. As the months passed, harassment and temporary detention of UNTAC personnel in PDK areas increased.

However, in the face of these obstacles and of lavish criticism in the foreign press of the corrupting effect of the UNTAC presence in Phnom Penh, Akashi and the (Australian) military commander, General Sanderson, pressed on. By January 1993, the Secretary-General reported that 4.4 million Cambodians, over 90 per cent of the electorate, had registered to vote and that most of the 360,000 refugees had returned safely. Politically motivated violence was increasing and UNTAC had taken powers to arrest, detain and prosecute persons suspected of serious human-rights violations. Neither the PDK nor the political party it had created in November 1992 had registered to participate in the elections which were due to be held on 23–25 May.

The elections took place as scheduled. On 10 June the Secretary-General reported to the Security Council. In the uninspiring prose for which the Secretariat has long been world-famous, he reported that, apart from some scattered incidents, 89.56 per cent of the registered voters had turned out in a 'peaceful and often festive atmosphere, with voters sometimes walking several miles to cast their ballots, apparently undaunted by threats of violence, of banditry, rough terrain or the heavy rain that swept much of the country.' Three of the four Cambodian parties which had signed the Paris Agreement had participated. 'The fourth Cambodian signatory party, the Party of Democratic Kampuchea (PDK), failed to register as a political party, took no part in the election and threatened to disrupt it with violence. As noted above, however, no significant disruption took place.'

The result, declared by the report to be free and fair, gave fifty-eight seats (45.47 per cent of the vote) to Prince Sihanouk's FUNCINPEC and fifty-one seats to Hun Sen's CPP (38.23 per cent of the votes). After some allegations of fraud, quickly squashed by UNTAC, all the participants accepted the result.

UNTAC progressively withdrew, the final component leaving on 15 November. It had stayed long enough to help the new Assembly to draft the Constitution which emerged as a constitutional monarchy with Prince Sihanouk as its head: the wheel had come full circle. Yasushi Akashi left in September to become the Secretary-General's Representative to the former Yugoslavia. A coordinated UN office remained in Phnom Penh mainly to work in the fields of human rights and economic rehabilitation. Cambodia is still beset by problems – banditry, occasional clashes between the National Army and Khmer

Rouge remnants, the lifting of mines which, according to General Sanderson, could be a forty-year problem, rehabilitation of refugees and rebuilding of the infrastructure. But the UNTAC operation, whatever the future may bring, must be accounted a notable success against heavy odds. It had cost fifty-two UNTAC lives and $1.5 billion.

The UN operations in Angola and Cambodia provide a telling contrast. It is true that Angola, for all the damage and casualties sustained in the liberation struggle, the subsequent civil war and the South African incursions, did not have to endure superpower carpet bombing and invasion, followed by systematic genocide. Cambodia is also a much smaller country and the suffering was more concentrated. Even so, the contrast is stark. In Angola, the UN, as I have suggested, was a peripheral participant in a settlement drawn up by others, with an inadequate mandate, operating with a few hundred personnel on a shoestring budget. In Cambodia, the Security Council and the Secretary-General were lead players from the outset in the formulation and the meticulous pre-planning of the largest operation ever undertaken by the UN, surpassing even the Congo in size and scope, carrying out an executive mandate covering almost all aspects of the country's life, all at substantial cost to the UN peacekeeping budget. If Angola was a lesson in how not to do it, Cambodia should be the basic text for future UN operations in analogous circumstances.

Why was so much time, trouble, manpower and expense committed by the international community to Cambodia, so little to Angola? Perhaps the answer lies in the deep sense of guilt felt at the wanton destruction of the country during the Vietnam war, at global indifference to Pol Pot's appalling massacres and, with imminent Vietnamese withdrawal in 1989, fear that South East Asia would be confronted with a replay of the killing fields.

CHAPTER THIRTEEN

Cyprus

Those of us who worked on the Cyprus problem in the 1950s had reason to curse Benjamin Disraeli for his vaunted master-stroke in acquiring the island on lease from the Ottoman empire in 1878 as the static guardship for the Suez Canal, the gateway to India. Four years later, Britain occupied Egypt itself, rendering the proposed role for Cyprus irrelevant. From that moment until the 1950s, the value of the island to Britain in imperial and strategic terms was more negative than positive. It was important to deny Cyprus to hostile powers during and after both world wars. But the annexation in 1914 and the proclamation of Crown Colony status in 1925 brought few positive benefits. It can be argued that, after the loss of the Indian empire in 1947, the island assumed growing importance because of Middle East oil, and that this gave it a fresh significance in the 1950s. Certainly military planners, scraping the barrel of argument to justify the retention of overseas bases in the immediate post-imperial epoch, were to make much of this argument. Cyprus also provided a useful jumping-off point for the invasion of Egypt in 1956 – a dubious bonus.

Disraeli acquired Cyprus, at no cost in lives and at a marginal cost to the British Exchequer, between 1878 and the annexation in 1914 – the bulk of the annual 'tribute' paid to the Ottomans being milked from the island's economy. The same cannot be said of his successors in the 1950s. One hundred British soldiers and probably five hundred Cypriots lost their lives in the campaign for Union with Greece (ENOSIS), spearheaded by the terrorist movement EOKA. At one stage nearly forty thousand British troops were in the island chasing the elusive EOKA hard core of probably no more than two hundred persons. In London, Nicosia, Athens and Ankara, a vast amount of time and trouble was spent by diplomats and politicians wrestling in the inextricable coils of the Cypriot octopus. And, even in the end, Britain did not get clean away. The unworkable settlement of 1959–60 left Britain with a responsibility as a guarantor which we have long since lost the power and the will to carry out, as well as a military base which even the most ingenious military mind could no longer justify were if not for its logistical and other importance for the UN peacekeeping force (UNFICYP), which this year celebrates its thirtieth anniversary.

The Cyprus problem reminds me of a symbolic Persian miniature painting, a representation on a tiny scale but in perfect detail of an abstract concept, in this case the word 'Insolubility'. Ethnically and in terms of religious faith the two communities – Greek and Turkish – cherish a mutual hostility going back to the last centuries of the Eastern Roman Empire when Christian Greeks were falling back before the advancing Moslem Turks. This mutual antipathy is shared in equal measure by the mainland champions of the respective communities – modern Greece, heir to Byzantium, and modern Turkey, heir to the Ottoman Empire which ruled Greece and Cyprus for over three centuries. Numerically, the proportion is such as to reduce to a minimum the possibility of mutual accommodation. If the ratio was close to 50:50 this might exercise pressure towards genuine sharing of power. If it was, say, 95:5 the small minority might be obliged either to leave or to accept subordination. But approximately 80:20 Greek to Turkish is large enough on one side to justify the Greek aspiration to dominate, but also large enough on the other side for the Turks to demand special guarantees amounting to a more decisive voice in government than their numbers merit. Furthermore, the solution eventually foisted on the communities in 1959–60 was one which neither wanted – independence. The Greeks had never wavered from their goal of ENOSIS; the Turks had been content with British rule, failing which they wanted partition, i.e. a return of the community and its lands to Turkish sovereignty – anything but ENOSIS.

Even before the Second World War, Britain had come into collision with the Greek demands for ENOSIS. Riots in 1931 led to the dissolution of the small elected Greek-majority Legislative Assembly: thereafter, until the end in 1960, Cyprus was ruled as an autocracy, the Governor having only appointed Advisory and Executive Councils to support him. There were occasions when British political leaders could have followed their instincts and presented the island to Greece without too violent a reaction from the less politically aware Turkish community: during the First World War, when the Ottoman Empire was an enemy; as part of the Treaty of Lausanne in 1923, which settled the international status of modern Turkey; and during or in the immediate wake of the Second World War, when Greece was an heroic victim of Nazi aggression and Turkey was neutral. But none of these opportunities was taken – not, as many Greeks believe, out of imperialist determination to retain control of a strategic asset, more probably for a series of lesser reasons which, when added together, outweighed the arguments in favour of a decisive step; a case of the familiar 'better not' syndrome.

Between 1947 and 1958 successive British governments made several attempts to reconcile a long chain of irreconcilables: to preserve Britain's strategic interests (imperialism as the Greeks interpreted it), with simultaneous recognition of the manifest ability of both communities to govern themselves; to protect the rights of the minority, without appearing implacably opposed to the notion of self-determination; to do so without precipitating civil war or, more serious, inter-state war between two NATO allies; and to combat terrorism effectively without alienating all forms of genuinely representative leadership of the Greek community.

It is scarcely surprising that these labours were unsuccessful: they would have defeated the god Hercules. The Greeks rejected all constitutional proposals which did not lead directly or leave the way open to ENOSIS. The Turks took precisely the opposite view. The Greek political leadership, the Ethnarchy headed by Archbishop Makarios, appeared blind to the example of the Zionists only a few miles away across the Mediterranean, whose policy of accepting whatever was on offer and then seeking more had won them a state and international recognition. He and his colleagues and their supporters in Athens were possessed by the mistaken belief that the British government was the stumbling block to ENOSIS, and that a raucous public campaign, recourse to the majority anti-imperialist vote in the UN and, from 1955, terrorism would do the trick.

I was in the Ankara Embassy from 1955 to 1959, the whole period of the endgame, from the start of EOKA terrorism, during the final three or four constitutional initiatives and the exile of Archbishop Makarios, to the consummation of the Zurich and London Agreements, which gave Cyprus its independence at the end of the decade. I do not believe that any of us who spent time on the problem doubted that mainland Greek and Greek Cypriot policy had ensured that, whatever else the future might hold for the island, it would not be ENOSIS.

The extravagance of the conduct of the ENOSIS campaign, combined
with EOKA terrorism, had aroused the one adversary the Greeks
could neither cajole, drive off or defeat – Turkey. It was plain to
anyone who knew the country and people that Turkey, that redoubtable
military nation of unyielding patriotism, would never allow the disliked
and despised Greeks to take possession of Cyprus, 'a dagger pointing
at Turkey's heart' as the saying used to go in the Turkish media, as
well as being the home of a substantial Turkish community. I never
doubted that, if the Turks believed that their community was in
serious danger or that ENOSIS was imminent, they would invade
Cyprus regardless of the consequences for NATO or for international
peace. Over those four years I saw the Cyprus problem permeate
Turkish public opinion at all levels and in all regions to an extent
comparable only to the permeation of the Palestine problem in Arab
societies. As a small example, I remember walking in Istanbul on the
day the pro-British Iraqi monarchy was overthrown and brutally
murdered in 1958. I overheard a Turk telling his companion – they
were reading a newspaper – that the Iraqi coup had been organized by
the British. Why? To divert attention from Cyprus, of course! I
mingled with mass demonstrations in 1958 when the Governor, Sir
Hugh Foot, and Archbishop Makarios were burnt in effigy and when
the inelegant slogan 'Ya taksim ya ölüm' (partition or death) was
endlessly chanted. These manifestations were of course governmentally
inspired, but the size and social variety of the crowds and their
unhysterical, resolute manner left a powerful imprint: it was not all hot
air.

The temperature rose with Sir Hugh Foot's appointment. Rightly
or wrongly, he acquired the reputation of being pro-Greek. Turkish
suspicion mounted and the settlement plan which he brought with him
did not allay it. I was present when he and the Foreign Secretary,
Selwyn Lloyd, unveiled it in Ankara to the Prime Minister, Adnan
Menderes, and his Foreign Minister, Fatin Rüştü Zorlu – powerful,
self-confident men, both hanged after the military coup two years
later. Writing from memory, the plan was based on self-determination
with the consent of both communities after mutual agreement on
progressive local autonomy. The preliminaries would be an end to the
State of Emergency and the return to the island of the exiled Makarios.
There were several reserved subjects which could be decided at the
Governor's discretion. I remember the Governor emphasizing how the

last word would rest with him. The Turks indicated dissent, and Sir Hugh appealed to them in emotional language. 'Don't you trust me?' he asked.

'No', replied Zorlu and fell silent.

The meeting was not a success. Sir Hugh (later to be my boss in New York when, as Lord Caradon, he was one of my most distinguished predecessors as Permanent Representative to the United Nations) told me afterwards that, never in a long career had he dealt with people like that!

Shortly afterwards serious rioting broke out in the Turkish quarter of Nicosia and the first half of 1958 was stained by more violent intercommunal clashes than at any time since Britain assumed control of Cyprus in the nineteenth century. My wife and I visited the island during the period: deserted streets and palpable tension.

In June Prime Minister Harold Macmillan launched a fresh plan which envisaged co-operation between London, Ankara and Athens, representative government qualified by communal autonomy, and unchanged international status for seven years. In August, Macmillan visited Athens and Ankara to sell the plan. At the first meeting in Ankara – I can still see the scene in the Turkish Government Guest House – Zorlu opened with a long and implacable harangue about the defects of the plan. When he finished, Macmillan said that, if this was the Turkish government's attitude, he was glad to have heard it. But, as a busy man, he saw no point in staying. He rose to his feet and announced courteously that he was leaving for the airport. There was a dramatic change of atmosphere. At Turkish pleading the meeting resumed: an hour or so later the Turkish government had dropped their earlier objections and had accepted the plan virtually wholesale. The Greek government and the Archbishop took a more reserved view.

This fresh approach, in which the direct involvement of Ankara and Athens was envisaged, combined with the dangerous rise in tension, made the Turkish and Greek governments realize that, unless they acted in unison, their two countries might drift into war. This, as I believed at the time, was the prime factor which stimulated the conclusion of the agreement at Zurich in February 1959 between the prime ministers of Greece and Turkey on the basis for a settlement, as well as the tactical conversion of the Archbishop to support for independence rather than immediate ENOSIS. The trouble was that the constitutional arrangements agreed at Zurich and confirmed in London shortly afterwards were unworkable without a measure of goodwill unlikely to be forthcoming from either community. The President (Greek) and Vice-President (Turkish) each had extensive veto powers. The legislature was proportional 70:30 but, in important fields, including taxation, a majority from each community was required. There were separate communal chambers dealing with religion, education and other personal matters. Public administration was based on the 7:3 ratio, with complex built-in veto powers over appointments. There were separate Turkish municipalities in the five main towns. ENOSIS and partition were excluded. In addition there were three treaties: one establishing two British sovereign base areas; one, the Treaty of Alliance, providing for the stationing in Cyprus of a prescribed number of mainland Turkish (about six hundred) and Greek troops (about nine hundred); and a third, the Treaty of Guarantee, under which Britain, Greece and Turkey undertook to maintain the independence of Cyprus and respect for its constitution. In August 1960, this cumbrous ship of state sailed into membership of the United Nations.

The ship sank three years later. The intervening period had been uneasy: the Greeks resented the Turks in the areas where constitutional powers were equally divided between the communities, as well as the disproportion in favour of the Turks of the 7:3 ratio (technically it should have been slightly less than 8:2) throughout the public administration. In 1963, President Makarios proposed a set of constitutional amendments, reasonable in terms of effective government but which would have seriously diluted Turkish rights. They were rejected by Ankara. Makarios announced in December his intention of implementing them unilaterally. Savage inter-communal clashes broke out and British troops from the Sovereign Base areas were deployed to keep the peace. Over the next few months the Turkish garrison in the island emerged from barracks to protect their community; fighting continued, and a Turkish invasion seemed imminent.

This was the first decisive turning point in the post-independence history of the island. The British troops, reinforced from Britain, could not be expected to keep the peace on their own in the face of Greek Cypriot hostility. The Guarantor Powers consulted but the common purpose of 1959 had evaporated. The constitution had collapsed, never to be restored. The Turkish Cypriot community became embattled in enclaves, suffered heavy casualties at Greek hands (George Grivas, the former EOKA leader, returned to Cyprus and immediately attacked Turkish villages which would have been overrun had they not been saved by Turkish air force bombardment of the Greek positions), and were plainly not prepared to resubmit themselves to junior partnership with the Greeks. In March 1964, while the fighting continued, Britain went to the Security Council. On 4 March, the Council unanimously adopted resolution 186 calling on member states (meaning Greece and Turkey) to refrain from actions or threats likely to worsen the situation in Cyprus, asking the Cyprus government to take measures to end the violence, calling upon the communities to act with restraint, recommending the creation of a peacekeeping force (UNFICYP) to 'use its best efforts to prevent a recurrence of fighting and, as necessary, to contribute to the maintenance and restoration of law and order.' The Secretary-General was invited to designate a mediator.

On the face of it this was a wholly correct procedure. Because of the involvement of Britain, Greece and Turkey, the crisis had international implications which warranted Security Council action. The parties had agreed to 'non-threatening' UN military intervention and the peacekeeping element was complemented by peacemaking in the form of the Secretary-General's mediator. The only peculiar feature was that the force had to be financed by voluntary contributions rather than assessments of the whole membership. The crisis had broken at the peak of the row about the financing of peacekeeping operations, which started with UNEFI in Sinai and had come to a head with ONUC in the Congo. The Soviet Union was prepared to support the establishment of UNFICYP only if contributions to it were voluntary. (Interestingly, this unique situation persisted until May 1993 when, following a rather odd Russian veto – the last one cast by any permanent member – the Council decided to fund UNFICYP in the normal way through assessments.) One thing is sure. Under the voluntary system, there would have been no UNFICYP had it not been for the prior existence of the British base both for logistical purposes and for the provision of the bulk of the operational forces – the first time on which forces from a Permanent Member state had participated in UN peacekeeping.

In spite of UNFICYP's presence, fighting continued sporadically until August 1964. In the view of those involved at the time the most that the force could do was to damp down outbreaks by means of patrolling between fixed posts and to act as a discouragement to large-scale intervention from the mainland powers. UNFICYP was neither armed nor mandated to restore order by force of arms against the determined Greek and Turkish Cypriot militias and the Greek Cypriot National Guard and police. By the time the shooting died down, the two communities were on the way to physical separation, and there was no hope of restoring the 1960 Constitution. The Turks regarded the Greek-Cypriot-only government as illegal: the Greek Cypriots saw their Turkish compatriots as rebels. The Secretary-General's mediator was helpless. Vigorous American diplomacy may well have discouraged Turkish invasion, but it failed to move the parties towards a settlement.

So began the saga of UNICYP, an unfinished historical episode. In the past thirty years all attempts to mediate a solution, by the UN and by successive American administrations, have run up against analogous roadblocks to those which frustrated British efforts over so many years. The only dynamic changes have been for the worse in terms of Greek aspirations and the international consensus. Every move on the Greek side has driven another large nail into the coffin of ENOSIS and has reduced to zero any faint possibility of a return to anything approximating to the Zurich and London Agreements of 1959.

In 1967, the Greek government in Athens was overthrown by the Colonels' coup, ushering in seven years of military rule. Over the previous three years Greece had infiltrated large numbers of mainland troops into Cyprus, and Greek Cypriot leaders had continued to preach ENOSIS, including a 1967 resolution of the Greek Cypriot Parliament. The advent of the Colonels sharpened the appetites of the apostles of ENOSIS and Grivas, now Commander-in-Chief of the Greek and Greek Cypriot forces in Cyprus, launched an attack on Turkish villages. An imminent Turkish invasion was averted at the last moment by American shuttle diplomacy on condition of the removal, to be confirmed by UNFICYP, of about ten thousand Greek troops from the island. This led to the proclamation of a Turkish Cypriot Provisional Administration.

The next blow, the second decisive turning point, fell in 1974. The Greek Colonels, via the mainland officers in the Cypriot National Guard, mounted a coup against President Makarios who, enjoying his status as the leader of an independent non-aligned state, had gone soft on ENOSIS and was on bad terms with the Colonels and with Grivas. Makarios narrowly escaped with his life, reaching Britain via the UN post in Paphos and the British base. The plotters installed the EOKA gunman, Nikos Sampson, in his place, Grivas having died a few months earlier. The Turkish Prime Minister sought British cooperation under the Guarantee Agreement to reverse the coup by force. Britain responded by calling a conference in Geneva! This time there was no stopping Turkey whose troops landed in Cyprus on 20 July. Two days later, Sampson fell and there was a cease-fire. But the Geneva Conference got nowhere and, in August, the Turks attacked again, halting on the line which they now hold.

The plotters had little to congratulate themselves about. Their action led to the immediate collapse of their nominal government, a Turkish invasion, the fall of the Colonels' regime in Greece, the de-facto partition of the island and the return of Makarios. The old schemer must have appreciated the irony of his indebtedness to the mortal enemy for his return to the Presidential palace. The Security Council passed resolutions calling for the withdrawal of 'foreign military personnel', a cease-fire and a resumption of negotiations.

The UN cannot be blamed for its impotence. UNFICYP had neither the mandate, the numbers, the arms, nor the defensive deployment to resist an all-out invasion by one of the most powerful NATO countries and, although Greece mobilized and withdrew from NATO's military structure, the Alliance was not going to fight Turkey with or without UN authority, because of a military move dictated by blatant Greek provocation. If there is blame to be distributed, apart from the Colonels and their henchmen in Cyprus, it must rest with the British government for failing to respond except with words to the request of its fellow Guarantor. Controversy on this question persists to the present day. I was observing events in Cyprus closely from Teheran at the time. It never crossed my mind that Her Majesty's Government, only recently returned to office, without a clear parliamentary majority and struggling with the swingeing economic and financial problems caused by the massive oil-price hike only a few months previously, would go to war in such a hopeless cause. Had Turkey and Britain combined to eject the Greek Cypriot local forces from power, the Greek community would have been totally alienated, there would been no possibility of restoring the constitution and Cyprus would have become an Anglo-Turkish condominium ruled by force. Common sense rather than international law or multilateral treaties (from both of which obligations there were copious loopholes) dictated Britain's unheroic policy.

Since 1975 the Security Council has reflected an international consensus, encouraging negotiations, and regretting separatist moves, such as the declaration of northern Cyprus as a 'Federated Turkish State' in 1975, and of the secessionist 'Turkish Republic of Northern Cyprus' in 1984. In August 1992 the Council reaffirmed that a Cyprus settlement must be based on the principle of a state with a single sovereignty and international personality and a single citizenship, comprising two politically equal communities in a 'bi-communal and bi-zonal federation'. Any settlement must exclude 'union in whole or in part with any other country or any form of partition or secession'. The Council optimistically anticipated that an overall framework agreement would be reached in 1992 with implementation in 1993. In November 1992 the Council urged the Turkish Cypriots to be more flexible and to agree the detailed 'set of ideas' for a settlement put forward by the Secretary-General. In May 1993, a new round of talks between the Greek and Turkish Cypriots began in New York in the presence of the Five Permanent Members. However, by the autumn no progress had been made.

Every expedient has now been tried without success – bilateral talks between President Makarios (who died in 1977) and his successors and the Turkish Cypriot leader, Raouf Denktas; proxy and direct negotiations under the aegis of the Secretary-General; urgings from the General Assembly and the Security Council; suggestions for confidence-building measures; American mediation, and much besides. Meanwhile, UNFICYP's task has become easier, maintaining a well-defined buffer zone between the area of Turkish occupation (about 37 per cent of the island) and the remainder of Cyprus. The force's numbers have been reduced from the peak of more than six thousand to around two thousand. However, at the time of the last mandate renewal – to June 1994 – the Council agreed with the Secretary-General that UNFICYP could not in present circumstances be reduced to the status of an observer force only. Meanwhile the Secretary-General doggedly continues his efforts to persuade the parties to agree to confidence-building measures.

In reviewing the Cyprus problem between 1959 and 1994 two principal questions arise. First, could the British, Turkish and Greek governments have done anything different at the outset which would have led to a more stable outcome? Secondly, should the United Nations have acted as it did in establishing and maintaining UNFI-CYP over three decades?

In reply to the first question, I believe the answer to be no. It is true that imposed solutions are undesirable and likely to fail, while agreements reached between the parties themselves have a better chance of lasting. In the case of Cyprus the settlement was unquestionably imposed by the three interested governments, in that it represented a solution which neither of the parties desired and which they would not have reached on their own. But, even with hindsight, London, Athens and Ankara had no choice. The parties were irreconcilable. This was clear from the failure of all previous initiatives. The danger of war between two NATO allies was imminent, with all the repercussions which this would have involved in the darkest days of the Cold War. An imposed solution with all its defects was the only serious option open. Even with hindsight, it is hard to imagine all concerned rejecting the Zurich/London formula on the grounds that it was unlikely to stay the course.

As I suggested earlier, the viability of the settlement depended on the goodwill of the parties, which was lacking, and on the continuing common purpose of all three guarantor powers, which did not long outlast the implementation of the settlement. When the constitution collapsed at the end of 1963 and inter-communal fighting broke out there was no question of Britain, Turkey and Greece acting jointly, if necessary with military force, to restore it. The mainland champions of the opposing parties had sided with their protégés, and it was too much to expect of Britain to shoulder single-handed the burden of putting Humpty-Dumpty together again in the teeth of all-out Greek-Cypriot opposition. This would in practice have meant the forcible re-colonization of Cyprus, an unthinkable step for any British government in the 1960s.

As regards the second question, I have always believed that the UN action in establishing UNFICYP and designating a mediator in 1964 was correct. It could not have been anticipated at the time that, over sixty renewals of mandate, eleven mediators, four Secretaries-General, and eight Force Commanders later, UNFICYP would be by far the longest lasting of all UN peacekeeping forces (as opposed to unarmed observer groups, where UNTSO in the Arab/Israeli theatre and

UNMOGIP in Kashmir hold the gold and silver medals). As early as 1969, when I was in the Security Council, I remember delegations grumbling that UNFICYP was becoming part of the problem, not part of the solution. I could never understand the meaning of this natty little epigram. If the idea is that, without a buffer between them, the parties would have to face reality and come to their senses, it is nonsense. The Greek and Turkish Cypriots have comprehensively demonstrated that, if left alone, they will enthusiastically fall on each other, regardless of the consequences. There can surely be no doubt that UNFICYP's presence from the beginning until the present day has defused dangerous local frictions, damped down outbreaks of fighting, negotiated local cease-fires and withdrawals – in short, saved lives and property within the limitations of a 'non-threatening' mandate. Nor can it be claimed that UNFICYP has been an intolerable burden on long-suffering Western, including British, taxpayers. Between 1964 and 1990 the overall cost of the force is estimated at about $635 million. This is roughly equivalent to the current cost of the Falklands garrison for one year.

Cyprus is about the only problem on the UN agenda which was to all intents and purposes untouched by the Cold War and which has been unaffected by its end. It remains as intractable as ever. Such problems, as I argued in relation to Southern Rhodesia, give way to peaceful negotiation only when all the parties, albeit each for a different reason, need a settlement simultaneously. Although agreement has on occasions seemed close in recent years, blocked only by disagreement on the percentage of territory to be given up by the Turks to reach agreed 'bi-communalism', it is difficult to detect the imperative on either party to make major concessions. Absence of international recognition is not a serious handicap to Northern Cyprus. The forty-five thousand Turkish Cypriots displaced from Greek areas by the 1974 upheaval have joined their compatriots and the whole community feels safe, and reasonably prosperous, behind the protective wall of the Turkish army. In the Greek Cypriot zone, the displaced persons (about 160,000) from 1975 are a problem but the country is thriving economically as a major tourist resort. Equally, from the prestige point of view, the official government is Greek and holds the seat in the UN. Why should either party launch itself into the unknown, especially the Turks, who have achieved their objective – partition – and would be very reluctant to see their mainland protectors sail away? At present it looks as though the status quo will persist without violence and loss of life in the island but with periodic incantations from the United Nations designed to encourage the parties and their champions to appease international concern by making concessions which neither wholeheartedly supports. Maybe it would be better to leave well enough alone, however diplomatically untidy it is.

PART FOUR

The New Agenda

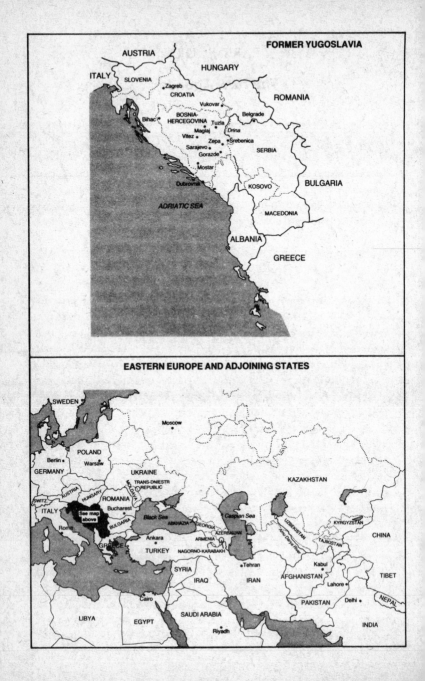

CHAPTER FOURTEEN

Introduction

History is a tiresomely untidy business. The coincidence of the end of
the Cold War and of the completion of decolonization of the Western
European empires should have wiped clean the Security Council slate
to make room for a pristine array of problems. But, as the last few
chapters have demonstrated, the blackboard is still smeared with the
markings of the past, which have overlapped and merged with new
preoccupations. There are other leftovers which I have not explored –
the almost imperceptible progress of the initiative of 1990 to organize a
referendum to decide whether the former Spanish Sahara (abandoned
by Spain in 1975) should secure independence or be absorbed into
Moroccan sovereignty; and the continuing presence of an observer
mission, UNMOGIP, with a strength of only thirty-nine personnel,
on the India/Pakistan cease-fire line in Kashmir, a reminder that, after
three major post-independence wars, there is still unfinished business
between the two major sub-continental powers. Also the shame of East
Timor shadows the Security Council. When Portugal decolonized this
small territory in 1975, Indonesia seized it before an independence
government could settle and seek membership of the UN. Indonesia
was too important and East Timor too insignificant in global, strategic
and economic terms to warrant an effective international response,
such as mandatory demands for withdrawal, let alone sanctions or
the use of force. The Security Council met twice, calling on all
states to recognize East Timor's territorial integrity and its peoples'
rights to self-determination, and 'calling for' Indonesian withdrawal.
On the second occasion the US and Japan abstained on the vote.
The Council has not met since and Indonesia has purported to
annex East Timor. This has not been accepted by the UN and
desultory talks continue between the Portuguese and Indonesian
governments, with occasional intervention by the Secretary-General;
resolutions are adopted in the General Assembly. The East Timorese
are still resisting and nearly one third of the population of six
hundred thousand are said to have been killed by the Indonesian

armed forces and security services. This is a sorry tale with no glimpse of a satisfactory ending.

However, it is possible to discern the pattern of a new agenda taking shape. Inter-state wars are out of fashion and, apart from the Baghdad regime and the successor to the late Kim Il Sung of North Korea, the originator of post-1945 aggression, there are no potential aggressors on the horizon. With the exception of Angola, Sri Lanka, the Sudan and Myanmar (Burma), the civil wars following the first wave of decoloniza-tion are dying down. But a fresh wave of civil and separatist conflicts has surged as a result of the last decolonization, that of the Russian empire, which had masqueraded for over seventy years as the Union of Socialist Soviet Republics. The most violent hostilities have erupted in the old sphere of influence with the disintegration of Yugoslavia, but warfare has also broken out in Azerbaijan (over the ethnic Armenian enclave of Nagorno-Karabakh), Moldova, Georgia and Tajikistan.

Secondly, over the past few years, several states (as well as Yugosla-via) have collapsed and now exist in name only and in the flags which adorn the kaleidoscope of bunting outside UN Headquarters in New York. Either because of a long period of rotten government, or through the exactions of civil war, or both, five countries – Afghanistan, Burundi, Rwanda, Liberia, Somalia and Zaire have imploded. Haiti is not far removed from the same condition and there could be more to come. This phenomenon constitutes a new category of problems confronting the Security Council.

There is of course no *prima facie* reason why the Council should engage itself with any of these problems. They all, or nearly all, fall within the definition of domestic jurisdiction into which the UN is not authorized to intrude except when 'enforcement measures under Chapter VII' are being taken (Article 2 (7)). All the purposes and principles of the United Nations as laid out in Chapter I relate to international relations. Why should the UN, except for purely humanitarian reasons, concern itself with the collapse of a weak, poorly governed state, or with the citizens of a state slaughtering and otherwise tormenting each other, provided that these happenings do not threaten regional or world peace?

The Five Permanent Members of the Security Council as well as other large and small regional states, have been long-standing devotees of this fundamentalist interpretation of the Charter. Article 2 (7) has protected many a government with skeletons in its cupboard from the intrusive prying of the Council, and its sacrosanctity was one of the

few principles on which East and West could agree throughout the
Cold War. Furthermore there was never any enthusiasm for miring
the Council in passionate, intractable and militarily confused civil wars
which lacked the simple certainties of inter-stage aggression in areas of
Great Power interest. This shared mind-set has enabled the Council
over the decades to turn a blind eye to at least twenty major civil wars
– some, such as Nigeria, Ethiopia and the Sudan, of grisly and
comprehensively destructive intensity. The membership has been only
too relieved to treat such events as 'man-made disasters' to be handled
by the economic and social agencies of the UN and by non-governmental organizations.

In today's world this hands-off doctrine has progressively become more
difficult to sustain for a number of reasons. First, with East/West
confrontation out of the way, there is a growing tendency amongst parties
to civil conflict to seek help from regional organizations or the UN to
rescue them from the abyss, something which, in previous years,
superpower patrons discouraged or which the parties themselves were
reluctant to initiate for fear of exacerbating their own problems by the
injection of Cold War rivalries. If there is a direct appeal to the Security
Council and the associated peacemaking and peacekeeping machinery, as
in the cases of El Salvador, Cambodia and Mozambique, it cannot be
rejected out of hand. Secondly, one of the few remaining shreds of the
tapestry of the vaunted New World Order is the notion that governmental
legitimacy and national stability are to an extent synonymous and thus to
be encouraged. This expressed itself originally in the linkage created by
certain donor governments between 'good governance' (whatever that
means) and the provision of aid. The most innovative manifestation has
been in Haiti where the UN had a hand in monitoring an unprecedented
'free and fair election'. When the newly elected President Aristide was
overthrown by military coup in 1991 (the normal method of changing
government in Haiti and in a large number of UN member states), he had
recourse to the Security Council and the General Assembly. Thirdly, the
world has gradually learnt the lesson that events in one state, however
domestic in origin, are likely if not checked to infringe on neighbours and
thus to assume an international dimension – South African apartheid is, I
suppose, the supreme example.

Finally, the communications revolution has conferred on the public
media a degree of power over the formation of public opinion, particularly through television, unknown and unanticipated when I was a

young man. The ability to stimulate public outrage and consequent pressure on governments to 'do something' is especially relevant to civil wars in which the innocent – women, children and old people – are invariably the principal sufferers. It has been said that 80 per cent of the casualties in civil wars are civilians and that, in a country like Angola, the safest occupation is that of soldiering. Had it not been for the heart-rendering television pictures, there would have been no coalition intervention in Iraqi Kurdistan in 1991 to rescue the inhabitants from the savage revenge of their own government, no American-led incursion into Somalia in 1992 to break the famine imposed by the warlords on the inland towns, probably no humanitarian deployment in 1992 of UN troops in Bosnia. In each case public reaction to the horrors brought into our living rooms overcame governmental caution.

For all these reasons, the rampart of Article 2 (7) of the Charter has been breached except where the threat or actuality of a Great Power veto can keep it intact, and the Security Council is going to find itself increasingly engaged in wrestling with domestic conflicts and anarchy of a kind which it would in the past have been able to ignore. It is enough to cite the case of Haiti to demonstrate this profound change in attitude. Who can imagine the Security Council in yesterday's world trying to restore a Head of State ousted by a military coup? It would have been impossible to match demand with supply in Latin America, Africa, and the Middle East!

The immediately pre- and post-decolonization outbreaks along the perimeter of the Russian Federation are more obvious candidates for Security Council action. The civil strife in Tajikistan has spilt over the border into neighbouring Afghanistan. In Gęorgia, Azerbaijan and Moldova, the spectre of separatisim is abroad, long regarded as anathema to the UN membership, as evinced by the belated attempts by the European Community and the United States to talk up the integrity of Yugoslavia in 1991 when it was clear to anyone who could read a newspaper that the state was doomed to fragment.

So far the response of the Security Council to this multiplicity of new challenges has been unimpressive. There have been instances when genuine prudence has tailored the UN's role to its limited ability and will to influence events. On occasions, however, especially when the public media has been dictating policy, over-impetuousness has been followed by embarrassing retreat and, in the case of the wars of the Yugoslavian Succession, errors of judgement by internally disunited covens of European Organizations have combined with political and military irresolution to land the United Nations with a mission which, from its outset in the autumn of 1991, was nearly impossible to carry out.

I am conscious that the following studies are aimed at moving targets which will have changed shape and direction by the time this book is published. The epilogue to this book, written in July 1994, will demonstrate to some extent the accuracy or otherwise of my assessment of likely developments, which at the time of writing (April 1994) lie hidden in the future. I can no longer enjoy the luxury of knowing how the story ended, which simplified the composition of some of the preceding chapters.

CHAPTER FIFTEEN

The 'Near Abroad'

This phrase, used by Russians to describe the independent states which were until 1991 part of the USSR, is emblematic of the difference between the decolonization of an overseas and a continental empire. For the roughly fifty UN member states which were in 1945 under British sovereignty or control, the departure of the imperial power was an irreversible act. There was no danger that Britain would re-cross thousands of miles of sea to reconstruct the empire and its spheres of influence. It is true that the retention of military bases, the perpetuation of the sterling area and, to some extent, the existence of the Commonwealth gave Britain a degree of influence greater than that of other medium-sized European states. But the newly independent states were on the whole free to pursue their own foreign, strategic and economic policies and to choose their own political systems regardless of the reactions of London.

The situation in the wake of Russian decolonization is qualitatively different and cannot even be compared with the fall in this century of the other two great continental empires, the Austro-Hungarian and Ottoman. These two were totally defeated in war, and the successors to imperial Vienna and Istanbul emerged as small, inward-looking states, shorn of external ambition. Russia, on the other hand, although ideologically and economically defeated by the capitalist adversary, is still one of the most powerful military nations in the world, perhaps the most powerful, with its heartland intact. There are substantial numbers of Russian troops based in the independent states which were born out of the wreckage of the USSR. Their economies are closely linked to that of the Russian Federation, a dubious legacy of seventy years of the communist system. In most cases, the political leadership comprises Brezhnevian wolves in nationalist sheep's clothing. In some instances, the Moslem states being the leading examples, the leaders had no desire for full independence, only to accommodate nationalist stirrings in the *glasnost* years. Moreover, about twenty million ethnic Russians are now inhabitants of the 'near abroad', one hundred times the number of white 'kith and kin' in Southern Rhodesia, ten times the number of white South Africans, nearly half the population of independent Kazakhstan. For all these reasons, the nature of the sovereign independence of the 'near abroad' is more akin to the backyard independence of Central America and the Caribbean *vis-à-vis* the United States than to the relationship of Commonwealth members to the United Kingdom or of the former French colonies to Paris. The 'Commonwealth of Independent States' (CIS) makes more stringent demands on its members than its London-based namesake. The notion that the independence of the six Moslem states (Azerbaijan, Turkmenistan, Kazakhstan, Uzbekistan, Tajikistan and Kyrgyzstan) would open floodgates of Islamic revivalism, with Turkey and Iran competing for influence, has for the moment turned out to be a chimera. In the first months of independence this tide looked like flowing. Now it has ebbed. The Moslem states are more conscious of the loom of the old motherland than of the attractions of Turkish ethnicity, Iranian zealots or Saudi money.

The present international conjuncture is also unfavourable to defiant assertions of independence from a still powerful ex-imperial power. Earlier decolonizations gave birth to the concept of non-alignment, propagated by commanding personalities such as Nehru, Nasser, Sukarno, Tito, and Nkrumah, who were able to play on the need of both superpowers for the support of the newly-independent majority of states in the world. This phase of history ended with the end of the Cold War: the militancy of non-alignment has dissolved as its purpose and *raison d'être* have dissipated. Cautious persuasion has replaced raucous browbeating as the means of inducing Great Powers to exert themselves to solve Third World problems or to conduct themselves within the confines of recognized international good behaviour.

There are other factors which have influenced the attitude of the UN membership to Russian policies towards, and actions in, the 'near abroad'. The unscheduled and wholesale nature of the dissolution of the empire in 1991 meant that there had been no opportunity to settle endemic ethnic, territorial and other disputes before independence; no time for the development of local military forces on the lines of, say, the King's African Rifles or the West African Frontier Force, which could simply serve or overthrow new political masters. Hence the new states floated off on the independence seas under converted communist leadership, replete with domestic problems and with Russian armed forces to provide external defence and internal security.

Against this overall background, the international community has adopted a cautious, conciliatory approach to Russian handling of crises and conflicts of a kind which, during British decolonization, would have been accompanied by fulminatory denunciation, tidal waves of suspicion and an innate refusal to give the benefit of any doubt. This approach has been conditioned by the knowledge that the states in question are helplessly vulnerable to Russian power, and that a harsher international attitude would provoke Moscow into excluding the UN and/or the main regional organization, the Conference of Security and Cooperation in Europe (CSCE) from any involvement in peacekeeping or peacemaking. No one who was involved at the time will forget how one Soviet veto eliminated the Security Council from the action on Afghanistan from 1980 until the Soviet Union was ready to withdraw in 1988. The only point at which the Security Council has made a stand has been to sidestep repeated Russian suggestions that Moscow should be granted a monopoly of 'peacekeeping' within the CIS and that the UN should fund such activities.

By the close of the 1980s, the Gorbachevian policies of *glasnost* and *perestroika* had demonstrated not that the Soviet system would respond positively to a less oppressive attitude to individual freedoms but that *homo sovieticus* was a myth: old-fashioned ethnic nationalisms were coming back to life everywhere and the Soviet Socialist Republics were asserting the sovereignty which had been theirs in name only under previous dispensations.

As the empire collapsed, the Russian and Ukrainian minorities in Moldova (annexed from Romania by Stalin in 1940) declared independence from the ethnic Romanian majority. Paramilitary units were formed, police stations were attacked and gun battles took place. By the summer of 1992 serious fighting had broken out with hundreds dead. The 14th Russian army, under command of General Alexander Lebed, waded in on the side of the separatists who had created the Trans-Dniestr Republic, cutting off the newly independent Republic of Moldova from its industrial base. In July a cease-fire was arranged between President Yeltsin and President Snegur of Moldova and an unorthodox 'peacekeeping' force of 3,800 Russians, 1,200 Dniester National Guards and 1,200 Moldovan troops was deployed to police what was in effect the new status quo created by the 14th Army. This short war did not figure on the Security Council agenda. The Secretary-General, at Moldovan request, despatched two fairly low-level fact-finding missions and urged a political solution in accordance with the UN Charter. The 14th army continues to shore up the breakaway republic rather as the Turkish army shores up the Republic of Northern Cyprus, but without international clamour for a definitive solution of the separatist problem.

Moscow has been more relaxed about international involvement in the crisis in Azerbaijan, perhaps because the Russian minority in that country is so small, between two hundred thousand and four hundred thousand, about 4.5 per cent of the population. Armenia and Azerbaijan were incorporated into the Tsarist Empire by conquest from the Persian Empire in the 1820s, including the predominantly Armenian enclave in Azerbaijan of Nagorno-Karabakh. The overwhelming majority (perhaps 90 per cent) of the Azeri population are homogenous with the population of Iranian Azerbaijan, namely Shia Moslems of ethnic Turkish extraction and language. The Christian Armenians of the enclave had always been restless citizens of a predominantly Moslem republic and, as local sovereignty was asserted in the *glasnost* era, made an unsuccessful appeal to Gorbachev for separate status. Skirmishing broke out as early as 1988, with the Azeris generally gaining the upper hand: with independence in 1991, it degenerated into warfare. In 1992 the situation became serious. The independence government in Azerbaijan had been pushed out by a Popular Front opposition, and the newly elected President Abu'l Faz Elçibey had forfeited Russian support by his pro-Turkish policies and determination to free Azerbaijan from Russian domination: he kept the country out of the CIS and the rouble zone. Without Russian military assistance of any kind, the embryonic Azeri forces fell apart. The Armenian fighters of Nagorno-Karabakh ethnically cleansed the Azeri villages in the enclave and, with help from the regular forces of the Armenian republic, seized large swatches of Azerbaijani territory and opened a corridor between Nagorno-Karabakh and Armenia proper. Hundreds of thousands of Azeris were displaced.

In June the Secretary-General reported to the Security Council on the findings of a fact-finding mission to Nagorno-Karabakh. The Council was already heavily embroiled with former Yugoslavia and was in no mood for another complex and perilous operation further east. The President affirmed that it was for the CSCE (already involved in an unsuccessful peacemaking operation) not the UN to take the lead and that the Secretary-General would be represented at the next CSCE meeting in Rome: the Council would then consider how it could assist the CSCE. Meanwhile the UN would open offices in Baku and Yerevan to observe developments and study ways of bringing humanitarian assistance to the refugees.

Even though this local crisis has evolved into something approximating to a medium-level war between two UN member states, the Council has only marginally modified this hyper-cautious approach. In October 1992 there was a Council appeal for implementation of a cease-fire mediated by the CSCE and in April 1993 the Council was bold enough to adopt a resolution demanding an end to hostilities between Armenia and Azerbaijan and withdrawal of forces: a further resolution condemning attacks on Azerbaijani territory from the enclave was passed in July. The fall of Elçibey and his replacement by Gaidar Aliyev, the most senior serving Brezhnevian in high office, reconciled Russia to the Azeri cause and the re-trained Azeri army began to perform more effectively. Some of the territory seized by the Armenians has been retaken. The Council returned to the charge in the second half of the year with resolutions calling for a Russian-brokered cease-fire to be made permanent and, in November, for a cessation of hostilities in accordance with a timetable laid down by the CSCE, in which the Russians, Aliyev having brought Azerbaijan into the CIS in September 1993, are playing a more vigorous role. So far, although this is the only active inter-state war in progress at the moment, no mandatory measures have been imposed, no UN military deployment contemplated. Unlike the former Yugoslavia, the UN is happy to leave Moscow and the CSCE in the lead position. In April 1994 fighting was still going on.

The ancient kingdom of Georgia, fought over for centuries by Russia, Turkey and Persia, was finally conquered from Persia by the Tsarist Empire in 1801. After the revolution of 1917 and Georgia's brief return to independence, it became a Soviet Republic incorporating as an autonomous republic within its boundaries the territory of Abkhazia at the eastern end of the Black Sea. Abkhazia had been annexed by the Tsarists in the nineteenth century. By the time of the collapse of the empire at the end of the 1980s, the Abkhazians, although retaining a lively sense of their identity, comprised only 18 per cent of the population of their territory, 45 per cent being Georgians with 14 per cent Russians and 14 per cent Armenians. Georgia's independence leader, the wayward and dictatorial intellectual Zviad Gamsakhurdia, was resolved to sever all subordinate links with the dying empire, and Georgia staggered into independence with no less than three minority separatist movements on its hands, namely Abkhazia, South Ossetia (adjoining North Ossetia in the Russian Federation) and, on a lesser scale, Adjaria. Abkhazia was destined to be the principal area of conflict. Russian 'peacekeepers' appear to have patched things up in South Ossetia since late 1992.

With the exception of Georgia, all the former Soviet republics were recommended for UN membership by the Security Council in January-February 1992. Georgia was so chaotic that membership was deferred until July by which time anarchy in Tblisi had led to the ousting of Gamsakhurdia and the accession to power of Gorbachev's old Foreign Minister and close friend of the West, Edward Shevardnadze. A kind of tranquillity returned to the capital, but Shervardnadze was not popular with the political and military establishment in Russia. He was regarded by many as one of the leading destroyers of the empire and he inherited from Gamsakhurdia a determination to keep Georgia independent of organic links with the Russian Federation.

In July 1992, Abkhazia was contemplating constitutional change which could have led to secession. In August, on the pretext of rescuing the kidnapped Interior Minister, Georgian troops invaded Abkhazia: there was fighting and casualties were sustained.

In November 1992, Shevardnadze wrote to the UN Secretary-General warning of the potential spread of war in the Caucasus and urging 'new practical steps to solve the conflict in Georgia'. The Secretary-General recommended to the Security Council that it call on the parties in Georgia/Abkhazia to resume peaceful negotiations and that it propose the UN as an observer and 'facilitator'. The Council should consider the deployment of UN observers to monitor implementation of any agreement reached. In January 1993 the Council decided to send a mission to assess the situation. The Secretary-General appointed a special envoy and, in July, the Council adopted a resolution requesting the Secretary-General to prepare to send fifty observers after a cease-fire had been established. In August the Council approved the despatch of a small advance team and, later in the month, created an

Observer Mission (UNOMIG) for six months with a strength of eighty-eight unarmed observers.

In the late summer, the Shevardnadze regime became seriously embattled. Gamsakhurdia, who had been lurking in the Caucasus, made a bid to return to power from his stronghold in western Georgia. The Russian garrison across the Black Sea border backed the Abkhazian rebels and the Georgian troops were driven out of the regional capital, Sukhumi. It looked as though the central authority of the state would collapse and grave human rights violations took place on all sides. A UN fact-finding mission in October reported arbitrary killings of non-combatants, torture, rape, destruction of property, abandonment of villages, the displacement of hundreds of thousands of people, in short all the horrors associated with civil war. In the same month UNOMIG, unable to fulfil its mandate, was reduced to a token presence and the Security Council condemned Abkhaz violations of the earlier cease-fire agreement.

In the late autumn Shevardnadze caved in to Russian pressure and agreed to join the CIS and to permit Russian bases to be established in Georgia in exchange for Russian support in creating stability. The Gamsakhurdists were routed with Russian help and the Abkhazians checked. In December a cease-fire was arranged and UNOMIG's mandate was extended with fifty additional observers to maintain contact with both sides and with Russian contingents.

In the first quarter of 1994 three rounds of talks have taken place in Geneva under UN auspices with the parties, the Russian Federation as 'facilitator' and representatives of the CSCE and the UNHCR. The two main issues have been the political future of Abkhazia and the return of refugees and persons displaced by the fighting. Little progress of substance has been made. The Security Council continues to insist on maintaining the territorial integrity of Georgia and has declined to deploy a peacekeeping force until political progress has been made, for fear of freezing the status quo on the lines of Cyprus. However, an increase in the number of UNOMIG observers was agreed in April.

The future status of Abkhazia remains unsettled and, as with the Trans-Dniestr Republic, the Russian Federation is clearly a key player in the negotiations, not only as a member of the Council but as a member of the CSCE as well. There is no apparent disposition in the Council to put Russia under any pressure.

*

The civil war which erupted shortly after independence in Tajikistan, the poorest of the new republics, is the only instance so far of the emergence of the bogey of Islamic revivalism. Although the Tajiks are mainly Sunni Moslems, they are Persian speaking and thereby regarded as vulnerable to the blandishments of the Teheran mullahs. Personally, I believe that the Islamic Republic of Iran is too conscious of the importance of its relations with the Russian Federation, now a principal supplier of military hardware, to indulge in political and subversive adventurism (offensive to Moscow) in the 'near abroad' and that their avowed concentration on cultural, commercial and communications links is probably genuine. Nevertheless the overthrow in September 1992 of the independence government in Dushanbe by a strongly Islamist grouping sent violent shock waves through the Russian leadership and through President Karimov of Uzbekistan (the most populous of the Moslem republics with large minorities in neighbouring states – 24 per cent of the population of Tajikistan and 13 per cent of the population of Kyrgyzstan are Uzbeks, not to mention the powerful Uzbek community in Afghanistan). Mayhem ensued and, in November, the Security Council called on the parties to stop fighting and reach a peaceful settlement. The Secretary-General sent a low-level 'goodwill mission' to Tajikistan and other Central Asian republics. In December the Islamists were overthrown and replaced by an old-fashioned ex-communist, Rakhmanov. Russian and Uzbek troops 'kept the peace' and the possibility that they had a hand in the change of regime would be excluded only by the naive. Inter-clan fighting persisted and the rebels were driven towards the Afghan border, creating a major refugee problem. The UN and the Afghans asked for emergency assistance to cope with ninety thousand Tajik refugees who had crossed the Amu Darya river.

In 1993, the Russian 201st Motorized Rifle Division and Russian border guards assumed effective responsibility for internal security and for the Afghan-Tajik border. The Secretary-General appointed a Special Envoy and a small UN monitoring mission (UNMOT) was created. UNMOT warned of escalation of fighting on the frontier and, in July, the Council again appealed to the parties to end the conflict. The Russian Federation protested to Afghanistan about a cross-border attack which killed several Russian soldiers and warned that Russia 'would use the entire arsenal of military means available' to protect the frontier and would provide all necessary assistance to

Tajikistan under their bilateral Treaty of Friendship. In August the Foreign Ministers of Russia, Kazakhstan, Kyrgyzstan, Uzbekistan and Tajikistan informed the Secretary-General that they had decided to form a coalition of defence forces for Tajikistan. Simultaneously President Yeltsin described the Afghan-Tajik border as being 'in effect Russia's' and it was revealed that there were as many as fifteen thousand Russian troops in Tajikistan: air strikes had been carried out against rebels across the frontier.

In April 1994 we find the Secretary-General warning of the explosive situation on the Tajik-Afghan border with continuing cross-border skirmishing and risk of Tajik-Uzbek ethnic confrontation exacerbated by the analogous problem within Afghanistan. The Special Envoy had contacted the governments of Iran, Pakistan and Uzbekistan as well as Moscow and agreement was reached to open talks, the first round to take place in Moscow, between the Tajik government and the opposition, with all the governments concerned participating as observers.

It is clear from these brief accounts that the Security Council has so far played only a peripheral role in the travails of the newly independent states along the southern rim of the former Soviet Union. The Council has shown itself even more reluctant to take risks in the ruins of Afghanistan. The UN returned briefly to the charge at the end of 1988 and the beginning of 1990 in the context of facilitating Soviet withdrawal from the disastrous and atrociously costly adventure which combined to destabilize both states, the Soviet Union and Afghanistan. Soviet withdrawal did not lead to peace. In 1991 the Secretary-General welcomed the American and Russian decisions to discontinue weapons supplies from January 1992 but the massive injections of military hardware to both sides in the ten years of civil war had done the damage. The attempts by the Secretary-General to consult all Afghan groupings in order to create a broad-based government following free and fair elections (imagine!) got nowhere and his calls for restraint and for an end to the fighting fell on deaf ears. The defection from the communist-led government of President Najibullah by the Uzbek militia, led by General Rashid Dostum, destroyed the last traces of order in the capital. An estimated one million dead, two million disabled and two million displaced had not appeased the Afghan predilection for inter-tribal warfare. By February 1993 the repatriation programme begun in 1990 had reversed itself and more Afghans were leaving the country than were returning to it. Appeals for humanitarian aid from the international community evoked a poor response. By the end of the year Kabul was in ruins and central government was non-existent as the Uzbek, Tajik, Islamist and other warlords fought it out with the modern weaponry supplied by their former superpower patrons. In January 1994 the Security Council called for an immediate end to the fighting and welcomed the Secretary-General's intention to send a special mission to consult with the leaders a.k.a. warlords. The Council plainly has no intention of doing more than emitting long-range exhortations. To impose sanctions on a country in Afghanistan's condition would be laughable, and there is no inclination to tangle militarily with the warrior tribes of Afghanistan who have successfully defied great empires over centuries.

I could perhaps have included the discussion on Afghanistan, per-haps Tajikistan also, in the next chapters which concentrate on the states which have disintegrated in all but name. But Afghanistan is historically and contemporarily so intimately tied up with the Soviet Union and its successor states that it would be artificial to separate it from the 'near abroad', particularly since cross-border ethnic ties are already infecting Uzbekistan and Kyrgyzstan in addition to the existing spread of the disease of tribalism and clan warfare in Tajikistan. I have analyzed these areas not because of the extent of UN involvement but for the opposite reason, to evoke the distinction between the aftermath in UN terms of British and other Western European decolonizations on the one hand, and that of the Russian Empire on the other. Moreover the future may show that we are now on the first rung of a ladder which will lead the UN into deeper involvement: the Council's careful, risk-free engagement may in retrospect seem like the record of a golden age. If the Russian Federation itself distintegrates; if the present pattern of ex-communist leaders and their nomenklaturas, ruling virtually all the states on the southern rim, changes radically as it briefly did in Azerbaijan, Georgia and Tajikistan; and if Moscow moves to encroach even further on the independence of the southern 'near abroad' in all but name, producing relationships akin to that of outer Mongolia with the old Soviet Union – any one of these 'ifs' could trigger off international crises which could present the UN with a more testing challenge than it has faced hitherto.

CHAPTER SIXTEEN

States of Anarchy – Somalia

In a world overflowing with centrifugal forces, it is an irony that Somalia, ethnically and linguistically as homogenous as almost any country in the world, should have destroyed itself in civil war thirty years after independence. Formed from the union of British and Italian Somaliland in 1960, the republic, strategically situated at the mouth of the Gulf of Aden on the Indian Ocean, had little chance of avoiding entanglement with the superpower competition of the 1970s and 1980s. The military dictator, Siad Barre, who seized power in 1969, turned first to the Soviet Union for arms and patronage. In 1977 he invaded the ethnically Somali Ogaden province of Ethiopia. This was a strategic mistake since the Soviet Union was busy establishing a 'special relationship' with President Mengistu of Ethiopia who had overthrown Emperor Haile Selassie in 1972. Moscow changed sides and the United States replaced the Soviet Union as Barre's patron: with Soviet support for Ethiopia, Barre's forces in the Ogaden were routed. What with copious supplies first of Russian and then of American military hardware, Somalia became the most militarized state per capita in the Horn of Africa. This was not unwelcome to the warlike Somali tribes and clans who had been fighting foreigners and each other for centuries.

When Siad Barre was overthrown in 1991, no single faction was able to consolidate power, and the country fell apart in an orgy of inter-clan fighting. The Organization of African Unity (OAU) and the Arab League, Somalia's parent organizations in the region, were helpless. In December 1991, the notional Somali Prime Minister and the Secretary-General of the OAU asked for the crisis to be considered by the Security Council. It was estimated that twenty thousand people had been killed in Mogadishu alone over the previous month and thousands were fleeing into neighbouring Kenya. The UN and non-governmental humanitarian agencies were being overwhelmed. The Secretary-General sent a senior representative to assess what was happening, which, in Mogadishu itself boiled down to a power struggle between the 'Interim President', Ali Mohammed, and the Chairman of the United Somali Congress, General Farah Aidid. Elsewhere in the country, clans were picking sides or acting independently of these two main factions.

On 31 January 1992, the Security Council adopted its first resolution, moving straight to Chapter VII to impose an arms embargo, calling for a cease-fire and requesting the Secretary-General to contact all parties to bring about a cessation of hostilities and a political settlement. In the next two months, the Secretary-General succeeded in negotiating a cease-fire and forty UN observers were sent to Mogadishu to supervise it. But seven hundred Somalis a day were fleeing to Kenya and the first World Food Programme ship to arrive at Mogadishu was fired on and returned without unloading to Mombasa. In spite of the arms embargo, the head of the UN team 'found evidence of continuing arms trade'.

In April the Security Council established a United Nations Operation in Somalia (UNOSOM) to facilitate the cessation of hostilities, to maintain a cease-fire, and to promote reconciliation and a political settlement as well as humanitarian aid. The Algerian diplomat Mohammed Sahnoun was appointed as the Secretary-General's Special Representative and fifty unarmed observers left for Mogadishu. By May a trickle of relief supplies was getting through but the daily aggregate of refugees crossing the border into Kenya was close to three thousand. In the summer the Council authorized a substantial increase in the strength of UNOSOM to escort humanitarian supplies. The first five hundred troops arrived in September and a further four units each of a strength of 750 were authorized (plus three logistic units totalling seven hundred personnel to guard supplies at the ports) to verify cease-fires and to escort supplies in four separate zones. The overall strength of UNOSOM exceeded four thousand. By that time, between four and six million people in the interior were suffering acutely from the effects of the fighting. Drought was an additional cause of mass starvation, and relief supplies were hampered by looting, and by attacks on incoming ships as well as on airports and airstrips.

By the early autumn, events had degenerated into near chaos and we, the public, were being treated to gruesome television footage of starving women and children in bleak interior towns, of the ruins of Mogadishu crisscrossed by careering 'technicals' (pick-up trucks mounted with machine-guns or light artillery) manned by wild-eyed

Somali teenagers, and all the detritus of civil anarchy. The UN effort was in disarray. A massive humanitarian relief programme was being frustrated by armed gangs, and no one could move without paying protection money to one or other faction. The military element of UNOSOM had no enforcement mandate and its 'non-threatening' role was treated with contempt by the clans. Even the large Pakistani unit guarding the airport was impotent against the blackmailing marauders. Mohammed Sahnoun had been sacked for criticizing details of the UN humanitarian effort. No progress had been made towards a political settlement. As many as three thousand people a day were dying of starvation.

In November there were intensive consultations between the Secretary-General and the Security Council against the background of mounting clamour from the American public media for something to be done to end the intolerable suffering of innocent Somalis dying of starvation in inland areas of which no outsider had heard before. At the time, equally dreadful, if not more dreadful, atrocities were being suffered by the women and children of Angola, the southern Sudan and elsewhere, but without the day-by-day accompaniment of television, radio and press coverage in the West. On 25 November, the US government (after President Bush had been defeated in the elections but still two months before President Clinton's inauguration) informed the Secretary-General that the United States would be ready, if the Security Council agreed, to command and control an operation to ensure the delivery of relief supplies. At the end of the month the Secretary-General put this option among others (which invited rejection in the circumstances) to the Council. On 3 December the Council unanimously adopted resolution 794 (1992) which bore a close resemblance to Resolution 678 (1990), which authorized the use of force to liberate Kuwait from Iraqi occupation. The resolution welcomed the offer by 'a Member State' of the establishment of an operation to create a secure environment for humanitarian relief operations. It authorized the Secretary-General and 'Member States cooperating to implement the offer' to 'use all necessary means . . .' and authorized the Secretary-General and the Member States concerned 'to make the necessary arrangements for unified command and control of the forces involved.' The substantive difference between this resolution and Resolution 678, arising out of agitation over the United States having 'hi-jacked' the Council over Desert Storm, was the inclusion of

STATES OF ANARCHY - SOMALIA

a link between the US-led military operation, the Secretary-General and the Council. Hence this operation, only the fourth instance of military enforcement authorized by the Council since the creation (Korea, the Congo and Desert Storm being the previous cases), amounted to a slight restriction on the absolute *carte blanche* enjoyed by the United States in Korea and the Gulf.

In retrospect, the resolution contained a fatal flaw which was to extract a heavy cost several months later. The impetus behind the resolution had not been the civil war as such. Apart from the refugee problem created for Kenya, the Somali mayhem had no serious international implications, and the Council was well accustomed to steering clear of equally bloody civil conflicts, including the next-door example in the Sudan which had been raging intermittently for thirty-five years. The Council already had a Chapter VI 'non-threatening' mandate, buttressed by a mandatory arms embargo (admittedly useless in a country awash with weapons), to help the regional organizations (OAU and Arab League) bring the parties together to settle their differences peacefully. If they failed to do so, that would be nothing new in UN history, as previous chapters of this book have indicated. The move to military enforcement was stimulated entirely by public pressure to ensure the delivery of humanitarian aid to the innocent victims. But the resolution made the mistake of linking this objective with the restoration of peace, stability and law and order, national reconciliation and a political settlement, although it paid lip-service to the 'ultimate responsibility' of the Somali people for achieving these aspirations. In the letter which formed the basis for the Council's action, the Secretary-General emphasized that it was time for forceful action to prepare the ground for peace-keeping and 'post conflict peace-building'. He dwelt on the need for the disarmament of irregular groups and for bringing the heavy weapons of the organized factions under international control. In their statements on the resolution, most members, with Desert Storm in mind, harped on the need for ultimate Security Council control of the military operation, although the British delegate stuck close to the humanitarian objective. The American delegate, while emphasizing the humanitarian aspect, and the temporary nature of the US deployment, observed that the 'international community was taking an important step in developing a strategy for dealing with the potential disorder and conflicts of the post-Cold War world.' All in all, this exercise revealed the Council straying from the prudent posture of mediating and blue-helmeted peacekeeping at the request of parties in civil wars, into forceful intervention to settle the conflict: the two strands became dangerously entwined.

To begin with, everything went according to plan. The United Nations Task force (UNITAF), comprising about thirty-seven thousand military personnel landed at Mogadishu and elsewhere in the face of opposition from massed television cameras. There were a few scuffles and shoot-outs and some arms were handed in or seized. The roads to the interior were opened and the famine was raised. Humanitarian aid flowed in. The warlords, replete with inherited knowledge of how to cope with better armed and more powerful outsiders, decided to lie low, propitiate the new gods and wait on events. Unlike their ancestors, they had been liberally provided with the Maxim gun, but not in the quantities and of the quality in the possession of their erstwhile donors, now the invaders.

In mid-December, the Secretary-General set out his thoughts on the transition from UNITAF to a second peace-keeping operation, UNOSOM 2. He suggested that the transition should await the establishment of a cease-fire, the control of heavy weapons and the creation of a new police force. He demurred slightly from the US view that the UNOSOM mandate, level of armament and rules of engagement should differ little from those of UNITAF. This would depend on the readiness of member states to support and finance 'a peace enforcement operation under UN command'. Minds were already moving beyond simply teaching the warlords an unforgettable lesson about humanitarianism, i.e. that Western public opinion and thence the international community would not tolerate the sight of the starvation and tormenting of innocent Somalis, and towards contemplating forcible attempts to end a civil war and reconstruct a collapsed state, when the most powerful local leaders, unlike in Cambodia, El Salvador and Mozambique, were demonstrably not ready for a peaceful settlement and were unawed by high-technology weapons.

In January 1993, the Secretary-General initiated a national reconciliation conference in Addis Ababa. Fourteen Somali political groups signed agreements on implementing a cease-fire, disarmament and the preliminaries for a further conference in mid-March. The humanitarian state of affairs improved and the March conference led to agreement on a transitional period of two years (until March 1995), during which a Transitional National Council, supported by regional and district councils, would run the country and prepare a new constitution. On 26 March the Security Council approved the Secretary-General's recommendations for the transition from UNITAF to UNOSOM 2 to take place on 2 May. In a nutshell, UNOSOM 2 would have enforcement powers to complete through disarmament and reconciliation the work begun by UNITAF for the restoration of peace, stability and law and order. This would involve preventing, by force if necessary, the resumption of violence, maintaining control of heavy weapons, seizing small arms from irregular groups, and securing communications, including forceful action to neutralize armed attacks. The operation would be in four phases: transition from UNITAF; consolidating UNOSOM control; assistance to civil authorities; and redeployment and reduction of the force as the tasks were completed. Humanitarian, economic and administrative assistance would continue throughout. UNOSOM would comprise at least twenty-five thousand personnel, making it, at the time, the largest ever UN-controlled operation. A retired American admiral, Jonathan Howe, was appointed as the Secretary-General's representative in Somalia, replacing the highly experienced UN and national diplomat, the Iraqi Ismet Kittani. UNOSOM's mandate was extended to October.

It soon emerged that General Farah Aidid, leader of the United Somali Congress/Somali National Alliance, probably the most powerful group of militias, was in no mood to be forcibly disarmed or to be corralled into a settlement process which meant sharing power with others. He had cultivated the Americans with some success in the UNITAF days but had scant respect for the UN, dating from the days of UNOSOM 1. Ambushes and attacks on UNOSOM in Mogadishu proliferated. On 5 June, twenty-five Pakistani soldiers were killed with ten missing and fifty-four wounded: there were heavy Somali casualties. The Security Council condemned the incidents and reaffirmed that the Secretary-General was authorized to 'use all necessary means'.

From then until October Mogadishu and its surroundings became the scene of continuing bloody skirmishes between Aidid's supporters and UNOSOM, with significant casualties on both sides. Active UNOSOM patrolling sparked off exchanges of fire but little progress towards disarmament. A manhunt complete with Wild West-style posters and a reward was launched to capture Aidid and bring him to justice (it was not clear whose justice would be imposed). It was unsuccessful and more lives were lost in the search. The Keystone Kops briefly took over in August when US Rangers from the American Quick Reaction Force (maintained offshore as back-up to UNOSOM) descended from helicopters through the roof of a building and seized eight staff members of the UN Development Programme! Rows developed within UNOSOM when it emerged that a major unit (the Italians) was referring for orders to its national capital rather than New York. American, Italian and Pakistani personnel were killed, and foreign journalists lynched by a mob. In all these incidents, most of which originated in the hunt for Aidid, Somali casualties were heaviest. In September Aidid's soldiers started mortaring UNOSOM positions.

In October matters came to a head. In a Quick Reaction Force operation which rounded up twenty-four suspects, including two close advisers to Aidid, two American helicopters were shot down by automatic fire and rocket-propelled grenades. In evacuating the detainees and the surviving helicopter crews, the Americans were fiercely attacked. Eighteen American Rangers were killed and seventy-five wounded. Bodies of American soldiers were gruesomely paraded through the streets. The Quick Reaction force was reinforced with tanks and armoured fighting vehicles but President Clinton announced that US forces would be withdrawn from Somalia by 31 March 1994. In November, the Security Council called off the hunt for Aidid and set up a Commission of Enquiry into responsibility for attacks on UNOSOM instead. Action was suspended against all those who might be implicated. France, Belgium and Sweden announced that their forces would withdraw by the end of the year. UNOSOM's mandate was extended to 1 May 1994. The Council decided to review the situation by 1 February in the light of three possible options put forward by the Secretary-General for the future of UNOSOM: (1) to continue with an unchanged mandate, but UNOSOM would not take the initiative to bring about coercive disarmament. This option would require UNOSOM to maintain its strength of twenty-nine thousand plus an additional brigade – total cost $1 billion a year. (2) To abandon coercive measures altogether and to rely on the cooperation of the Somali parties. Disarmament would be voluntary. This option would require about 18,500 troops and the financial burden would be significantly reduced. (3) To limit its operations to securing ports and airports and to maintain open supply routes for humanitarian aid. This would require about five thousand troops and a considerably reduced budget.

In his reports to the Council at the beginning of 1994 the Secretary-General was able to point to substantial progress with the Group of Twelve (Somali parties) in the creation of district and regional councils and to a start in recreating police forces and judicial services; as well as improvements in the humanitarian and social areas – agriculture, nutrition, schools, health – some resettlement of displaced persons, and so on. But he conceded that there was no sign of reconciliation between the Group of Twelve and the SNA of General Aidid (now operating from an hotel in Nairobi), the essential pre-condition for a political settlement. (Moreover, former British Somaliland in the north-west had quietly separated itself from the ruined republic and was reconstructing as a separate state). Mogadishu was quieter and attacks on UNOSOM had almost ceased since Aidid declared a cease-fire in October, and was absolved from the 'wanted man' category. His captured aides were released later. However, with continuing insecurity the clans were rearming, and inter-clan fighting was resuming. He recommended the adoption of his option (2) described in his November report. On 4 February the Security Council accepted his recommendations, which downgraded the enforcement functions of UNOSOM to defensive tasks, protecting ports, airports and safeguarding lines of communication for humanitarian relief and reconstruction, and to defending its own personnel. At the end of March UNOSOM II consisted mainly of Pakistani, Indian and Egyptian troops. All the Western contingents had withdrawn and little weight was placed on a peace agreement signed in a Nairobi hotel between the two principal warlords. By that time UNOSOM 1 and 2 had cost about $1.2 billion.

It is easy to criticize after the event and this operation has over a year to run before a final judgement can be made. But there is no question that, in combination with the fiasco in Haiti, the successful defiance by a local warlord of the might of the United States combined with that of the United Nations had dealt a severe blow to international authority. There is of course no question that the UN operation has saved many lives and that, overall, Somalia is in less dire straits than it was when the original appeal to the Security Council was made at the end of 1991. But, in geo-political terms, the country has perhaps irrevocably split into two and there is no immediate prospect of a restoration of central government.

The lessons, as with Haiti, are obvious enough. In the bad old days, Chapter VII of the Charter was seldom invoked for a whole series of reasons. When it was, measures such as sanctions were adopted only when their failure would not lead the UN deeper into a mire. Otherwise, Chapter VII resolutions were confined to demands, as with the cease-fire resolution on Palestine in 1948, the Falklands crisis in 1982, and the Iran/Iraq war in 1987. On the very few occasions when force was resorted to under the aegis of the UN, it was either unequivocally used under genuine UN command and control – the Congo in the early 1960s – or fully delegated to the United States – Korea 1950–54 and the Gulf 1990–91. Now an unfortunate habit has developed of combining Chapter VI (mediation and peacekeeping with the consent of the parties) and Chapter VII (mandatory sanctions and the use of force). This practice led in Somalia to a confused mandate which combined seeking Somali cooperation and acquiescence with forthright coercive measures. UNITAF set out to break a famine but its mandate infected UNOSOM 2 with the impossible task of forcibly disarming an undefeated group of militias and pacifying a ruined country. No wonder disaster ensued and the UN had to backtrack in a humiliating U-turn. The command and control was also tragically confused. In spite of the existence of a Security Council resolution (794 of 1992), UNITAF was perceived as an American operation. The appointment of Admiral Howe transfused that coloration to UNOSOM 2. Was Washington the prime mover from start to finish with the UN as an instrument of American policy? Most Somalis, I would imagine, believe this to be the case, as do some troop contributors, judging by statements in Security Council debates. If so, the reputation of the only superpower has taken a hard knock. If not, the whole international community must accept the blame for the continuing failure to agree on a genuine system of UN command and control of enforcement operations which have not been delegated to the authority of a single power or group of powers.

These observations will inevitably recur in discussion of the UN operation in the wars of the Yugoslavian Succession. In a nutshell, Somalia illustrates the folly of reaching impetuously for too many objectives at once, most of which turned out to be beyond grasp, especially when a firm hold on the nettle looked like involving more casualties and a long-drawn out campaign. Perhaps Washington was not told that the mighty British empire pursued the so-called Mad Mullah of Somaliland for thirty years until his death from natural causes in 1920!

CHAPTER SEVENTEEN

Haiti

The Security Council's Haitian adventure, particularly when combined with Somalia, is likely to discourage further incursions by the international community into the domestic affairs of badly governed or collapsed states when there is no public or other pressure to do so. The upshot so far has been to add to the subversion of the authority and reputation of the United Nations, and to make a laughing stock of the Security Council. It would have been better from the outset to leave the manipulation of Haiti's domestic policies to the regional organization, the OAS, with encouragement from the General Assembly.

I remember reading a despatch from the British Ambassador in Port au Prince in the early 1960s, which opened with the lapidary sentence, 'Cruel, corrupt and incompetent, the government of Haiti must be the worst in the world', or words to that effect. A similar characterization could have been made with comparable accuracy at many periods in Haitian history. The oldest independent state in the Western Hemisphere except for the United States of America, Haiti has an almost unbroken history of revolutions, coups, assassinations and other such bloody upheavals. In July 1915 the President was forcibly removed from his place of asylum in the French legation to be lynched and physically dismembered by the mob outside. The same day 300 US Marines were landed to protect American and foreign interests. They were to restore order and to 'professionalize' the Haitian Army. They stayed for nineteen years. From 1957 to 1986 the country first endured the evil and brutal regime of Papa Doc Duvalier, who died in 1971, followed by his grotesque son, Baby Doc, who was thrown out in 1986 to be followed in turn by a procession of vicious military and police bosses. Their incompetence was such that, in the late 1980s, a semblance of civilian constitutional rule was restored. Throughout this long period, these macabre rulers had escaped retribution at the hands of the neighbouring superpower by skilful deployment of the anti-communist card and its corollary, fear of the spread of Castroism. The fact that they reduced the mass of the population to grinding poverty – Haiti is one of the poorest countries in the world – and a state of terrorized deprivation remarkable even by Central American standards, was of secondary importance. Misrule only became an issue when, by the late 1980s, large-scale illegal flight to the United States began. Many of the rickety boats with their sad cargoes have been turned back: God alone knows how many people have drowned. But the question of Haitian misrule could no longer be ignored as being 'essentially within the domestic jurisdiction of any state' (Article 2 (7)).

Pressure was brought to bear and, in 1990, a genuine election was held with UN observation authorized by the General Assembly, which returned to the presidency the dauntlessly brave and immensely popular (with the wretched masses) Father Jean-Bertrand Aristide, survivor of assassination attempts, whose church had been burnt and whose congregation had been machine-gunned and hacked to pieces before his eyes in 1988. The ecstasy of the populace was short-lived. A little over six months later the army struck and Aristide had to flee the country. He appealed to the Security Council which, fearful of breaching Article 2 (7), responded not with a resolution but with a presidential statement condemning the coup. The General Assembly, less diffident in the light of its involvement in Aristide's election, inscribed the question on the agenda and adopted a resolution condemning the coup, affirming the unacceptability of the military junta and appealing to all member states to support action being taken by the OAS to redress the situation.

In January 1993, the Secretary-General appointed Sr. Dante Caputo, former Argentinian Foreign Minister, as his Special Envoy to assist his opposite number in the OAS to solve the crisis. In April a joint UN/OAS Civilian Mission was established. In June, to buttress measures already taken by the OAS, the Security Council imposed a mandatory Chapter VII oil and arms embargo on Haiti.

The following month there was a breakthrough. After discussions on Governor's Island in New York, agreement was reached on a political truce for six months. President Aristide would return to Haiti on 30 October and appoint a new commander-in-chief. There would be an amnesty for the military and police junta, whose leaders would retire. Aristide would appoint a prime minister, after which sanctions would be lifted. In August the Secretary-General sent an advance team to Haiti to assess detailed requirements. The Council suspended sanctions.

All seemed well when the Secretary-General reported to the Council at the end of September. He recommended the creation of a UN Mission to Haiti (UNMIH) to be led by S. Caputo. UNMIH would coordinate its activities closely with the Civil Mission. Its principal purposes would be to establish and organize a national police force separate from the armed forces and to re-train the armed forces, especially in civil-assistance tasks. The Secretary-General assessed that 567 police monitors and seven hundred military personnel would be needed, all for a period of six months, with the possible extension of the police team for another three months. On 23 September the Council adopted a resolution approving the recommendations: the military element was to provide non-combat training and a military construction unit was to work with the Haitian military to carry out specified civil-assistance projects.

During the next week or so the junta leaders, the army general Raul Cedras and the police chief Colonel François, had second thoughts about retiring from their lucrative positions. They may well have been encouraged by the successful defiance of the American-led UN force in Somalia by a local warlord, and by the unpopularity in important sections of the American political establishment of the left-wing populist Father Aristide, not to mention the irresolution shown by the Great Powers in the face of the intransigence of the Bosnian-Serb militia of General Ratko Mladic.

On 12 October the troopship USS *Harlan County*, carrying the military component of UNMIH, arrived off Port au Prince. It was met by a group of pistol-waving civilian 'attachés', the lineal successors of Papa Doc's Tontons Macoutes. The *Harlan County* beat a retreat and the 'armed thugs' danced in the streets. Two days later Aristide's Minister of Justice in Haiti was gunned down in broad daylight with his driver and bodyguard. The assassins dragged the corpses to the pavement and arranged them in a bloody tableau. President Clinton ordered six American warships into Haitian waters and sent a company of Marines to the American base at Guantanamo Bay, Cuba. The Security Council reimposed sanctions on 13 October and, three days later, threw a UN umbrella over the American and other national warships which have been enforcing the sanctions ever since.

In November the Security Council fired off a verbal condemnation and the Secretary-General reported unsurprisingly that UNMIH was unable to carry out its functions. In December the General Assembly supported Aristide and demanded his return. Negotiations between Aristide and Haitian parliamentarians have devised plans for the resumed implementation of modified versions of the Governor's Island Agreement but the junta remains firmly in the saddle, disseminating disinformation designed to assassinate President Aristide's character, since they cannot do so physically. Conditions on the island continue to deteriorate, with murder and police oppression a commonplace.

There are clear lessons to be drawn from this tragicomic fiasco to which only the pen of the late Graham Greene could do full justice. Who rules Haiti and how is not a question relating to international peace and security unless the Haitians stir up trouble with the neighbouring Dominican Republic, with which they share the island of Hispaniola. If the behaviour of the regime is so intolerable as to demand external attention – as it has been for decades – the Organization of American States, of which Haiti is a founder member, is the best placed to take action. If it requires further international involvement, the General Assembly of the United Nations, with its array of persuasive mechanisms, is the appropriate forum. If all these expedients fail, and public outrage demands that the Security Council takes decisive action, the Council must either refuse to do so and refer the case back to the Assembly and the OAS or, if the membership fears the wrath of the public media to the extent that it has to 'do something', it must be prepared to follow through as the President of the United States did when he landed the US Marines in 1915. To move to Chapter VII, impose sanctions, and then have a ship full of armed soldiers driven off by a handful of pistol-waving civilians, succeeded in securing the worst of all worlds not simply for the US and the OAS – that is their affair – but for the whole UN, which is our affair as well.

CHAPTER EIGHTEEN

Burundi, Rwanda, Liberia

Security Council involvement in the affairs of these three states presents an interesting contrast to the impulsiveness of the international rush into the domestic collapse of Somalia, the internal affairs of Haiti and the wars of the Yugoslavian Succession. It is not that the human scale of these disasters has been any less. It has been reliably estimated that the civil war in Liberia between 1989 and 1993 cost 150,000 lives (6 per cent of the population, the equivalent in Britain of over three million dead) and seven hundred thousand refugees (about 20 per cent of the population). In Burundi, as a consequence of the military coup of October 1993 and the resulting anarchy, the UN High Commission for Refugees (UNHCR) mounted an emergency programme to succour the eight hundred thousand (a little under 15 per cent of the total population) who are now refugees in neighbouring countries. Tribal massacres have been on a comparable scale. And, in April 1994, Rwanda was submerged by a blood bath which cost tens, if not hundreds, of thousands of lives.

The Burundian tragedy derived from the same cause which has bedevilled the politics of the country and of neighbouring Rwanda ever since independence from Belgian-administered Trusteeship in 1962. In both countries the majority of the population belong to the agriculturalist Hutu tribe, but historically power has rested with the pastoralist Tutsis who, in Burundi, have dominated the armed forces. In October 1993, Tutsi soldiers overthrew and murdered the democratically elected (Hutu) president. But the coup was unsuccessful: members of the government went into hiding, massacre and counter massacre erupted between Hutu and Tutsi townsmen and villagers; the country sank into chaos. But there has been little or no pressure from regional or sub-regional organizations or from the public media for international intervention, except for humanitarian purposes. The Security Council has confined itself to verbal condemnation of the coup, a tribute to the dead president and murdered ministers and a call on the Secretary-General to monitor developments, bring the murderers to justice and to assist the parties in returning the country to constitutional legality. A further statement encouraged the Secretary-General to continue using his 'good offices' and to consider despatching a small fact-finding team to facilitate the efforts of the Burundi government and the OAU!

The Council has adopted a less detached attitude towards the civil war in neighbouring Rwanda which had cross-border implications, and which originally prompted a request from the parties which could not be ignored. Fighting first broke out between the predominantly Hutu Rwandese armed forces and the Tutsi-dominated 'Rwandese Patriotic Front' (RPF) across the Ugandan border in 1990. Cease-fires were arranged and broken and warfare resumed in early 1993 while OAU and Tanzanian sponsored negotiations were in progress between the combatants. Rwanda and Uganda addressed the Security Council, requesting the deployment of UN observers along the border. A fresh cease-fire was arranged and, after reconnaissance missions by the Secretary-General's representatives and an exhortatory Council resolution, a UN Observer Mission Uganda-Rwanda (UNOMUR) was deployed on the Uganda side of the border to discourage the transit of military equipment to the RPF. By September UNOMUR was fully operational with eighty-one observers.

Meanwhile, a second Security Council exercise was under way. OAU/Tanzanian negotiations with UN representation succeeded in negotiating a comprehensive peace agreement between the Rwanda government and the RPF in August. The parties asked for a UN peacekeeping force to guarantee public security, especially for the delivery of humanitarian aid, to help in discovering weapons caches, in the neutralization of armed bands, in de-mining, and to assist in the creation of a new National Army and Gendarmerie. In October the Council authorized the establishment of the UN Assistance Mission for Rwanda (UNAMIR), which in effect subsumed UNOMUR. Its overall mandate was to 'contribute to the establishment and maintenance of a climate conducive to the secure installation and subsequent operation of a transitional government.' It would assist in ensuring public security in the capital, monitor the cease-fire, DMZs and demobilization, and assist with mine clearance. It would provide security for repatriation of about nine hundred thousand (out of a total population of about six million) Rwandese refugees and displaced persons, and would escort and protect humanitarian activities until the new Rwandese forces could take over. UNAMIR would function in four phases, the last one leading to elections which would complete the transitional period (scheduled to end in October 1995). UNAMIR took the field in the autumn of 1993 with a peak strength of about 2,500 military personnel plus a civilian police unit. By the end of 1993, about six hundred thousand of the displaced Rwandese had returned home.

On 6 April 1994, the aircraft carrying the new Burundian President and the long-standing (Hutu) President of Rwanda on return from negotiations in Tanzania was shot down by a missile on approach to the Rwandan capital, Kigali. Both were killed. Kigali exploded in a holocaust of slaughter. The (Tutsi) Prime Minister was murdered by the Presidential Guard along with ten Belgian soldiers of UNAMIR who were protecting her. For days the streets literally ran with blood and corpses were piled high. Belgian and French paratroops landed to evacuate the expatriate communities: apart from the killing of the Belgian UNAMIR soldiers, the savagery of the Presidential Guard and other ill-disciplined soldiers and plain thugs was directed against Rwandans. The old enmity had boiled over. The RPF forces left their cantonments and marched on the capital. Belgium withdrew its contingent from UNAMIR (was it wise to include the old imperial power in the first place?) and the Force Commander could do no more than offer protection to some terrified Rwandans, and to try to mediate a cease-fire between the 'government', which quickly fled the capital, and the advancing RPF. On 22 April the Security Council decided to withdraw virtually the whole of UNAMIR whose mandate had become irrelevant as fighting continued across the country between the RPF and government troops.

The collapse of this operation cannot be blamed on the UN. No one could have anticipated the shooting down of the presidential aircraft and the blood bath which destroyed the carefully formulated peace settlement which UNAMIR was supervising. Equally the lightly armed UN force had neither the mandate, the numbers nor the equipment to quell what amounted to a nation-wide explosion of internecine violence. Nor, without television coverage of the atrocities, had there at the time of writing been public pressure on governments to do anything more than wring their hands.

*

Liberia, the second oldest (after Haiti) independent black republic in the world, survived the decolonization of its neighbours – Côte d'Ivoire, Guinea and Sierra Leone – without disturbance. Colonized between 1820 and 1865 by freed American slaves, it secured independence in 1847. The Americo-Liberian elite maintained a state of nineteenth-century grandeur, complete with stiff protocol, top hats and tail coats. American influence was paramount, enhanced in the 1920s by the acquisition by the Firestone Rubber Company of a one million acre concession, the backbone of the economy. But the writ of the True Whig Party never extended far into the multi-tribal interior. In 1980 the Americo-Liberian rulers were overthrown by a bloody military coup led by Master Sergeant Samuel Doe. The late twentieth century had caught up with Liberia at last. Doe turned out to be an unpleasant military dictator and, nine years later, some of his colleagues rebelled: the subsequent civil war destroyed central government, law and order throughout the country. In September 1990, Doe was tortured and killed by Prince Johnson, leader of the so-called Independent National Patriotic Front of Liberia (INPFL). At the time the greater part of the country was in the hands of Charles Taylor, leader of the National Patriotic Front of Liberia (NPFL). The remains of Doe's army, about a thousand troops, formed a group called the Armed Forces of Liberia (AFL). None of the factions controlled substantial armed forces. In 1989, before the overthrow of Doe, the army strength was only 7,300 comprising seven infantry battalions, plus armoured personnel carriers and some towed artillery. The airforce was tiny, a few reconnaissance aircraft. The navy consisted of four patrol boats and there was a paramilitary police force of about two thousand personnel. It is a feature of civil war that even limited fire power is capable of wiping out a significant proportion of the population.

I do not know what negotiations took place between the United States, still the most important external power, the various factions and the governments of the neighbouring and near-neighbouring West African states. However, the UN showed no disposition to involve itself in the bloody struggle as Liberia tore itself to pieces. The lead was taken by the Economic Community of West African States (ECOWAS), which created a 'Military Observer Group' (ECOMOG) and set about the task of peacemaking and peacekeeping (ECOWAS consists of sixteen states, including Liberia, the most important in this context being Liberia's three neighbours plus Nigeria, Ghana and Senegal. Côte d'Ivoire was the only ECOWAS state to be a non-permanent member of the Security Council [1990–91] during the main period of the crisis). The title 'Observer Group' did ECOMOG scant justice, just as 'peacekeeping' in the UN sense of the word has been inadequate to describe the activities of the Russian 201st Motorized Rifle Division in Tajikistan. At its peak in mid-1993, the strength of ECOMOG was close to twenty-five thousand, including tanks, artillery, combat aircraft and warships. It has in practice acted as an enforcement force, dominating battlefields as well as policing truces and cease-fires. This function has inevitably led to accusations of taking sides, particularly against Charles Taylor's NPFL and National Patriotic Reconstructional Assembly Government (NPRAG), which still controls parts of the countryside, and in favour of the United Liberation Movement (ULIMO) of Al Haji Kromah, which joined the fray in 1992 and occupies some rural areas, and the Interim Government of National Unity (IGNU) led by Amos Sawyer, which emerged from the ECOWAS-sponsored All Liberia Conference of March 1991 and controls the capital, Monrovia. It is difficult for an outsider with no intimate knowledge of Liberian politics to judge between the innate democratic or other credentials of this weird array of personalities and acronyms who crowd the ruined stage of the country. However the truth is that enforcement, as opposed to peacekeeping, means taking sides. This is accepted in inter-state confrontations such as the Gulf crisis, but it leads inexorably to controversy in civil wars, as when the UN took on the Katangese separatists in the early 1960s; as when UNOSOM 2 pursued General Farah Aidid in 1993.

Whatever the rights and wrongs between Taylor, Johnson, Sawyer, Kromah, and the AFL, the Security Council has thrown its weight unequivocally behind ECOWAS/ECOMOG. In January 1991, the President of the Council commended ECOWAS's efforts – a cease-fire had been arranged two months earlier – and, in May 1992, made another statement supporting the agreement, known as the Yamoussoukro IV Accord, mediated by ECOWAS, which outlined a peace plan including disarmament under ECOMOG supervision and the establishment of transitional institutions leading to elections. In November 1992, at the request of ECOWAS, the Council imposed a mandatory arms embargo on all parties and invited the Secretary-General to despatch a representative to evaluate things. In March the Secretary-General reported that there was consensus that the UN should play a larger part in the search for peace, and reaffirmed his commitment to 'a systematic operation between the UN and a regional organization, as envisaged in Chapter VIII of the Charter.' Following this intriguing observation (Chapter VIII – Regional Arrangements – had not hitherto played much of a part in Security Council operations, although it was beginning to feature in the Yugoslav crisis), he proposed a Summit Meeting to reaffirm commitments to implement Yamoussoukro IV. The Council requested the Secretary-General to convene such a meeting and to discuss with ECOWAS and the parties the contribution the UN could make, including the deployment of observers.

In July 1993, the Secretary-General's Representative, the Executive Secretary of ECOWAS and the President of the OAU co-chaired a meeting at Cotonou (the capital of Benin) at which the parties signed an agreement on a series of steps leading to elections, starting with a cease-fire on 1 August to be monitored by ECOMOG and UN observers. Politically there would be a single Transitional Government with elections to take place seven months after the signing of the Agreement (a timetable which has not been met). On 10 August the Council authorized the despatch of thirty military observers and, by Resolution 866 of 22 September, established the UN Observer Mission in Liberia (UNOMIL) to work with ECOMOG for the implementation of the Cotonou Agreement. UNOMIL now comprises roughly five hundred personnel, including three hundred military observers. Its headquarters are in Monrovia, with four regional sub-headquarters, one in each of ECOMOG's sector commands.

For the moment the worst of the fighting has died down, although there were reports of clashes in mid-March 1994 along with reports of some voluntary disarmament by Taylor's forces. Overall, progress towards peace has been snail-like and, in February, the Council, while welcoming another agreement reached in Monrovia, called on the parties to adhere to the timetable, underlining the importance of disarmament and the link between ECOMOG's discharge of its responsibilities and UNOMIL's ability to carry out its mandate.

This relationship distinguishes the Liberian operation from all others mounted by the Security Council and may well constitute a precedent for international involvement in future civil wars. In the debate leading to the adoption of Resolution 866, speakers mentioned the unique nature of this joint effort involving the Council and a regional organization. The French delegate specifically mentioned

Chapter VIII of the Charter. Article 53 of the Charter (Chapter VIII) states that 'The Security Council shall, where appropriate, utilize . . . regional arrangements or agencies for enforcement action under its authority. But no enforcement action shall be taken by regional agencies without the authorization of the Security Council.' No such specific authorization was delegated by the Council to ECOWAS/ECOMOG, nor is ECOWAS a 'regional agency' on a par with the OAS, OAU or Arab League. However, Article 52 (3) states that 'The Security Council shall encourage the development of pacific settlement of a local dispute . . . by . . . regional agencies either on the initiative of the states concerned or by reference from the Security Council.'

There is plenty of scope for legalistic argument about whether an economic sub-regional organization (ECOWAS) constitutes a 'regional agency' as defined by Chapter VIII, whether ECOMOG is an enforcement or peacekeeping force, or both, and whether the Security Council's unswerving support for ECOWAS/ECOMOG since 1991 constitutes the authority required by Article 53. Whatever the outcome of such debate, the Security Council has in Liberia taken the pragmatic step of operating in tandem with a regional organization in a civil war which combined observation, lightly armed peacekeeping, and heavily armed enforcement, all for political and humanitarian objectives.

What makes the relationship potentially attractive to those governments which shrink from Somali-type entanglements is UNOMIL's mandate. The resolution and its associated documentation clarify that UNOMIL and ECOMOG will cooperate closely but with separate chains of command, UNOMIL's being via the Secretary-General's Special Representative to the Secretary-General and thence to the Security Council. ECOMOG has the primary responsibility for ensuring the implementation of the Cotonou Agreement while UNOMIL will monitor the implementation procedures to verify their impartial application. If ECOMOG has to engage in enforcement operations to deal with, for example, cease-fire violations reported either by UNOMIL or by ECOMOG, UNOMIL observers would not participate in such actions and would be temporarily withdrawn from the area of operations. In a nutshell, UNOMIL is to advise, to train, to verify, to observe, to investigate, to monitor, i.e. to shadow ECOMOG across the spectrum of its activities, but, if and when it comes to combat, ECOMOG will take over. In addition, since ECOWAS represents a far from rich part of the world, the Council has established a voluntary Trust Fund to defray part of ECOMOG's expenses.

If this combined operation works, there will be strong temptation to repeat it in other civil wars where there is a major regional power or regional/sub-regional organization which would be prepared to do the dirty work under Security Council supervision. Indeed, in his report of 3 March 1994 to the Security Council on Abkhazia/Georgia, the Secretary-General suggests either that the UN establish a peace-keeping force (as opposed to the unarmed observers of UNOMIG) under UN command and control, or the Council could 'authorize a multi-national military force not under UN command and consisting of contingents made available by interested Member States.' UNOMIG would monitor the operations of such a force, which would presumably be drawn from the Russian Federation and others in the CIS. Interesting idea.

CHAPTER NINETEEN

The Wars of the Yugoslavian Succession

During the past forty-eight years British troops have fought and died in about a dozen wars, many of them 'emergencies', in the course of decolonization – Palestine 1945–48 and Cyprus 1955–59 being good examples. One or two have been bilateral inter-state wars – Suez 1956 and the Falklands 1982 – others have been in support of UN-authorized multilateral enforcement operations – Korea 1950–54 and the Gulf crisis 1990–91. I can remember bitter parliamentary and public controversy over Palestine and the Suez operation, as well as unity to all intents and purposes over Korea, the Falklands and the Gulf crisis. But I cannot recall any operation which has generated such an intensive, continuing and wide-ranging public debate and so strong a day-to-day interest as the civil war which erupted in Yugoslavia in June 1991, first in Slovenia and Croatia and thereafter in Bosnia-Herzegovina. This is all the more remarkable when it is considered that the United Nations military deployment has been for the most part of a 'non-threatening' blue-helmeted peacekeeping nature, and that only two to three thousand British troops have been involved over the past two years – with very few casualties.

I pretend to no specialized knowledge of Yugoslavia and can only comment as one of 'we, the people'. To me Yugoslavia first meant the partisans who gave the Germans such a hard time between 1941 and 1944. But I also remember how, during the same period, the country was embroiled in violent internecine strife, with royalists ranged against communists and a Nazi puppet state in Croatia inflicting appalling atrocities on Serbs: there were contemporary rumours in Italy that even the Germans were sickened by Croatian butchery. Then Yugoslavia was, under Tito, the gallant and successful bulwark of resistance to Stalinist expansionism in the late 1940s, when the spread of Soviet imperialism was a reality, not the pantomime demon which it became after the construction of the Berlin Wall and the Cuban missile crisis of a year later. For most of my diplomatic career, Yugoslavia was more than anything else the leading light of the Non-

Aligned Movement, the bridge between the worlds of Western capitalism and Soviet communism on the one hand, and the Third World of
Asia, Africa and Latin America on the other. Yugoslavia ranked
among the European neutrals who were acceptable as troop contributors to UN peacekeeping operations, from which NATO and Warsaw
Pact countries were excluded. In New York Yugoslavia always fielded
a skilful team of diplomats and, to borrow a phrase from our Foreign
Secretary, they punched above their weight across a wide field of UN
activities. Yugoslavia served four times as a non-permanent member of
the Security Council representing the East European Group. In a
sentence, Tito's Yugoslavia was communism with a welcome
difference.

After Tito's death in 1980, few people expected the complex structure of rotating presidencies which he bequeathed to last, although
radical change seemed unlikely so long as the Cold War menace hung
over Europe: let us not forget that Yugoslavia, the grey area between
NATO and the Warsaw Pact, always seemed the most probable flash
point for the Third World War. Indeed General Sir John Hackett
chose it for this role in his compelling book *The Third World War*,
published in 1982.[1] After the collapse of European communism, the
demolition of the Berlin Wall and the unification of Germany, the only
hope for communist politicians was to jump onto the nationalist
bandwagon. It was therefore no surprise when the Serbian leader,
Slobodan Milosevic, started to beat the Greater Serbia drum, nor
when the component parts of the Federation launched their bids for
independence.

Knowledgeable people have argued that the break-up of the Federation was bound to lead to war unless the international community took
effective pre-emptive action. The geographical divisions between the
six component republics as laid down by Tito had been administrative
rather than political: there was free movement throughout and the
capital of the Serbian republic, Belgrade, was also the capital of the
state. However, one third of ethnic Serbs were living outside the
Serbian republic and, given the paranoid nature of Serbian nationalism,
Belgrade would not allow the federal structure to collapse without a
fight and, even if the Serbs could not prevent disintegration, they

---

[1] *The Third World War: The Untold Story* by General Sir John Hackett, Sidgwick
and Jackson, 1982

would not abandon compatriots to the alien sovereignty of potentially hostile Croats or others. Hence, the argument ran, the major European powers and institutions should, after the Slovenian plebiscite of December 1990 resulted in an 88 per cent vote in favour of independence, have taken vigorous action either to stem the tide of independence or to ensure that it took place peacefully, for example by insisting on public, cast-iron guarantees of Serbian minority rights in those republics which decided irrevocably to break away. Instead, the European Community continued to support Yugoslav integrity after it was plainly a lost cause. The Conference on Security and Cooperation in Europe (CSCE) managed only to express 'friendly concern', and the American Secretary of State, James Baker, visiting Yugoslavia shortly after the CSCE had pronounced, also spoke out in favour of Yugoslavian integrity. This attitude was naturally interpreted by Belgrade as meaning that, if Serbia decided to hold the state together by force of arms, the European Community and the United States were unlikely to kick up much of a fuss.

Perhaps the trouble was that the international community had too much else on its plate to give the necessary attention to the burgeoning crisis. The European Community was preoccupied with the Maastricht negotiations and with the Gulf crisis which exploded in August 1990. Minds were focused on the terminal sickness within the Soviet Union. American attention was ineluctably concentrated on Desert Shield and Desert Storm and their immediate aftermath. As a result Yugoslavia was relegated to minor-league status. Nothing decisive was said or done *vis à vis* President Milosevic to persuade him to abandon chauvinistic policies such as the removal of the autonomy of the Kosovo province, and whipping up anti-Croat emotions, policies which were provoking separatism. Nor was it impressed on President Tudjman of Croatia, after the referendum on independence in 1991, that Croatia could not expect international recognition unless he could provide Serbia with satisfactory guarantees for the treatment of the six hundred thousand-strong Serbian community – in fact anti-Serbian activity in Croatia had already led to the formation of para-military groups in Serbian communities. Perhaps none of these expedients would have worked without the buttress of international military force on the borders between Serbia, Croatia and Slovenia. But this was something which neither the EC, still less the UN at that stage, would have contemplated.

Ironically, the balloon went up in June 1991, only a few days after the UN Secretary-General had submitted to the Security Council the document 'Agenda for Peace', with its strong accent on the need for preventive action 'to ease tensions before they result in conflict – or, if conflict breaks out, to act swiftly to contain it and resolve its underlying causes.' At the end of June the Yugoslav federal army (JNA) moved into Slovenia to impose its authority. The following month fighting began to spread across Croatia. Hostilities were accompanied by a frantic bustle of European diplomacy involving principally the European Community plus the CSCE (which included Yugoslavia plus all other European states as well as the United States and Canada). Washington was content to leave the burden of restoring peace to the EC which, after its unimpressive collective showing in the Gulf crisis, was straining to demonstrate that it had a coordinated foreign policy and that it could match words with action. The 'troika' (past, present and future EC presidents, in this case Italy, Luxembourg and the Netherlands) dashed about, extracting signatures for cease-fires, waving sticks and carrots at Belgrade, and occasionally issuing confident statements which demonstrated that expectation was in danger of becoming a substitute for achievement. The Italian Foreign Minister, whose public persona was conspicuously lacking in gravitas, succeeded in giving the impression that the EC needed no help from Washington and/or Moscow and was happy to deal with the situation on its own. This suited the United States well enough, and the Soviet Union, by then at its last gasp, had more pressing matters on its mind. More agreements were signed and broken, EC monitors were deployed in concert with the CSCE and the EC even considered the despatch of a military force. By the beginning of September, the fighting in Slovenia was ending as the JNA realized that their task was hopeless: in any case Slovenia was ethnically homogeneous, virtually Serb-free and closer in all respects to Austria and Italy than to its Slav compatriots. By this time Serbia was fighting not so much to preserve Yugoslavia, but to protect and further the interests of their community in Croatia. Serb forces of the JNA, in conjunction with paramilitary formations from Serb-dominated areas of Croatia, had by the end of August occupied one third of Croatian territory. As the Serb/Croat war intensified, a more rational diplomatic forum than the antics of the troika was established – the International Conference on Yugoslavia, chaired by the former British Foreign Secretary, Lord Carrington.

More truces, cease-fires and wider agreements were negotiated with the combatants: none of them held, although Lord Carrington extracted from Milosevic the crucial admission that the republics had the right to self-determination.

In September the UN was belatedly brought into the act. This was a less dramatic development than it would have been in the case of a similar domestic conflagration in, say, Africa or Latin America. Seven of the fifteen members of the Security Council are also members of the CSCE, including four of the five Permanent Members, and the three European non-permanent members at the time had a close interest in the crisis (Romania and Austria for obvious reasons of geography and history, plus Belgium, an EC member). Hence the discourse in the European forums could be smoothly transferred to New York. Too smoothly, perhaps, since the first act of the Security Council was to universalize the measure adopted by the European Community in early July namely the imposition of a mandatory arms embargo on the whole of Yugoslavia. This move, reached with little opposition, must have had the champagne corks popping in Belgrade. Since 1990 Belgrade had been systematically impounding weaponry which should have gone to the territorial forces in the republics and, of course, Belgrade controlled the JNA itself as well as nearly 80 per cent of Yugoslavia's military industries. A comprehensive arms embargo would therefore do nothing to weaken Serbia but would have a catastrophic impact on the military potential of other republics. This action by the Council amounted to confirmation of the European view that the crisis was still a civil war. It is normal in civil conflicts to adopt an impartial attitude to all sides, i.e. either sanctions on none or on all. In inter-state wars, with the exception of Arab/Israeli conflicts, it is customary to distinguish between attacker and defender, and to impose sanctions on the former without impairing the ability of the latter to exercise its right of self-defence under Article 51 of the Charter. A few months later, with Slovenia, Croatia and Bosnia-Herzegovina internationally recognized as independent states and with Bosnia trying to defend itself with small arms against Serbian tanks and artillery, Resolution 713 would not have been put to the vote. But the damage had been done. The precedent, established with the lifting of Rhodesian sanctions in 1979, that only the Council can cancel what it has imposed has precluded the possibility of lifting the arms embargo from the Bosnians only. The Russians would, if necessary, veto an act so clearly directed against the Serbs. A half-hearted attempt by the Americans in June 1993 secured only six favourable votes, Britain, France and Russia being among the nine abstainers. Western governments have been obliged to counter public clamour to enable the Bosnians to exercise their right to self-defence with unconvincing bromides about not wishing to prolong or intensify the fighting, thus prompting a hypothetical response of Winston Churchill to an American embargo on arms supplies to Britain after Dunkirk on similar grounds!

Resolution 713 of 1991 was the first snowflake in what was to develop into a blizzard of Security Council resolutions and presidential statements, still blowing as I write in April 1994. In the space of two-and-a-half years, the Council has adopted nearly half as many resolutions as it has adopted over the forty-five years of the Arab/Israeli problem in all its aspects, more than twice as many as it adopted over thirty years on apartheid, or over seventeen years on Southern Rhodesia, to select some of the Council's principal preoccupations of earlier times. It is tempting to conclude that, as I used to say so often about the General Assembly, the Council's effectiveness is in inverse proportion to the number and length of its resolutions on a specific subject. But it is only fair to examine more closely the various avenues opened up by the Council in conjunction with the EC before reaching such a conclusion.

Through the autumn, Lord Carrington soldiered on with the thankless policy of trying to formulate political settlements acceptable to all parties, while the Secretary-General's newly appointed Special Representative, the former American Secretary of State Cyrus Vance, cautiously explored the prospect of UN peacekeeping in Croatia if and when the fighting died down. It was at this point that Serbian military policies for the first time created a stir in Western public opinion. The savage siege of the city of Vukovar and relentless bombardment of the Dalmatian coast of Croatia, including the historic port of Dubrovnik, were widely televized, the latter evoking emotional reactions among millions of Western European holiday makers. The classic symptoms of civil war were appearing on our screens – atrocities committed mainly against innocent civilians, trails of sad refugees, the reduction to rubble of towns and villages; all this not in alien surroundings such as black Africa or South East Asia, but happening to people who looked like us in environments which could have been ours and in an area where we believed that such abominations were part of a forever buried past in our history. In December the Secretary-General reported that five hundred thousand people, two thirds of them women and children, had been driven from their homes and that forty thousand had taken refuge in neighbouring Hungary. The UN humanitarian agencies and the ICRC were already hard pressed.

I wondered at the time whether the whole imbroglio could be ended if the US Sixth Fleet in the Mediterranean spent half an hour, all that would have been required, destroying the puny Yugoslav navy bombarding Dubrovnik and if NATO knocked out with air attacks the Serbian artillery which was smashing up Vukovar. But governments were in no mood for trenchant action, and public opinion was not sufficiently aroused to force a change of attitude. There was no disposition to go beyond 'non-threatening' peacekeeping, about which the UN was being extremely cautious, and diplomatic negotiation, to a quest for UN authority for the use of force before war escalated beyond the point of anyone's control. Reluctance was compounded by a probably exaggerated respect for Serbian military prowess deriving from the partisan activities in the Second World War, a rubric of which we were to hear much in the months to come.

Cyrus Vance, operating in close touch with the parties, with Lord Carrington and with the EC/CSCE leaderships, focused on forging a cease-fire and creating a UN peacekeeping force to police it. With encouraging resolutions from the Council, he picked his way through conferences, meetings and false starts to a signing ceremony, ironically held in Sarajevo (still technically a Yugoslavian city), on 2 January 1992. By that time a small group from the UN peacekeeping machine was already testing the ground and, in February, the Council formally established UNPROFOR to 'create the conditions of peace and security required for the negotiation of an overall settlement of the Yugoslav crisis within the framework of the European Community's Conference on Yugoslavia.'

The Serbs and their local community had by this time secured their objectives in Croatia and heavy fighting was dying down. UNPROFOR was able to deploy with a strength of about thirteen thousand plus civil police in a series of UN Protected Areas (UNPAS) and adjoining 'pink zones'. Their task was to ensure the withdrawal of the JNA, in which they were eventually successful, the continuing function of local authorities, and demilitarization. Progress has been patchy, to say the least: the local Serb authorities circumvented demilitarization by creating new militias under the guise of police. For all its efforts, UNPROFOR has been unable to prevent these units from continuing to terrorize and drive out non-Serb communities. There have also been sporadic outbursts of fighting, mainly precipitated by the Croatian army, with heavy Serb reaction. There has been no progress towards a political settlement of the problem of the breakaway Serb-controlled third of Croatia and the local leaders have been able to consolidate their hold in the so-called Serb Republic of Kranjina. It was in unsuccessful efforts to end this stalemate that Croatian forces attacked a dam at the southern end of the zone in early 1993, and rebuilt a bridge – the Maslenika bridge – in July, prompting the Serbs to recover use of weapons handed in for storage. It took three months to calm the second round of fighting. It has to be borne in mind that UNPROFOR's mandate, although the enabling resolution was peppered with 'Chapter VII language', was strictly 'non-threatening' with no enforcement provisions. It has been regularly renewed in spite of Croat complaints about lack of political progress.

As a kind of sporadic calm (certainly not peace) returned uneasily to Croatia, the waters had already been muddied by the question of recognition, i.e. of international acceptance that the old Yugoslav Federation of six republics was dead. The EC had established a commission to examine criteria for recognition of the four (Slovenia, Croatia, Bosnia-Herzogovina and Macedonia) which, unlike Montenegro, wanted to break from Belgrade. Germany had been badgering its EC partners for some time in regard to Slovenia and Croatia, thus fuelling Serb paranoia about a renaissance of German imperialism, and had with difficulty been dissuaded from jumping the gun and unilaterally recognizing in advance of the rest of the EC. In the event, in January, Slovenia was recommended for recognition without difficulty, as was Croatia, even though President Tudjman's policies had not met all the criteria. Macedonia was deferred because of Greek opposition, and Bosnia-Herzegovina was told to hold a referendum first. German insistence, which had already strengthened Croatia's determination to opt for total independence, had overridden the misgivings of most of the EC membership: the Bosnian decision was to prove fatal. It is hard to envisage now that the Serb/Croat cease-fire agreement was concluded in Sarajevo, still harder that Sarajevo was chosen as the most appropriate city for the original Headquarters of UNPROFOR.

The referendum in Bosnia-Herzegovina was held at the end of

February 1992. It was totally boycotted by the Serb community (the proportions at the time were 44 per cent Moslem, 32 per cent Serb and 17 per cent Croat). Even so the resulting independence constitution was regarded as sufficient to merit recognition under the presidency of the Moslem Alia Izetbegovic. This decision compounded the bungle over Croatian recognition, i.e. the failure first to extract binding commitments on treatment of the Serb community (six hundred thousand out of a total population of 4.5 million), which had contributed to the outbreak of the war. Surely Izetbegovic should have been told by the EC that it was madness to proceed to independence on the basis of a constitution rejected by a powerful minority which controlled virtually all the heavy weaponry in the country and had the military backing of the JNA itself. He should have been refused recognition until he could demonstrate that the structure of the new state was acceptable to all three communities, including the Bosnian Serbs. To go ahead on the basis of a majority vote without regard for the glaring reality of military power was frivolous. But the EC momentum was too strong, and its influence on the UN too great. In May, Slovenia, Croatia and Bosnia-Herzogovina were all admitted to UN membership. In September, the Council disallowed Serbia/Montenegro from continuing in the UN seat of the Federal Republic of Yugoslavia: the General Assembly decided that the so-called Republic of Yugoslavia must reapply for membership, the first time the Assembly had voted to remove a member state from its seat: South Africa in 1974 was only suspended. Hence the net effect of the EC's policy was to arrange for UN membership for the breakaway states while ejecting the parent unit!

The new republic of Bosnia-Herzogovina quickly learnt that international recognition did not mean international protection. In April fighting had broken out between Bosnian Moslems and Croats on one side, Bosnian Serbs on the other. At the end of the month, forty UNPROFOR observers were sent to Mostar. Pages of statements and resolutions emanated from the Council, appealing, noting with concern, demanding and urging. The parties must stop fighting: the JNA must withdraw, as must the Croatian army; irregular forces must be disbanded; forcible expulsions and attempts to change the ethnic composition of the population (ethnic cleansing) must cease, etc., etc. Fighting continued and unarmed observers as well as part of the UNPROFOR Headquarters began to withdraw.

At the end of May the Secretary-General reported to the Council in grim terms. Displacement of civilians in Bosnia was on a scale not seen in Europe since the Second World War. Well over five hundred thousand persons had been driven from their homes and civilians trapped in besieged cities were in a grievous state. In Sarajevo alone, three to four hundred thousand people needed emergency relief. UNHCR relief convoys were being seriously hampered by militias and humanitarian supplies were being commandeered. The ninety remaining UNPROFOR personnel in Sarajevo were mainly engaged in mediating cease-fires, arranging exchanges of prisoners and war dead and were themselves becoming the deliberate targets of mortar and small-arms fire. The withdrawal of JNA units was proving difficult and Bosnian Serb citizens in the JNA had joined the so-called army of the 'Serbian Republic of Bosnia and Herzegovina' under command of General Mladic, who was taking control of the heavy weaponry and was shelling Sarajevo. Croatian army personnel were also operating as part of militia formations.

In short, another classic civil war had developed, with the army dividing in support of the three factions, the Bosnian Serbs being immeasurably the strongest.

The Secretary-General confronted the Council squarely with the military option if agreements for the protection of humanitarian relief could be neither negotiated nor respected. Armed protection would require the deployment of troops in force to clear the route in advance of each convoy and protect it as it passed. Road blocks would be easily dealt with, the danger coming from mortar or artillery fire from further back. As regards guaranteeing Sarajevo airport for humanitarian supplies, UN troops would have to secure the surrounding hills. These combat missions would be 'extremely difficult and expensive': UN troops would have to secure several hundred kilometres of roads and a zone with a thirty-kilometre radius round Sarajevo. Moreover, hostile or coercive action against 'certain factions' in Bosnia could make it more difficult to secure continuing cooperation for UNPRO-FOR in Croatia. The Secretary-General concluded that a more promising course would be to persuade the warring parties to sign and honour agreements permitting the unimpeded delivery of relief supplies.

The Western-dominated Security Council was for the first time confronted by a brutal civil war in the heart of Europe in which a

panoply of horrors was daily being enacted. Land-locked Bosnia-Herzegovina, with its mingling of Catholic Croats, Orthodox Serbs and
Moslems, was probably the least intrinsically viable of the breakaway
republics. The war was about territory. Backed by Belgrade, the
Bosnian Serbs were out to grab as much land as they could and to
create an ethnically pure statelet, probably to be joined with Serbia, by
driving out non-Serb communities. Hence the civilian population was
a prime target of the attackers. Persecution, destruction of property,
terror, rape, medieval siege, and concentration camps were all used in
the service of ethnic cleansing. For the first time in Europe, such
atrocities were displayed in detail, as they happened, in the living
rooms of millions of ordinary people through the intrepid reporting of
television journalists. At the heart of the picture, an elegant, cosmopoli-
tan European city, Sarajevo, was being systematically pulverized from
a safe distance by cigarette-smoking, *slivovitz*-drinking gun and mortar
crews while they and the snipers leisurely targeted schoolchildren,
bread queues, housewives doing their shopping, funeral ceremonies
and the like. In Western countries the cry of 'something must be done'
rose. This was a *Daily Telegraph* headline on 5 August 1992, with the
supplementary question – 'BUT WHAT?'

   We now know how far governments were prepared to go in response
to this most vivid of crises. On 30 May 1992 a comprehensive array of
mandatory economic sanctions was imposed by the Security Council
on Serbia and was subsequently tightened. In August the diplomatic
effort was re-launched at the London Conference which appointed
Cyrus Vance and Lord Owen as the 'Co-Chairmen of the Steering
Committee', the joint UN/EC negotiators. The military response was
more tentative, even timid. Through the summer UNPROFOR's
mandate was progressively extended geographically to cover the opening of Sarajevo airport and functionally to cover the delivery of
humanitarian relief in and around Sarajevo and throughout the
country. Gradually a kind of *modus vivendi* by which UNPROFOR
took control of Sarajevo airport was achieved, but attempts to place
Bosnian Serb heavy weapons under UN control came to nothing. In
August the state of affairs in Sarajevo was so bad that the Council
adopted Resolution 770, under Chapter VII, which called upon states
'to take nationally or through regional agencies or arrangements all
measures necessary' to facilitate the delivery of humanitarian assistance.
This proved to be the high-water mark for nearly a year of willingness

to use force. It sank rapidly. It was agreed that the task would instead be entrusted to UNPROFOR, whose strength was greatly enlarged in September by the addition of several infantry battalion groups (including a British contingent). It was made clear that UNPROFOR would follow normal peacekeeping rules of engagement. Resolution 776, which subsumed Resolution 770 in passing the responsibility to UN-PROFOR, made no mention of Chapter VII. The will to use force had dissipated: General Mladic no doubt took note. In October Bosnia-Herzegovina's airspace was declared a 'no-fly zone' without authority for enforcement in the air, only for observation on the ground.

By the end of the year, UNPROFOR was heavily involved with the demanding, frequently humiliating but vital task of negotiating UNHCR aid convoys through road blocks and war zones to the citizens of besieged towns and villages. UNPROFOR had been deployed as a traditional peacekeeping force with blue helmets in white painted vehicles, albeit with heavier than usual deterrent weaponry. It had no supporting arms such as artillery, nor significant heavy armour, nor close air support. It was therefore formidable enough to make hostile militiamen think twice before denying passage, but in no way equipped to fight a campaign were its mandate to be changed from 'non-threatening' to enforcement in mid-stream. Equally the no-fly zone was ineffective without air patrolling on the lines of the equivalent zones in Iraq. What all this amounted to was a message to the aggressors that the United Nations, in practice the major Western European and other NATO powers, with the most awesome military force of all arms ever known in peacetime at their disposal, were not prepared to engage in combat and thus risk being drawn into a messy civil war on hostile terrain. If they were not ready to fight even to convey humanitarian supplies, there was no risk that they would use force to influence the course of the war itself. This meant that General Mladic and, to a lesser extent, the Bosnian Croats, had a more or less free hand to continue with land grabbing and ethnic cleansing subject only to the constraint of Bosnian Moslem resistance, Security Council verbal condemnation, and the need to avoid provocation of UNPRO-FOR so outrageous as to oblige even the most cautious governments, such as London, to change tack.

Should, or could more have been done in those first six months or so before it was too late to reverse the damage? I believed so at the time and still do, although there is no way of proving it. I would never have advocated full-scale enforcement to end the war: this would have needed an operation on the scale of Desert Storm, with no guarantee of a quick or successful outcome. However, having made it impossible for the state of Bosnia-Herzogovina to acquire the arms needed to defend itself (there was no shortage of manpower), the United Nations owed it to the government to do more than mediate and engage in non-threatening peacekeeping. This was not just a moral obligation. Morality is an uncommon ingredient in international decision making. It is more that the concept that acceptance into the international community carries with it a degree of security becomes meaningless if Great Powers are unwilling to lift a finger to protect a new member who has immediately come under attack. If Resolution 770 had been followed through by its principal sponsors, France, Britain, Russia and America and if the Serbs besieging Sarajevo had been given an ultimatum to lift the siege and hand over all their heavy guns and mortars, or else . . . and if the threat had been carried out, I have a feeling that the consequences would have been salutary, as perhaps would have been the case if the bombardment of Dubrovnik had been similarly checked. The high-technology weaponry and delivery systems were there for both contingencies without putting troops on the ground: by the time UNPROFOR was deployed throughout Bosnia it was too late; the argument that the lightly armed peacekeepers would become in effect hostages following air strikes carried too much weight. As I see it the only opportunity to secure the limited objectives of breaking the sieges and facilitating the passage of humanitarian aid had been lost. However, as T. S. Eliot says, 'What might have been and what has been point to one end which is always present.'

At the end of 1992 UNPROFOR's activities were extended to yet another republic, Macedonia, or the 'Former Yugoslav Republic of Macedonia' (FYROM), as it is ridiculously known in order to meet Greek objections. President Gligorov asked in November for UN observers on his borders in view of the possible spread of the fighting. Vance/Owen supported the proposal and the Secretary-General recommended it to the Council as a valuable exercise in preventive action. Accordingly one thousand all ranks, including at a later date three hundred American troops, have been deployed on the Macedonian side of the Macedonian/Serbian and Macedonian/Albanian frontiers. So far these frontiers have been quiet but the Serbian side comprises the volatile Albanian ethnically dominated Kosovo province, which could at any time explode.

Also in 1992 the Security Council opened the road to an International War Crimes Tribunal, the first since Nuremberg. Notwithstanding the rhetoric during the Gulf crisis about Saddam Hussein being a latter day Hitler and about how Iraqi war crimes would be punished, this issue was not pursued in the comprehensive cease-fire resolution which followed Desert Storm.

At a special session of the Human Rights Commission in Geneva, the former Polish Prime Minister, Tadeusz Mazowiecki, was appointed a Special Rapporteur to investigate human rights in the former Yugoslavia. Mr Mazowiecki's first report, presented on 28 August, amounts to a blood-curdling litany of atrocities. He opens with the following passage:

> Most of the territory of the former Yugoslavia, in particular Bosnia and Herzegovina, is at present the scene of massive and systematic violations of human rights, as well as serious, grave violations of humanitarian law. Ethnic cleansing is the cause of most such violations.

The report describes the various methods of persecution, violence and terror designed to force communities to leave their homes: torture, 'disappearances', inhuman conditions of arbitrary detention, and systematic executions are mentioned, although the report is careful to distinguish between first- and second-hand sources. It also makes the point that all parties were perpetrating violations but that the Moslems alone felt threatened by extermination. The report recommends a far larger international presence to investigate and monitor human-rights violations, that irregulars must be disarmed, that local authorities be warned of their responsibilities, and of the need for an investigative commission to determine the fate of the thousands of persons who disappeared after the capture of Vukovar and elsewhere.

Resolutions had already condemned ethnic cleansing and demanded its cessation as well as emphasizing obligations under humanitarian law. In the late summer stories and horrifying television pictures of the 'detention centres' began to circulate and the Council demanded immediate access for the ICRC to all such places. This demand was repeated and, with the Mazowiecki report available, the Council adopted a very tough resolution (780) in October requesting states to make information available and establishing a Commission of Experts to report on breaches of the Geneva Conventions and other violations of humanitarian law. More condemnatory statements followed, with further warnings of the individual responsibility of those committing violations. In December a resolution strongly condemned the 'massive, organized and systematic detention and rape of women, in particular Moslem women', and demanded the closure of all detention camps.

In February 1993, the Council, having studied the report of the Commission of Experts, decided to establish an International Tribunal to prosecute persons responsible for serious violations of international humanitarian law committed in the territory of former Yugoslavia since 1991. In May the Secretary-General submitted his detailed report which made clear that the Security Council authority for the establishment of the Tribunal did not relate to the creation of an international criminal jurisdiction in general nor the creation of a permanent international criminal court, only to events in Yugoslavia since 1991. He proposed that a Chapter VII resolution should provide its legal basis. The Tribunal should apply existing humanitarian law and would try grave breaches of the 1949 Geneva Conventions, violations of the laws and customs of war, genocide and other crimes against humanity. It should consist of two Trial Chambers, an Appeals Chamber, a Prosecution and a Registry. The Chambers would comprise eleven judges. Penalties should be limited to imprisonment, including life imprisonment, confiscation and return of criminally acquired property. Sentences would be carried out away from Yugoslavia in states designated by the Tribunal, which had indicated their willingness to accept convicted persons. The Court should be situated at the Hague. (The full report and statutes are in document 5/25704 of 3 May 1993.) The Council confirmed the recommendations in Resolution 827 (1993) on 25 May. The eleven judges were elected by the General Assembly in September and the Security Council appointed the Venezuelan Attorney-General as Prosecutor in October. The first session of the Tribunal opened in the Hague on 17 November.

While American forces were storming into the deserts of Somalia to break the famine, UNPROFOR was continuing with the arduous, albeit less spectacular, task of negotiating UNHCR and other UN agency and non-governmental humanitarian convoys through the harsh, wintry mountains of Bosnia. For all the delays and frustrations, probably more than $1 billion worth of aid was delivered through the winter of 1992–93, thus averting what would have been an even greater human disaster. But UNPROFOR was protecting the aid, not the recipients and the fighting and ethnic cleansing continued unabated regardless of the flood of Security Council condemnations and demands. Nor did the sanctions, although disastrous for the Serbian economy, seem to be having more impact on President Milosevic's general attitude than the equivalent had on that of President Saddam Hussein.

For a brief moment it looked as though this pessimism might be misplaced. The Co-Chairmen (Vance/Owen) had been indefatigably shuttling between the parties and were close to completion of a plan to secure a peaceful settlement. From February to March 1993 the action moved to New York and the Council urged the negotiators forward with encouraging statements. In March President Izetbegovic and Mate Boban, leaders of the Bosnian Croats, signed all the documents. The plan, which was as complex as the problem which it set out to solve, envisaged a decentralized state comprising ten semi-autonomous provinces with a six-monthly rotating presidency. It involved some withdrawal by the Bosnian Serbs, who had seized about 70 per cent of the whole state, the territory from which withdrawal took place to be occupied by UNPROFOR for an interim period during which transitional arrangements would be converted to a final settlement. A large UN military presence would be deployed to monitor the agreements. The map of the provinces with corridors, access routes, etc, was labyrinthine but, all in all, it is hard to see how any negotiating team could have done more or better. In order to bring pressure to bear in Belgrade, and on the Bosnian Serb leadership, the Council adopted in late April a long, detailed resolution setting out a series of sanctions-tightening measures, including blockade, which would be adopted against Bosnian Serb-held areas and against Serbia if the peace plan was not accepted and if the Bosnian Serbs did not stop their military offensives.

On 2 May Dr Radovan Karadzic, the Bosnian Serb leader, signed the documents at a meeting of all the parties with the Co-Chairmen outside Athens. His acceptance was made subject to confirmation by the 'Assembly of the Republic of Srpska' (The Bosnian-Serb 'Parliament', which had its headquarters at the ski-resort of Pale near Sarajevo). My scepticism took a jolt. Dr Karadzic, a frequent interviewee on British television, had long since earned the nickname 'The Liar' in my family for the wide-eyed candour with which he gave

assurances immediately to be broken, signed documents immediately
to be repudiated, and made statements which even outsiders could see
to be demonstrably untrue. But this time it looked as though Milosevic
had decided that enough was enough, especially when he went on to
Pale ostensibly to sway the 'Parliament'. On 6 May the 'Parliament'
rejected the plan, and a 'referendum' produced the same result. My
suspicion was that the key player was in fact General Mladic, who was
not prepared to surrender any conquered territory and knew that the
outside world did not have the stomach to coerce him into doing so.
The Vance/Owen Plan was dead.

   This setback came at a fresh phase in the military operations which
led to a partial strengthening of UNPROFOR's mandate. Early in
1993, the Serbs launched an offensive to capture and cleanse Bosnian
Moslem territory along the Drina valley in Eastern Bosnia. Names of
towns such as Srebenica, Cerska, Gorazde and Zepa soon became
familiar to TV viewers as, crammed with refugees who had fled from
or been driven out of villages in the countryside, they were subjected
to the merciless siege tactics which the Serbs had perfected. Humanitarian relief became almost impossible and by March, in Srebenica alone,
thirty to forty civilians a day were dying of starvation, cold or lack of
medical treatment. Although there had been 465 reported violations of
the 'no-fly zone' no aircraft had been used in combat until, on 16
March, three aircraft dropped bombs on villages near Srebenica. After
inconclusive investigation, the Council authorized member states
'acting nationally or through regional arrangements' to take 'all necessary measures' to enforce the ban. In early April, after consultation
with NATO, the aircraft of several nations started to enforce the
zone. This had little military significance but it was a portent of
mounting Western exasperation. Then, with public opinion pressing
hard for something to be done to relieve the agonies of the Drina
valley towns, the Council demanded that Srebenica and its surroundings be treated as a 'safe area' and that it be demilitarized with an
UNPROFOR presence. This status was extended in May to Sarajevo,
Tuzla, Zepa, Gorazde, Bihac and their surroundings. Resolution 824
declared that 'safe areas' should be free from armed attacks, that
Bosnian Serb units should be withdrawn and that UNPROFOR
should monitor compliance. In the event of non-compliance, the
Council would 'consider immediately the adoption of any additional
measures necessary ...' On 4 June the Council in Resolution 836

authorized UNPROFOR to take necessary measures, including the use of force, in reply to bombardments of the safe areas, or to armed incursions, or to deliberate obstruction of the freedom of UNPRO-FOR, or of protected humanitarian convoys. Supporting air power was also approved. An additional 7,600 troops for UNPROFOR were authorized.

The international worm had turned a little at last and there is no doubt that these measures saved the whole area from being grabbed and ethnically cleansed.

After the collapse of the Vance/Owen plan, the fighting spread. The Bosnian Croats began to consolidate their 'Herceg-Bosnia' statelet. Mostar in the south-west came under siege. The Bosnian government mounted an offensive against the Croats in central Bosnia and captured towns. The Bosnian Serbs drove the government forces off high ground around Sarajevo. Bosnian Serb operations in the north-east continued. Security Council appeals, including a demand for the cessation of fighting round the 'safe area' of Sarajevo, were ineffective and UNPROFOR showed no disposition to implement its new forceful mandate. In July the Secretary-General reported on the difficulties of the humanitarian effort: UNPROFOR was being delib-erately targeted and casualties were mounting. UNPROFOR had incurred fifty-one fatalities (including one British) and nearly five hundred wounded. Resources and equipment were under strain.

The Co-Chairmen, now Lord Owen and the Norwegian ex-Foreign Minister Thorvald Stoltenberg – Cyrus Vance had retired in May – tried again in the summer to negotiate a fresh plan which drew heavily on the detail of Vance/Owen. This plan envisaged a confederal state with a single international identity comprising three mainly ethnic republics, with access to the sea for the Moslems who would have at least 30 per cent of the territory of Bosnia-Herzegovina. Sarajevo would be put under temporary UN administration and Mostar would similarly be administered by the EC. As with Vance/Owen, it looked briefly like winning the assent of all the parties but, on 2 September, the attempt foundered: the Bosnian government found the proposed boundaries unacceptable.

Through 1993 a gap had been opening between the European troop contributors to UNPROFOR, particularly Britain and France, and the United States. President Clinton favoured a more robust policy of support for the Bosnian government. 'Lift and strike' became a

watchword, i.e. lift the arms embargo on the Moslems and break the
Serbian siege of Sarajevo by air strikes. This policy was opposed by the
Europeans, in particular Britain and France, on the grounds that
lifting the embargo would only intensify the fighting (apart from the
procedural obstacle which I have mentioned), while air strikes would
leave the relatively lightly armed peacekeepers of UNPROFOR exposed to retaliation: they would become the hostages of the Bosnian
Serbs. The fact that the US was prepared to engage in risk-free air
strikes while refusing to deploy ground troops except as part of a
monitoring force of a final peace settlement added a harsh tone to the
debate. An element of 'those behind cried forward, while those in
front cried back' informed the proceedings. Until the end of 1993,
European opposition prevailed: the only positive outcome of Washington's policy was the conviction of the Bosnian government, who felt
betrayed by the Europeans, that they had a friend in the White House.

At the end of 1993, UNPROFOR comprised over twenty-seven
thousand military, police and civilian personnel, twelve infantry battalions in Croatia, nine in Bosnia-Herzegovina, a thousand observers in
Macedonia, and seventy-five observers at various airfields. The rough
annual cost was $1.2 billion, met by assessed contributions from
Member States.

In January 1994, the Secretary-General submitted a gloomy report
to the General Assembly. The Co-Chairmen had negotiated agreement
with all three parties on core areas: the few problems remaining could
be resolved with goodwill on all sides. But, while innumerable cease-
fires had been agreed on, practically none had been implemented. A
Christmas truce had been violated and the military state of affairs was
likely to deteriorate further. Some 1,470 shells had been fired at
Sarajevo on one day (4 January). Of the 7,600 troops requested by the
Secretary-General to monitor the 'safe areas' only three thousand had
arrived. The Bosnian Serbs had been deterred from further incursions
into 'safe areas' but no withdrawal of heavy weapons from Sarajevo
had taken place. Only 50 per cent of necessary humanitarian aid was
getting through, in spite of an agreement (negotiated by Mrs Ogata,
head of UNHCR) to stop fighting along the main supply routes.

In February there was a sudden and unexpected change. Some of
the *dramatis personae* were new. In December Yasushi Akashi, fresh
from his Cambodian triumph, had been appointed Special Representative of the Secretary-General, replacing Thorvald Stoltenberg who

had combined this post with his Co-Chairmanship. A dynamic British general, Sir Michael Rose, unwearied by the frustrations of Bosnia, had assumed command of UNPROFOR in Bosnia. There were signs of new American and Russian interest in the negotiating process. But the latest effort of the Co-Chairmen to revive the confederation/three-mainly-ethnic-republics concept was making little progress, the Bosnian Moslems being the main stumbling block to what seemed to them, and to Washington, as an unjust and thinly disguised partition plan which would lead quickly to the creation of Greater Serbia and Greater Croatia with the Moslems stranded in an unviable rump micro-state in the middle.

On 5 February a mortar bomb exploded in a crowded market place in Sarajevo killing sixty-eight people and wounding well over 100. This was by no means the first such atrocity and the Croat massacre of Moslems in Stupni Do the previous October had been of comparable proportions as a single act of terrorism. But the political impact was dramatic. General Rose took advantage of the resulting atmosphere to arrange a cease-fire in Sarajevo. Four days later, after consultation with the Secretary-General, NATO issued an ultimatum that, unless heavy weapons were either withdrawn to a twenty-kilometre radius round Sarajevo or grouped under UN control, air attacks would be launched against them. This initiative, promoted by France with US support, came as a shock to the Bosnian Serbs and to the Russian Federation, Serbia's historical ally. NATO air attacks in support of UNPROFOR deterrence of attacks against 'safe areas', which specifically included Sarajevo, were unequivocally authorized by Security Council resolutions 824 and 836 of 1993 but, although this authority had deterred further incursions into the other, smaller 'safe areas', the Bosnian Serbs had long since assumed that NATO lacked the nerve to apply them to Sarajevo.

There followed a few days of Serbian bluster and Security Council debate. The Russians called a Council meeting in an attempt to establish that further Council authority was needed before air strikes were launched. A Russian statement referred to a 'one-sided ultimatum to the Bosnian Serbs'. Speaker after speaker in the debate confirmed the authority already granted in resolutions 824 and 836, and the Secretary-General informed the Council that he had delegated authority to Mr Akashi to approve a request from the UNPROFOR Commander to call up the air strikes. For once, the Council forbore to adopt a resolution, perhaps a sign that it at last meant business! As the fatal date of 19 February drew nearer, the Russians sent an envoy to Bosnia and the Serbs were presented with the face-saving escape ladder that Russian troops of UNPROFOR would occupy positions evacuated by their militia. Just in time, the guns and mortars were withdrawn. For the first time Serb bluff had been decisively called; and they had climbed down.

Thereafter events moved quickly. The United States took a lead in the peace negotiations, using its friendship with the Bosnian Moslems and economic sticks and carrots on the government in Zagreb, whose compatriots in Central Bosnia were on the defensive against the Bosnian army, to mediate a new-style agreement under which Croatian and Moslem Bosnia Herzegovina would federate and simultaneously form a confederation with Croatia proper. A Bosnian Moslem/Bosnian Croat cease-fire and cessation of hostilities was signed on 23 February, heavy weapons were withdrawn or put under UNPROFOR control and UNPROFOR units were interposed: the horrendous siege of Mostar and the bitter fighting in Central Bosnia were over. On 28 February NATO's seriousness of purpose was demonstrated when NATO jets shot down four Serb aircraft which were bombing an ammunition factory in a Moslem area – the first ever active enforcement of the no-fly zone.

At the beginning of March, the Council approved measures to return normal life to Sarajevo and to extend the safe areas concept to Maglaj (under siege by the Serbs for months), Mostar and Vitez. By the end of the month, although Bosnain Serb bombardment of Moslem enclaves continued, more routes had been opened for the passage of humanitarian aid and the overall level of fighting was probably lower than at any time since early 1992. A kind of normality was returning to Sarajevo. Negotiations had also begun in Zagreb under Russian auspices in an attempt to solve the problem of Croatian Krajina: a comprehensive cease-fire was concluded. At the time the main complaint of the Secretary-General was the shortage of additional troops to enable UNPROFOR to carry out its much extended responsibilities. A vigorous recruitment campaign initiated by Britain in the Council produced some results, including an additional British battalion, but UNPROFOR was still several thousand troops short of requirement as March turned to April.

Nascent optimism was shattered by an all out Bosnian Serb assault on one of the UN safe areas, Gorazde. Heavy artillery and armour had been moved from Sarajevo and Gorazde was subjected to merciless bombardment. Bosnian Serb forces entered the city. For two or three weeks the UN failed to react in spite of standing authority to use force to protect the safe areas against bombardment or incursion. Eventually a few NATO aircraft dropped a few bombs, only enough to encourage General Mladic in the belief that he had little to fear. Russian diplomacy failed to restrain the Serbs and, on 22 April, Russia joined in voting for a tough Security Council resolution demanding a cease-fire, disengagement of military forces and withdrawal. This was followed by a resolute decision in NATO to use air strikes if the Bosnian Serbs did not comply. By the deadline they appeared to have done so, although a row between the UN and NATO over the question of compliance exposed the inadequacy of the chain of command. In any case General Mladic had achieved his objective of neutralizing the strategic value of Gorazde and terrorizing its population: there were several hundred civilian deaths and thousands wounded during the siege. At the end of April a fresh peace initiative was launched by the US, the Russian Federation, the European Union and the UN. The Bosnian Serbs were moving towards fresh military objectives.

I shall touch on several of the issues raised by the UN handling of the Yugoslav crisis in the concluding chapter. There is no point in harping back to the specific blunders which compounded the difficulties facing the international community, such as the premature recognition of Croatia and Bosnia-Herzegovina and the imposition of a blanket arms embargo with no skilfully drafted paragraph foreshadowing review if the Council found itself dealing with an assault on a independent member state following the break-up of the Federation.

By the time this essay is published, it will be apparent whether the current stir of activity heralded the advent of peace. Even if it does I hope that the governments most closely concerned will engage in self-examination rather than self-congratulation. There is no escaping the fact that there has been a dismal, tragic failure of international management. Two hundred thousand people are dead and two to three million displaced as a result of the fighting of the past two-and-a-half years. Neither the UN nor the EU, nor the US, nor the Russian Federation has been able to do much to prevent a massive campaign of ethnic cleansing with all its attendant horrors, an atrocity which arouses especially poignant memories in people of my generation.

I do not blame the Co-Chairmen, who have been skilful and indefatigable in trying to bring the parties to their senses. I do not blame the people on the spot – UNPROFOR, UNHCR and the other humanitarian agencies – who have performed heroically and whose labours have averted an even greater disaster. What strikes me most forcibly is the contrast between on the one hand the square jawed firmness of the rhetoric of Security Council resolutions and statements (the condemnations, the demands, the appeals, on cessation of fighting, free passage of humanitarian aid and adherence to humanitarian law), and on the other the unwillingness to translate this torrent of words into action on the ground. Why did the Council back away from Resolution 770, adopted as early as August 1992, which authorized the use of force to ensure the delivery of humanitarian supplies? Why did the Council not implement the authority to defend the 'safe area' of Sarajevo by force, as authorized in resolutions 824 and 836 of May/June 1993 respectively, until the United States and France lost patience seven months later? Why was there a six-month gap between the imposition of the 'no-fly zone' and authority to enforce it in the air? Why was there a lapse of weeks between the opening of the siege of Gorazde and even a half-hearted move by the UN and NATO to confront the Serbs? These and other similar questions point to one answer, especially when it was clear from the outset that the Western members of the Council were in more or less unfettered control of its deliberations and decisions.

Even though the public media had, quite rightly, brought Western public opinion to a high temperature of indignation and distress at the atrocities inflicted by the Bosnian Serbs and to a lesser extent the Bosnian Croats, governments were obsessed by the need to avoid casualties and possibly indefinite embroilment in a bloody civil war. The public was clamouring for something to be done but governments feared that this ardour would quickly dissipate once the body bags started arriving at the airport. But no one was asking for a comprehensive, Desert Storm-type operation to fight all the combatants to the ground. The demand was for an unequivocal message that the world would not tolerate the worst of the atrocities. Such a lesson could have been administered at any time with limited risk and little danger of permanent embroilment. But it was not. I shall always believe that the governments concerned underestimated the steadfastness of their own electorates, and that the excessive timidity was unnecessary. The net effect has been to undermine international authority and to encourage warlordism. I am not suggesting that Messrs Milosevic, Karadzic and Mladic have Hitlerian ambitions in Europe, but, if NATO with all its power plus the backing of the UN Security Council could do so little about a conflagration on its borders, the credibility of these institutions in the eyes of other potential disturbers of the peace is unlikely to be enhanced. The international community had a choice between shutting up or putting up. It tried to do both and achieved neither.

CHAPTER TWENTY

Conclusions

A panoramic survey of the principal preoccupations of the Security Council from the creation to the present day discloses a surprising fact, namely that the effectiveness of the Council's activities, both persuasive (Chapter VI) and coercive (Chapter VII), has changed less than many people might imagine with the end of the Cold War and the advent of a climate of unprecedented international cooperation. The notion has proved fallacious that the failure of the Council to live up to the expectations of the Charter was solely due to the Cold War and associated divisions in the international community. Indeed, over the past two or three years, the UN had experienced as many fiascos and failures as at any time in its early history.

A glance at the table of contents of this book reveals that the bulk of the conflicts and disputes on the Council's agenda originated in the rapid decolonization of the European empires since the end of the Second World War, a consummation which the Founding Fathers at Dumbarton Oaks and San Francisco did not anticipate. Few of these crises related to the ideological struggle between American-led capitalism and Russian as well as Chinese-led communism, which was called the Cold War, although many were vicariously affected by it. In fact, on all but one of the occasions on which the main antagonists came closest to collision – the Berlin blockade of 1948, the Korean War of 1950–54, the Cuban missile crisis of 1962, the Vietnam War and the 1973 Arab/Israeli war – the Security Council played little or no part except for validating the American-led military response to the Korean invasion, and a valuable initiative by the Secretary-General to help the Soviet Union to climb down in 1962 without unacceptable loss of face: a Western resolution on the Berlin blockade of 1948 was vetoed by the Soviet Union.

All my case studies had local causes, namely ethnic and/or religious hostility, the implantation in Asia and Africa of alien communities, the creation by imperialism of artificial states which, on independence, were racked by centrifugal forces or by that restlessness which sublimates in a desire to dominate or to expand. A few derived from the abysmal quality of government over a long period. Where strong regional powers or the superpowers intervened, the consequences were dire – witness the bloody anarchy of Angola and Mozambique, the destruction of Cambodia – while the championship by the United States and the Soviet Union of opposing sides in so-called 'regional' disputes succeeded in exacerbating and prolonging them as the protégé states hardened their attitudes, secure in the support of their respective patrons. On occasions, this configuration threatened world peace as the uncontrolled policies of the clients dragged the patrons close to direct confrontation – the October War of 1973 is the most vivid example, an occasion when the deployment by the Security Council of a UN peacekeeping force defused the crisis hours before superpower units were due to arrive on the battlefield.

Fortunately the end of the Cold War has eliminated this wider danger – far greater in my judgement than the likelihood of a Soviet onslaught on the Central Front – and the withdrawal of championship from rival parties has led to old enemies having to face up to the sterility of their policies, the first step towards mutual accommodation. If the champions were still in the lists giving more or less unqualified backing to their clients, the civil war in Ethiopia would still be going on, apartheid would not have been abolished in South Africa, Namibia would not be independent, there would have been no peaceful solution to the tragedy of Cambodia, and the glimmer of hope which is visible on the Palestine-Arab-Israel horizon would not be visible. Probably Washington would have been reluctant to give the peacemaking Central American presidents and the UN so much latitude. In some, not all, of these cases this evolution provided the persuasive machinery of the UN – mediation and non-threatening military peacekeeping – with the opportunity to capitalize on the more flexible attitude of the parties. Even so, as indicated in Part Three, there is unfinished business from the past still on the agenda.

What is to me most significant about the new agenda is its similarity to the old. To a great extent it is dominated by the decolonization of the Russian Empire, which masqueraded so successfully in the eyes of the Non-Aligned Movement as the anti-imperialist champion of national liberation for most of the life of the UN. The new agenda is already littered with the debris of this last decolonization and the release of the periphery from the old sphere of influence – conflicts arising out of ethnic, sectarian and religious hostilities; separatist tendencies within states artificially created by the imperial power, some purely domestic, others spilling across internationally recognized borders. This familiar landscape provides a continuum rather than a break with the past.

It is true that the Security Council has been vastly more fecund in terms of the production (and length) of resolutions with the passing of the Cold War. For example, between 1980 and 1983 the Council adopted eighty-three resolutions and nineteen drafts were vetoed (sixteen by the US, sometimes in company with Britain and France, and three by the USSR). Between 1990 and 1993, 246 resolutions were adopted and only three drafts were vetoed (two by the US and one by the Russian Federation). However, the key questions which I address in this chapter are the following: does this increased output represent increased effectiveness or simply increased activity? How much of the great arsenal of ammunition being discharged by the Council is blank, how much live? Is the end of the Cold War the sole reason for the expansion of Council activity?

It is an over-simplification to blame the negative impact of Permanent Member vetoes for the arduous and frustrating nature of the Council's operations in the past. Furthermore, relatively few of the 195 draft resolutions killed by vetos were victims of the Cold War. Of course the superpowers brusquely disposed of Security Council involvement when they were directly concerned – Soviet actions in Czechoslovakia in 1948 and 1968, the Berlin blockade of 1948, Hungary in 1956, Afghanistan in 1979, the American invasions of Grenada in 1983 and Panama in 1989. But the majority of vetoes concerned membership applications (fifty-four) and what I call demonstration vetoes, namely negative votes cast to wrong-foot adversaries, to show the non-aligned membership that the West could be pushed so far and no further, to demonstrate loyalty to protégé and client states, and to satisfy domestic opinion. Going over the list, the only clear case where the Council could have played a valuable part in substance had it not been for vetoes was the turbulence in the Balkans between 1946 and 1947 when the Soviet Union blocked action on six occasions.

The fact that the achievement of a positive result in the Council was more often than not akin to towing a recalcitrant brontosaurus through a glutinous swamp was a function of the Cold War in that, without it, there would have been no tripartite division of the Council into East,

West and Non-Aligned. On stock subjects like the Middle East and Africa, the six or seven non-aligned members (three African, two Asian and two Latin American) could count on automatic support from the Soviet Union, China and the Eastern European non-permanent member. But they first had to get their act together within their own group, in which some were more non-aligned than others – Cuba and the Sultanate of Oman being examples of the two ends of the spectrum – and clear their deliberations with the relevant geographical group, say African or Arab. Then they had to decide whether to go for a demonstration veto from the West, or to try to nudge the West a little further than they had gone on the previous occasion, or to seek quick unanimity. Should they also try to divide the far from monolithic West – give or take the government of the day, the United States was regarded as the unambiguous champion of Israel but more inclined than Britain to take a tough line with South Africa; France was known to yearn to show its independence of the Anglo-Saxons and its sympathy with non-aligned positions, especially where the Arab world was concerned; and the two non-permanent Western Europeans and Others (Australia, Canada, New Zealand) often included an idealistic Scandinavian or a Southern European who were not easy targets for American or British persuasion.

The ensuing process was absorbing to those of us, myself included, who enjoy pure negotiation. But it was time consuming as working paper followed working paper, draft resolution followed draft resolution, group and bilateral consultations pullulated until the moment of voting at last arrived, sometimes weeks later. The journey to the centre of the maze was complicated by the fact that, like mythical monsters, features of the landscape kept changing as the overt and hidden motivations and objectives of the players altered with the shifting pattern of reactions to successive formulations. It was not a *modus operandi* which encouraged doubters to take their problems to the Council, still less to expect results which would have immediate impact on the ground. The Council could act quickly and decisively in emergencies, as demonstrated in the Falklands crisis of 1982. However, by the 1980s Western governments in particular were becoming wary of resorting to this cumbrous and unrealiable mechanism as a place in which to conduct serious business.

Now, as I suggested above, the spirit of cooperation within the Council is closer than at any time since the creation, the old political divisions and caucuses have become largely irrelevant and the hidden agendas have for the moment at least disappeared. There must have been an unimaginable (to my generation of UN diplomats) streamlining of working methods: otherwise only a race of supermen could manufacture the volume of resolutions and presidential statements which flood out of the Council these days. But is this torrent having any greater effect in the world of reality than did the laboriously achieved trickle of earlier days?

As I have explained in the previous chapters, there are essentially two types of Security Council operation which go beyond the mere adoption of declaratory resolutions (useful though these can be in helping to quieten agitated public opinion – for example, the most recent resolution on the Hebron massacre), sometimes, increasingly in today's world, they intermingle. The first is what is called a Chapter VI (Pacific Settlement of Disputes) operation where the Council acts in a persuasive capacity with at best the full consent, at worst the acquiescence of the parties to the dispute or conflict. The form of such operations is normally a combination of diplomatic mediation and 'non-threatening' military peacekeeping. The second is chapter VII (Action with Respect to Threats to the Peace, Breaches of the Peace and Acts of Aggression) where the Security Council resolutions are mandatory and measures adopted are coercive – either sanctions or, if the worst comes to the worst, military force.

Over the past forty-six years, the UN has acquired considerable experience and expertise in Chapter VI operations, and the following conclusions can be drawn from earlier chapters in this book. Such operations are successful only when certain requisites are present from the outset and maintained throughout: the basic williness of the parties to stop fighting and/or to settle their differences; their acceptance of the negotiating and peacekeeping mandate of the UN; and adequate financial and manpower resources for the military/civil side of the UN operation. The previous case-studies show how, when all these conditions are met, the UN can achieve remarkable successes, as in the Congo (although non-threatening peacekeeping had to be escalated to enforcement at one stage), in Namibia, Cambodia, El Salvador and, fingers crossed, in Mozambique After the October War of 1973, UNEF II kept the peace until American mediation secured a settlement between Egypt and Israel. On occasions, success is only partial, as in Cyprus where UNFICYP has helped to maintain the peace, but the intransigence of the parties has resisted thirty years of mediation. And on the Golan Heights, UNDOF continues to hold the line while the parties negotiate. Sometimes the operation works for a time, but fails when the consent of a party is withdrawn – the Egyptian expulsion of UNEFI in 1967 and the Israeli invasion of the Lebanon in 1982 are examples. On one recent occasion – Angola – the UN presence was too small and its mandate too weak to exercise enough authority to maintain the cooperation of both parties when the going got rough; the result has been a bloody fiasco. In Somalia, the Chapter VI mandate was inadequate to control the anarchic frenzy of the clans. In the Arab/Israeli dispute as a whole the negotiating acceptability of the UN has been destroyed by the one-sidedness of the majority view.

These examples, dating from 1960 to the present day, demonstrate that the same premises govern today's operations as governed those of the past. The difference is quantitative and horizontally extended rather than qualitative and vertically extended. Military peacekeeping used to be mainly a matter of a thin blue line of unarmed observers or lightly armed forces monitoring a recognizable cease-fire line or demili-tarized zone between two armies. The Congo was an exception and today's operations – Cambodia, Mozambique, El Salvador, Somalia, even Bosnia – are closer to the Congo in quality than to UNEF I and II, UNFICYP, UNIFIL and the like. Like the Congo, they are engaged in a more all-embracing set of tasks, escorting humanitarian aid, organizing elections, reconstructing the administration of shattered states, de-mining, rehabilitation of discharged soldiers, economic and social development, as well as the more traditional tasks of verifying and monitoring cease-fires, now in civil war situations where recogniz-able front lines are often non-existent. This is the main reason why so many more UN peacekeepers are now deployed worldwide, why it takes between ten and thirty thousand personnel for each operation (if, unlike Angola, it is to have a chance of success). It is not that their power is greater, only that the demands on them have broadened. To put this in proportion, UN figures published for January 1994 reveal that there were at that time about seventy-one thousand peacekeepers deployed in seventeen operations (five pre-dating 1991). Over sixty thousand were in three operations only – Somalia, Mozambique and former Yugoslavia – representing 75 per cent of the total annual cost to the membership of $3.2 billion.

Coercion (Chapter VII) is a different story altogether. Chapter VII was at the heart of the Charter, providing the Security Council with powers and the 'teeth' which the League of Nations had lacked. In practice its provisions have never worked as they were designed to. Certain lessons have emerged which will probably be as valid for the second half-century of the UN as they have been for the first.

Mandatory sanctions of all kinds do not work as a coercive device short of military force designed to oblige a transgressor state or faction to change its policy. Sanctions are either circumvented, or they take so long to bite that the circumstances for which they were imposed have changed, or they punish the innocent while leaving the guilty un-scathed, or they heighten the determination of the victim to resist. Before 1990 they were only imposed twice, on Southern Rhodesia and the arms embargo on South Africa. I have drawn attention to their failure in the relevant case studies. Since 1990, in the veto-free world, they have become a commonplace. It is almost a reflex action for the Council to move to Chapter VII and to impose arms embargoes, oil embargoes and wider economic measures. They have failed to do the trick in Iraq, in Somalia, in Liberia, in Haiti, in Angola, and in the wars of the Yugoslavian Succession. Ironically they have been effective on the only occasion when they have been maintained and strengthened *after* rather than *before* the use of military force. The stringent military and other measures imposed on Iraq in the cease-fire Resolution 687 have not produced change in the inherently aggressive nature of the Baghdad regime, but they have substantially reduced the threat posed by Iraq to its neighbours.

The second lesson is that the military structure built into Chapter VII is inoperable. The philosophy of the founders was, as I have earlier suggested, that states were authorized to use force only in self-defence (Article 51), 'until the Security Council has taken measures necessary to maintain international peace and security.' States were enjoined (Articles 43 and 45) to earmark forces for use by the Council which (Article 46) was to be responsible for plans for the application of armed force while (Article 47) the Military Staff Committee (the Chiefs of Staff of the Five Permanent Members) was to be responsible for the 'strategic direction of any armed forces placed at the disposal of the Security Council.'

The Cold War strangled this mechanism at birth, although it was a portent that, even with a free hand in the temporary absence from the

Council of the Soviet Union in 1950, the United States showed no disposition to involve the Council in the command and control of the forces fighting the war in Korea. A simple validation by the Council of an American-led military campaign was enough. Forty years later, when responding to Saddam Hussein's invasion of Kuwait, there was no serious question of reviving the military articles of the Charter, although the Soviet Union made a half-hearted attempt to mobilize the Military Staff Committee. As with Korea, the Council delegated authority to an American-led coalition. With minor modifications, the same principle was applied to UNITAF in Somalia two years later. It is clear that national governments are not prepared, even in a propitious international climate, to commit their forces to dynamic warfare (as opposed to static or semi-static peacekeeping) under the ultimate command and control of a discrete multilateral structure of committees such as the Military Staff Committee and the Security Council. They will either insist on national command and control or delegation to a coherent organization such as NATO. Indeed NATO has become the chosen instrument of the UN for air strikes in Bosnia. I foresee no change in this situation.

Previous chapters, especially in Part Four, illustrate the most acute problem facing the UN when it comes to the use of military force. Straightforward inter-state aggression in areas of Great Power national or strategic interest is rare. Indeed inter-state warfare of any kind is at the moment out of fashion. At present and in the future the Security Council is confronting and will continue to confront mainly civil wars in which there is no direct national interest of major powers and in which, as often as not, there are not even recognized governments to deal with. The UN can no longer afford to ignore all such conflicts on Article 2 (7) grounds, and the Council has devised many ways of circumventing this constraint. If neglected, some of these wars might spread, and the new power of the public media, particularly television, focusing on the suffering of the innocent, which is a prominent feature of all civil conflict, is demanding from governments something more than paper resolutions, diplomatic mediation and 'non-threatening' peacekeeping. This has already led to the involvement of the UN in places such as Bosnia, Somalia and Haiti with mixed mandates combining Chapter VI mediation, Chapter VII mandatory sanctions, Chapter VI peacekeeping and Chapter VII authority for the use of force.

Inevitably this commingling has led to irresolution, and to confusion in chains of command.

Moreover, the travails of the UN in Somalia and Bosnia have demonstrated with cruel clarity that impartiality (the essence of UN success in Chapter VI) is incompatible with the use of force, which requires taking sides. This contradiction has underlined the need not to mix persuasion with military coercion in the same operation. Most important, the humiliations suffered by the UN in 1993 have revealed a fact of crucial importance on which I have touched, namely that Western governments, although prepared to commit their armed forces to combat in pursuit of national or patriotic interest (the Falklands), or for wider strategic reasons (Middle East oil), are not prepared to risk casualties and long drawn-out warfare to stop Bosnians from killing Bosnians, Somalis from killing Somalis, Haitians from tormenting Haitians and so on.

This may not be heroic but it is a fact which has to be faced. Some of the studies in Part Four suggest that this timid tendency is intensifying. In the 'near abroad' the UN response has been mainly conditioned by the need not to provoke the Russian Federation. In Liberia the UN has settled for a non-combatant role. It will keep as clear as it can from the slaughter in Rwanda and, if it resumes, in Burundi. There is no inclination for forceful intervention to stop the civil war in Angola. All the Western contingents are now out of Somalia. Other ghastly civil wars – the Sudan, Afghanistan – are being treated only as man-made disasters to be dealt with by humanitarian agencies. The current attitude is best summed up by President Clinton in his address to the UN General Assembly on 27 September 1993 (with my italics):

> In recent weeks, in the Security Council, our nation has begun asking harder questions about proposals for new peacekeeping missions: is there a real threat to *international* peace? Does the proposed mission have clear objectives? Can an end point be identified for those who will be asked to participate? How much will the mission cost? . . . The United Nations simply cannot become engaged in every one of the world's conflicts. If the American people are to say yes to UN peacekeeping, the United Nations must know when to say no.

Subsequent statements from Washington and from European capitals have done nothing to dim the clarity of this message. Local warlords and potential aggressors would be justified in assuming that, if they can minimize television coverage of their atrocities; if they can steer clear of Great Power national interests; if they can promise the outside world an indefinite, uncomfortable stay with the certainty of casualties, they stand a reasonable chance of being left alone to get on with whatever horrors they may be contemplating. The risk of the cavalry suddenly appearing over the hill will be slight.

The United Nations is half-a-century old and the Security Council has functioned against a backcloth of seismic change in the international scenery – the decolonization of all the European empires leading to a more than three-fold increase in the number of independent states comprising the international community, an elephantine ideological clash, an arms race unprecedented in peacetime, recurrent threats to world peace deriving from some of over 100 wars which have cost the lives of over twenty million people, an acceleration of technological discovery, especially in the field of communications, which makes the world of 1945 seem archaic. The Security Council has reflected these changes in its output, its agenda, its rhetoric and its inner relationships. But the Council's power to influence events diplomatically and militarily, by means of persuasion, coercion and the use of force has remained more or less constant even now that the constellation of international relations is in a more propitious conjuncture than at any time in the present century. Hence I would not expect any radical change for better or for worse in the years to come. However, there are incremental possibilities for improvement.

The end of the Cold War, the Gulf crisis and the premature acclamation of a New World Order have brought the UN, for the first time for many years, to the forefront of Western governmental thinking in a positive rather than a hostile sense. The advent of the fiftieth anniversary has merged with these factors to stimulate a massive re-examination of the Organization in all its aspects. The Security Council Summit meeting (a British initiative) of January 1992 led to the publication in June of the same year of the Secretary-General's report 'Agenda for Peace', which has formed the basis for a flood of suggestions for enhancement of the functioning of the Security Council. The General Assembly followed up in 1993 by creating a working group to examine possible restructuring of the Council membership, a hardy perennial of many years standing. Today the ground is blanketed with think tanks and planning groups, both governmental and non-governmental, and the air is thick with their proposals on such matters as expanding the number of Permanent Members (there is a strong case for including the two economic superpowers, Japan and Germany, as well as representative African and Latin American states), solving the financial crisis, elimination of waste, increasing efficiency in the peacekeeping organization, better training for peacekeeping forces, more effective preventive action and much more.

I will concentrate on three topics which seem to me to be the basis for any improvement which may be achieved. The first is money. The endemic UN financial crisis is not about the amounts in question. A $3 billion annual peacekeeping budget may be two to three times what it was in the past, but it is still less than 10 per cent of the British defence budget, about 1–2 per cent of the American equivalent, and about the same as the US annual aid budget for Israel. The crisis is caused by the disproportionate sums paid by certain countries. Roughly speaking, the United States (30 per cent) the European Union (30–35 per cent) and Japan (11 per cent), pay about 75 per cent of the total, leaving only 25 per cent to be subscribed by about 170 member states, including some of the richest per capita in the world. This has a particularly negative impact in the US where Congress and influential elements in public opinion argue that America should not have to pay one third of the cost of a series of operations in almost all of which there is no threat to world peace and no direct American national interest. Or, if Washington is to pay so much of the piper's wages, it should have a proportionate say in selecting the tune. In a democratic environment where governments formulate their foreign policies and overseas expenditures with national interest and public opinion as the first two priorities and internationalism a poor third, this is an attitude which is unlikely to change. Several complicated cures have been advanced, such as interest charges on late payers (mainly the US), the flotation of bonds, a peacekeeping insurance scheme, the creation of emergency funds, borrowing on the commercial market, and others. Most of these expedients are, in my view, false trails. I believe that the crisis can be solved only by reducing the gap between the American contribution and the rest. This would mean altering the equation on which assessments are based so that the richest per capita countries, many of which are small, thinly populated and surrounded by predators, pay more, with a ceiling of, say, 10 per cent of the total paid by any single member state, including the United States. For example, the six states of the Gulf Cooperation Council at present pay only 1.6 per cent of the total; Singapore and Malaysia only .2 per cent between them. All of these – there are others – could easily afford to pay ten times their present contributions, and it is such countries which are for obvious reasons in the greatest need of international protection. If a system were developed under which the US paid 10 per cent, Japan 10 per cent, and the European Union its present 30 per cent to 35 per cent this would leave about 45 per cent to be paid by the remainder, which includes not only the affluent countries I have mentioned but also major powers such as China, the Russian Federation, India, Brazil, Canada, and Australia, to name a few. Something on these lines would be my solution, leading to the avoidance of more Angolas, of more bitter arguments about the inadequate strength of UNPRO-FOR, all of which weaken Chapter VI and Chapter VII operations alike.

My second topic is the need for more effective preventive action, a drum which I and others have been beating unheard for over a decade and which has now become received wisdom among governments and the UN Secretariat. The importance of taking action to defuse mount-ing crises, inter-state and civil, before they explode into warfare has grown with the increasing reluctance of the UN to involve itself in military enforcement in the kind of conflict which it is most likely to have to face in the future – new Somalias, new Bosnias. If the Great Powers are unwilling or unable to dowse the flames, all the more reason to forestall ignition.

Agenda for Peace and the Secretary General's Annual Report for 1993 focus strongly on this topic, stressing the need for confidence-building measures, improved fact-finding and early-warning systems and preventive peace-keeping military deployments. I have no quarrel with these propositions. But the truth is that elaborate fresh diplomatic machinery is not necessary. It did not need the CIA or MI6 to deduce that Saddam Hussein was planning to invade Kuwait, that Somalia was dissolving into chaos, that Yugoslavia was breaking up, that North Korea is aggressive. Any newspaper reader could come to the correct conclusions, as he or she could have months in advance of the June War of 1967, or of Saddam Hussein's invasion of Iran in 1980. It has not been lack of information or analysis which has precluded preventive action, although governments for obvious politi-cal reasons have to pretend to total surprise when wars break out which they have failed to prevent. It is more that governments, and thereby the Security Council itself, are gripped by a kind of inertia, or in some cases self-deceiving complacency, which inhibits strong collective diplomatic action by regional organizations or by the UN itself in advance of shots being fired. The fear of alarmism, or of courting unpopularity, or simply the 'better not' syndrome, so often appears to overcome common sense, or resistance to obviously wrong-headed policies, as in the summer of 1990 *vis-à-vis* Iraq and the summer of 1991 *vis-à-vis* Yugoslavia. With the lessons of the past few years before them and with no longer a fear of preventive action provoking an East/West crisis, the hope is that the Permanent Members and the rest of the Council, in close cooperation with the Secretary-General, will improve on their previous track record.

The ultimate in preventive action is of course military. A UN force could be deployed on a potential victim's side of an inter-state frontier only with the consent of that government, or within a state verging on civil war or disintegration only with the consent of the government in power or, in the absence of central government, with the acquiescence of as many political leaders as could be mustered. However, I do not believe in the effectiveness of unarmed observers or lightly armed peacekeepers in such roles. If for example one or the neighbouring states is determined to violate the Macedonian border, I doubt that the UN observer presence will act as a deterrent any more than the seven thousand-strong armed force of UNIFIL did when the Israelis invaded Lebanon in 1982. However, if a potential aggressor or warlord knew that his forces would be met by a UN force armed, equipped and mandated to fight, with Great Power air or naval support available as relevant, this would constitute a powerful disincentive. Such a force, not necessarily larger than, say, three or four battalion groups with supporting weapons, if deployed on the Kuwaiti side of the Iraq/Kuwait frontier in 1990 or on the Croatian side of the Serbia/Croatia border in 1991, might well have prevented hostilities from breaking out.

Judging by recent events, it does not look as though the will exists within the international community or regional organizations to act in this way. I understand that the Secretary-General's proposal in Agenda for Peace that member states should earmark forces to be on call for 'peace enforcement' operations has been turned down. This means that the only option is for the UN to have a volunteer force of its own available to act as such a deterrent under the control of the Security Council and the Secretary-General. This proposal was advanced in 1993 by Sir Brian Urquhart, the doyen of UN peacekeepers. It received some support, including from myself, and a barrage of criticism – where would the volunteers come from, on what military philosophy would it be trained, where would it be based, who would pay for it, what would be the system of command and control, etc? There are positive answers to all these and other questions and I believe that those who make the decisions would be well advised not to dismiss the 'Urquhart initiative' out of hand. If it is not followed up, the deterrent, preventive capability of the UN will remain close to its present low level.

My last topic is that of command and control of military forces authorized by the Security Council in circumstances where, unlike Korea or Desert Storm or UNITAF in Somalia, such authority has not been delegated to a member state or group of states. There is no problem where traditional Chapter VI peacekeeping is concerned, such as UNIFIL, UNFICYP or UNDOF. These are static deployments and the chain of command running from the Security Council through the Secretary-General and his peacekeeping staff to the Force Commander has worked well. It is not so easy when the duties of the peacekeeping force are more multifarious, including, say, escorting humanitarian supplies, disarming militias, de-mining, supervising elections and so on. Even so, provided the operation remains within Chapter VI, the difference should be incremental rather than qualitative, demanding, as is happening, a larger and more highly trained staff at UN Headquarters. The qualitative change comes when Chapter VII enforcement is involved, particularly when it is combined with Chapter VI peacekeeping. So far, to an outsider, the result has been a shambles. In Bosnia there have been public arguments about exactly whose finger is on the trigger even after ultimata have been delivered. In Somalia, some contingents have referred to their national governments for orders or for confirmation of orders descending from New York. I have the impression that Washington is not prepared to commit American forces to combat except under command of an American officer. If the UN is to recover military credibility beyond that of a facilitator for others to act, something must be done to redeem this unmilitary situation. If there are governments which will not allow their forces to go into action except under national command they should be confined to a logistical role, leaving less sensitive nations to operate at the sharp end. If, as I believe to be the case, there is no question of activating the mechanism in the military articles of the Charter, it would be best to revert to the *modus operandi* developed by Dag Hammarskjold for the Congo crisis. The Security Council remains in political and strategic command and delegates day-to-day control of operations to the Secretary-General who deals through a Special Representative in the field with the Force Commander. The Secretary-General establishes a permanent advisory body for each crisis, comprising representatives of the principal regional states and the main troop contributors. Something of this kind happens already, I am told: if so, it does not seem to be working very well.

When the fiftieth anniversary celebrations are over, the speeches, re-dedications, pledges, collective statements and reports have been delivered, the authority and power of the United Nations will not have changed much. The Organization will still be the quintessence of the Lowest Common Denominator, most effective when parties wish to settle but cannot do so on their own, or as a convenient ladder down which governments can climb when their national policies have led them into dangerous places; least effective when persuasion fails and the Security Council resorts to enforcement, except on the rare occasions when it acts as a rubber stamp approving military action by a Great Power.

As regards the Security Council agenda, there will be more civil wars and more states of anarchy which the Council will not be able to ignore. But the approach of the membership, especially the major Western powers, will be characterized by growing caution and reluctance to become involved except on a risk-free basis. The scars of 1993 will not heal quickly.

I prophesy that two fundamental issues will cast a lengthening shadow in the years to come. The most sacred of UN cows has been the integrity of states within existing frontiers, however artificial the states and unrealistic the frontiers. Separatism has been the devil incarnate. These articles of faith are being challenged. In recent years, new entities such as the Turkish Republic of Northern Cyprus, the Republic of Somaliland and independent (universally recognized) Eritrea have taken root. Now we have the Trans-Dniestr Republic, Nagorno Karabakh, Abkhazia and the divisions and sub-divisions of former Yugoslavia to add to the list. The rebel movements in the southern Sudan are edging away from the quest for local autonomy towards a demand for sovereign independence. The notion of confederations of sovereign states is gaining popularity while internal autonomy is regarded with increasing suspicion. Slovakia has broken with the Czech Republic, velvet divorce following velvet revolution. As central government fails, as in Afghanistan or Zaire, and what used to be provinces have to get on with life on their own, this trend will accelerate. For how much longer will the UN be able to ignore this sea-change, and insist on withholding recognition, except when it is agreed by all parties?

Secondly there is the future of the 'Near Abroad'. This may present the Security Council with its most delicate challenge. Questions abound to which there are at present no answers. Will some of the former imperial territories, particularly the Slav states, return to mother Russia on a genuinely voluntary basis? What does the international community do if, for example, the Ukraine splits on such a question? Will economic, political and military pressure from the Russian Federation oblige some of the weaker states to renounce sovereign independence in all but name, becoming what Outer Mongolia used to be *vis-à-vis* the Soviet Union? Or will some of the Moslem states rid themselves of Brezhenevian overlords and seek to join the wider Islamic embrace? Will a time come when CIS 'peacekeeping' becomes indistinguishable from Russian imperialism? Will the well-being of Russian communities in the Near Abroad become a pretext for military intervention for more sinister reasons?

So far, the Council has played its hand cautiously and, in the present international climate, Moscow would be reluctant to cast vetoes as it did to cut off discussion of Cambodia and Afghanistan. There is therefore room for manoeuvre. Russian foreign policy in its former empire is of far-reaching importance to the Far East, the Indian sub-continent, the Middle East, as well as to the whole of Europe and, of course, the United States. It is thus appropriate that it be monitored in the United Nations, as was British policy in the immediate post-imperial years, and that the discourse should not be confined to the outdated East/West forum, except on nuclear matters, or to a limited and inchoate body such as the CSCE. The United Nations did not hesitate to sound off about the perils of neo-imperialism after the first round of decolonizations. It should not hesitate to do so again if the last decolonization looks like going wrong.

EPILOGUE

Since I finished writing the preceding chapters, I have scanned the horizon for signs of dispersal of the clouds of doubt and uncertainty surrounding the Security Council, and for evidence that my somewhat less than enthusiastic prognosis in Chapter 20 was too pessimistic, a symptom of the disillusionment of old age. I have detected no such portents. Indeed, as I write in the autumn of 1995, the overall level of activity in the Council seems to have declined, and there is reluctance to assume fresh responsibilities or to intensify involvement in disputes and conflicts already on the agenda unless success, or the absence of failure, is more or less guaranteed, or unless, as in the case of Bosnia, there is overwhelming political pressure to 'do something'. Moreover, the Congressional victory of the Republicans in November 1994 has produced an American legislature whose pronouncements make the Reagan Administration in the 1980s seem positively enthusiastic about the United Nations by comparison.

It took the Council nearly a month to pronounce on the civil war in the Yemen in the late spring of 1994. Tension had been building up for some time between the leadership of the traditionalist North and the formerly Marxist South in the Yemen, the country which, against all expectations, united in early 1990 and subsequently carried through one of the rare genuine multi-party elections in Arab history. But the armies of the previously separate states had not been united and, in spite of vigorous efforts by individual Arab leaders to defuse a burgeoning crisis, full-scale warfare broke out in early May. The Security Council looked the other way for some weeks: there was little television coverage of the fighting and, unlike most civil wars, it comprised principally battles between regular forces, although there were substantial civilian casualties resulting from air and ground bombardment of towns and cities, mainly the port of Aden. On 20 May the Southern leadership announced secession and, at the end of the month, the Council met at last at Arab instigation. On 1 June a mild Chapter VI resolution emerged 'calling for' a cease-fire and 'urging' cessation of arms supplies. The fighting died down of its own accord with the defeat of the Southern forces.

At the same time, all other events were engulfed by the ghastly tragedy of Rwanda. The Secretary General put it well in his report to the Security Council of 31 May. 'The magnitude of the human calamity that has engulfed Rwanda might be unimaginable but for its having transpired.' The massacres which were beginning when I completed Chapter 18 at the end of April developed into the most brutal, comprehensive, and clearly long pre-planned holocaust of ethnically based genocide since the Second World War. Figures are unreliable but it seems possible that up to five hundred thousand Tutsis and their Hutu supporters were bludgeoned, hacked or shot to death, while the total of displaced persons and refugees in neighbouring countries passed the million mark. The carnage was perpetrated by government forces and the Hutu militia in a manifest effort to eliminate the Tutsi population. It is the supreme irony that the same government was the holder of Rwanda's seat as a non-permanent member of the Security Council!

What about the reaction of the international community? In Chapter 18 I wrote that the Security Council could not be blamed for withdrawing the bulk of the lightly armed peacekeeping force, UNAMIR: its peacekeeping and peacemaking mandate was demonstrably in ruins. Apart from the massacre of civilians, the civil war itself had resumed in earnest, and UNAMIR had only a Chapter VI mandate. By mid-May, the sickening nature and horrendous scale of the holocaust had created a tidal wave of public outrage and a tempest of criticism was directed at the UN decision to withdraw. It is from this point that the Council merits the Secretary-General's rebuke in his report of 31 May that, 'The delay in reaction by the international community to the genocide in Rwanda has demonstrated graphically its extreme inadequacy to respond urgently with prompt and decisive action to humanitarian crises entwined with armed conflict.'

On 17 May the Security Council reacted to the situation with a wordy resolution which, setting aside the rhetoric, delegated responsibility to UNAMIR to establish secure humanitarian areas and to provide security for the distribution of relief supplies and for relief operations. For these purposes, an expansion of UNAMIR to a strength of 5,500 was authorized and the force was permitted to take action 'in self-defence'. Over six weeks later, not one of the 5,500 troops had appeared on the ground. African governments had offered contingents but lack of resolve, haggling over costs and availability of equipment, on the part of the US and others prevented the operation from getting under way. While this lukewarm dithering went on, tens of thousands more innocent people were massacred, hundreds of thousands were displaced and the few hundred remaining UNAMIR personnel, plus non-governmental agencies, notwithstanding their heroic combined efforts, were able to protect only a tiny proportion of the potential victims.

While the haggling continued, it was reported, over the terms and conditions of the lease or sale to the UN of fifty American armoured personnel carriers from stocks in Germany, the Rwandese Patriotic Front continued its offensive against the forces of the interim government and made clear that it did not want the UN to step in and block the total conquest of Rwanda, the quickest way in the view of the RPF to bring the massacres to an end.

In late June there was a new twist to the plot of this Grand Guignol. France decided that public outrage, honour and French prestige in Francophone Africa demanded action: it was announced that French forces would be sent to Rwanda, preferably with authority from the Security Council, to protect civilians in danger of massacre. This bold move evoked a variety of reactions. The Great Powers were cool but felt unable to oppose openly. The RPF, mindful of twenty years of French support for the Hutu government of the late Juvenal Habyarimana, including the arming and training of Rwandan armed forces and the militias, the perpetrators of the massacres, declared that French forces would be treated as enemies, since they were clearly coming to frustrate the victory of the (anglophone) RPF and to maintain the murderers in office. The states of the OAU were divided, with reactions varying from unenthusiastic support from some Francophone governments to the disapproval of leading Anglophones. French representatives insisted that their motives were purely humanitarian: there was no intention of disturbing the military balance; the expedition would last only two months and the troops would be confined entirely to protecting civilians in areas still under government control. The non-governmental agencies involved in humanitarian relief work in Rwanda were vociferously opposed and the Francophone African members of the remaining UNAMIR contingent were withdrawn.

On 22 June, France secured a Security Council resolution by the narrow margin of ten favourable votes to five abstentions (including Nigeria) for the deployment. The following day about two thousand French troops arrived in Eastern Zaire and small numbers crossed the border into Rwanda to be welcomed with flowers and flags by the Rwandan government and the Hutu militias. The first question to be asked was: if France could achieve this logistical feat at such short notice, why could this capability not be put at the disposal of the African contingents which had volunteered to make up the enhanced UNAMIR authorized by the Council over a month previously? There was no answer.

The French left on time and Rwanda is now ruled by a government of the RPF. UNAMIR's strength has risen to over 5,000 but this figure will be halved this autumn. There has been no settlement. Hundreds of thousands of refugees remain in Zaire and Tanzania: the Hutu militias are rearming and training for a counterthrust. The government has brutally cleared the refugee camps within Rwanda at the cost of several thousand civilian lives. In neighbouring Burundi, which the Security Council is watching closely, there have been sporadic massacres of Hutus by the Tutsi-dominated army.

Elsewhere in Africa, the formal obsequies of apartheid were performed to universal rejoicing. On 10 May 1994 President Nelson Mandela was inaugurated. Two weeks later the Security Council arms embargo was lifted, and South Africa was admitted to the OAU and readmitted to the Commonwealth. By mid-June the international anti-apartheid apparatus was finally dismantled and, on 23 June, it was announced that South Africa would be welcomed back to its seat in the General Assembly. *Nunc dimittis.*

The new government will have little time, money or manpower to spare from the titanic task of reconstructing the country after nearly fifty years of apartheid. But it is clear that much is expected of President Mandela in relation to the myriad problems besetting other African states. He has played an influential part in the peace settlement operations in Mozambique and Angola.

The large-scale UN operation in Mozambique was a success. Elections took place on schedule in October 1994 and the country is now settling to the task of reconstruction, all the refugees having returned. In equally tragic Angola, a ceasefire was negotiated in the same month and a peace accord was concluded in Lusaka in November. With great caution and on stringent condition of the good behaviour and co-operation of the parties, the Council is now slowly deploying what will be a 7,000-strong UNAVEM III (a British logistics battalion is already in place) to monitor the establishment of a coalition government, UNITA (which was doing badly on the battlefield) having belatedly accepted the results of the 1992 elections. These positive achievements have been offset by the failure of the UN and ECOMOG to stop the civil war in Liberia (although a fresh cease-fire has led to the establishment of an interim government), by the blind eye turned by the Security Council to an almost equally bloody conflict which has broken out in Sierra Leone – the Security Council is happy to leave the initiative to the Commonwealth – and to the humiliation of UNOSOM in Somalia. The force in Somalia withdrew in March 1995, leaving the clans to their own devices. In the Sudan, the civil war splutters on, ignored by the Security Council.

In the 'Near Abroad' (Chapter 15) the Russian Federation, with Security Council compliance, is tightening its grip on those weak states which have proved incapable of managing post-decolonization instability and separatist movements. Without CIS, a.k.a. Russian/Uzbek 'peace-keeping' forces, the domestic situation in Tajikistan would be liable to collapse, and there has been more fierce fighting on the Tadjik–Afghan border. The CSCE 'Minsk Group' ploughs on with its negotiations between the parties in Azerbaijan (a 1994 ceasefire has held) and there has been no increase in the marginal role of the UN. The Secretary-General has recommended against deploying a full UN peacekeeping force in Georgia. Instead there is general agreement that the 'Liberian solution' should be used, i.e. an expanded version of UNOMIG monitoring the activities of a largish CIS (Russian) 'peacekeeping' force mandated to separate the parties and create conditions, with UN participation in the mediation exercise, for a general settlement.

I wrote in Chapters 11 and 12 about the two most striking successes for UN mediation combined with Chapter VI peacekeeping – El Salvador and Cambodia respectively. The former, following parliamentary and presidential elections which gave victory to the ruling Arena party, is still holding and the UN presence has been wound up. Cambodia is paying a price for the failure either to suppress or to co-opt the Khmer Rouge during the transitional period. King Sihanouk's health is increasingly fragile and fighting grumbles on at a low level between forces of the coalition government and Pol Pot's troops. There is, needless to say, no disposition within the Security Council to return to the charge.

In 1994/5 the United States redeemed the Haitian fiasco of 1993 (Chapter 17). In July the Security Council authorized a US-led force to use 'all necessary means' to bring about the departure of the military junta and the return of President Aristide. In September, preceded by a persuasive mission by ex-President Carter, a force of over 20,000 combat-ready American troops landed in Haiti. The junta departed and President Aristide returned in October. On 31 March 1995 the Americans felt able to hand over to a UN force of about 6,000 personnel of which over 2,000 are Americans. The internal situation is quieter than could have been anticipated and elections have taken place.

In the Eastern Mediterranean the Secretary-General has failed, mainly on account of Turkish-Cypriot intransigence, to deliver even limited progress in the form of 'confidence-building measures'. As predicted in Chapter 13, the Turkish-Cypriot leadership, comfortable with the well-protected status quo, is not prepared to take any risks simply in order to please the UN and tidy up a long outstanding international dispute. There are reports that a fresh initiative is in the offing but I would not put much money on its success.

Pressure mounts to lift sanctions from Iraq, emanating from governments which believe that Saddam has fulfilled the terms (or most of them) of Resolution 687, from others who see sanctions as a perpetual punishment for the innocent Iraqi people while Saddam and his clique live high off the hog and, most important, from those who see a cornucopia of potential business contracts building up behind the sanctions dam. Fortunately, in my view, the US and Britain are demanding more comprehensive proof of Saddam's genuine compliance with Resolution 687 and have, as I understand it, moved the goalposts by insisting that Saddam comply also with Resolution 688 (oppression of his own people) before sanctions are lifted. The likelihood is remote that Saddam will stop oppressing the Shi'a south where his programme of draining the marshes continues to give readier access for his tanks and infantry, or that he will fail to seize an opportunity to reoccupy 'liberated' Kurdistan and resume the massacres. He did not improve his international standing by moving troops towards the Kuwaiti border in October 1994. The Council reacted with a resolution demanding their withdrawal and coalition forces rushed to the area. Iraqi troops withdrew. Subsequently Iraq formally recognized Kuwait within the borders approved by the UN. But sanctions remain in place. Meanwhile, squabbling has broken out with accompanying bloodshed between the political groupings in 'liberated' Kurdistan. The Security Council did nothing about the Turkish drive into Northern Iraq in pursuit of Kurdish rebels early in 1995.

In July 1994 the Gaza Strip and Jericho lurched into limited autonomy in accordance with the Oslo Agreements and Yasser Arafat established his headquarters in Gaza (Chapter 2). In September 1995, agreement was finalized on the next phase, Israeli 'redeployment' from urban areas on the West Bank leading to elections for a Palestine National Council. So far events have conspired to bolster the extremists on both sides who oppose the Oslo Agreements. The incompetence of the PLO administration and the reluctance of investors have inhibited the flow of aid. The misery has been intensified by periodic closures of the crossing into Israel to the tens of thousands of Palestinians who normally work there, on account of the suicide bombings by Islamic extremists which have caused serious Israeli casualties. These outrages have in turn prejudiced Israeli public opinion against concessions to the Palestinians. Arafat's response to Israeli pressure to crack down on the terrorists has led to his being characterized as an Israeli surrogate by his own people while he has proved incapable either of persuading the Israelis to withdraw some of the settlements in the Occupied Territories, even from the Gaza Strip, or of preventing continuing expansion of existing settlements in the West Bank and the Jerusalem area. The Islamist movements have fed on the mounting disillusionment. The Jewish settlers on the West Bank are now up in arms about the latest agreement.

On the inter-state front, there has been little or no progress on the Syria/Israel sector – the Golan Heights – and opposition to withdrawal grows inside Israel: the government's willingness to take bold steps will evaporate as the 1996 elections loom closer. In October 1994, Jordan and Israel signed a Peace Treaty and relations have to a significant extent been normalized.

The Security Council has played no part in these events. The United States, resolved for domestic and other reasons not to offend Israel, has taken the line that, with the parties in direct negotiations, there is no justification for intervention by outsiders. Although the UN peacekeeping and observer forces remain in place, the Americans prevented the Lebanese, in late 1994, from bringing to the Council a series of savage Israeli retaliatory bombing attacks in response to Hizbollah guerrilla activity in South Lebanon. In May 1995, the Israelis confiscated Arab land in East Jerusalem and the non-aligned members brought the question to the Council. The result was an American veto (the seventieth in all and the first by the Clinton Administration) of a mild resolution declaring the act illegal and seeking its rescindment. The remaining fourteen members voted for the draft. Ironically the Israelis suspended their decision when the government was in danger of being defeated in the Knesset by an improbable combination of Arab members (opposing the confiscation) and the opposition Likud (seeing an opportunity of bringing the government down).

The lull in Bosnia in the early summer of 1994 did not last (Chapter 19). From June onwards fighting resumed, intensifying in the autumn in the Bihac pocket, punctuated by isolated pin-prick NATO airstrikes. In September a new Contact Group (Russia, the US, Britain, France and Germany) tried unsuccessfully to persuade the Bosnian Serbs to accept a peace settlement which would involve their disgorging about 20 per cent of the 70 per cent of Bosnia which they were occupying. Meanwhile President Milosevic of Serbia sealed Serbia's border with the Bosnian Serbs and agreed to international monitoring, in exchange for the suspension of some sanctions. At the turn of the year the parties accepted a four-month ceasefire, the harshness of winter probably being the determining factor.

By the end of January the ceasefire was being regularly broken and, in March, the Bosnian government, having acquired fresh weaponry, launched tactical offensives in Central Bosnia with some success. The Contact Group failed to persuade Milosevic to recognize Bosnia-Herzegovina in exchange for a general suspension of sanctions. Further efforts in May and June were unsuccessful.

In March, President Tudjman of Croatia withdrew a threat to expel UNPROFOR from the Serb-occupied districts of Croatia. After some comic-opera bargaining, agreement was reached on a much-reduced force named the UN Confidence Restoration Operation (UNCRO!). In May a Croatian government offensive retook Western Slavonia (UN Sector West) while the Security Council emitted squawks of disapproval.

By the end of April, the ceasefire was in ribbons and fighting intensified around Sarajevo and elsewhere with UN peacekeepers being deliberately targeted by the Bosnian Serbs. UN collection points for heavy weapons were plundered and the exclusion zone around Sarajevo was ignored.

On 25 May the crisis exploded. Following the expiry of an ultimatum to withdraw heavy weapons from the exclusion zone or return them to the UN, NATO aircraft bombed an ammunition depot near the

Bosnian Serb Headquarters at Pale. This clearly hurt. The Bosnian
Serbs responded by shelling civilian targets in five of the six UN 'safe
areas', one shell killing over seventy people and wounding over a
hundred in Tuzla. After a further NATO strike the next day, the
Bosnian Serbs started to abduct UN Military Observers and to use
them as human shields, à la Saddam Hussein, close to the ammunition
depot. They then either blockaded or abducted a large number of
UNPROFOR troops, nearly 400 in all, including many French and
over thirty British from the Royal Welsh Fusiliers. The UN weapons
collection points were taken over. The exclusion zone round Sarajevo
and the monitoring of heavy weapons ceased to exist. Fighting spread
round the lines of confrontation and the Bosnian Serbs maintained that
the military hostages would be released only on guarantee of no further
NATO airstrikes: they had already closed Sarajevo airport and were
blocking the passage of humanitarian aid. UNPROFOR lapsed into
virtual impotence.

By late June, the overall landscape had changed. The UNPROFOR
hostages, following intense pressure on the Bosnian Serbs from President
Milosevic, were released in batches, the last group emerging on 18
June. On 15/16 June the Bosnian Government launched a series of
offensives to relieve the pressure of the Sarajevo siege, with minimal
success. Meanwhile the hostage-taking had generated a tempestuous
media and domestic political reaction in the West. In the US, which
had encouraged the NATO airstrikes, the attitude of the Administration
chopped and changed with the Congressional and public wind. Britain
and France, in the context of NATO rather than the UN, decided to
deploy a Rapid Reaction Force of about 10,000 personnel, including a
British Air Mobile Brigade, in Bosnia: its chain of command and
mandate were initially unclear but, by the end of June, significant
numbers, including artillery, had arrived in Bosnia. The Security
Council was for two or three weeks a spectator and the Secretary-
General's options (ranging from total withdrawal to the creation of a
fighting force not under UN command on the lines of Somalia and
Haiti) were ignored.

On 16 June the Council, after long deliberation, adopted Resolution
988 authorizing the increase of UNPROFOR by 12,500 personnel to
form a rapid reaction capacity 'to enable UNPROFOR to carry out its
mandate'. The Rapid Reaction Force would form an 'integral part of
UNPROFOR'. Two-and-a-half thousand personnel were already in

the theatre. However, this belated confirmation of what had already been decided in NATO capitals was vitiated by the American refusal to pay their share of the costs of the force in spite of the Anglo-French argument that it should be treated as a normal peacekeeping operation. Whatever President Clinton's view, Congress would not play.

In July these humiliations were compounded when the Bosnian Serbs overran two of the 'safe areas', Srebenica and Zepa. The customary horrors of ethnic cleansing followed. On 21 July a conference in London decided to resist strongly if the Serbs attacked Gorazde (no mention of Srebenica and Zepa) and the Rapid Reaction Force moved on to Mount Igman to defend UN aid convoys to Sarajevo.

In August the Americans began to take a lead. With US connivance Croatian forces drove the Serbs out of the Krajina (except for the sliver of land in Eastern Slavonia): about 200,000 Serb civilians fled. British and Ukrainian peacekeepers withdrew from Gorazde, minimizing the risk of further hostage-taking. A mortar attack on a Sarajevo market was the straw which broke the back of the camel of UN/NATO timidity. For nearly three weeks from 30 August NATO carried out systematic bombing and Cruise missile attacks on the Bosnian Serb military infrastructure until Bosnian Serb heavy weapons were withdrawn from Sarajevo. Simultaneously the Americans led vigorous peace negotiations, which continue at the time of writing. Taking advantage of these events, Bosnian government and Croatian forces swept into Western Bosnia, expelling the Serbs from much of the territory seized since 1992. Over 50 per cent of Bosnia is now in government hands. After four years of bloody warfare and massive displacement of innocent civilians, optimism is at a discount. But it is just possible that, for the first time, all the parties are ready to settle simultaneously. Again, after four years of dithering, it seems that Washington has at last decided to pull out the stops to secure settlement.

To sum up, nothing has happened to invalidate the trends which I adumbrated in Chapter 20. On the contrary they are coming into stronger outline. The reservations expressed by President Clinton in his statement to the General Assembly of 27 September 1993 regarding American participation in and support for UN operations have been sharpened by the Republican landslide of 1994. Unless a clear United States national interest is engaged, Washington will be even more laggard than before in the face of further demands from other members

of the Security Council on its purse, and above all for military involvement on the ground.

There is a paradox here. Imperial responsibility and latterly the
ideological coloration of the Cold War engendered a kind of internationalism. Now that both these influences have dissolved and multi-party
democracy has taken a stronger hold, governments, even in the most
powerful states, are more inclined to formulate their foreign and
defence policies on the basis of short-term national interest than they
were previously. It is no longer possible to invoke, for example,
responsibility for subject peoples or the struggle against international
communism in support of domestically unpopular decisions. The quest
for domestic popularity is a dominant factor and, with the communications revolution, public opinion wields hitherto unimagined power.
Hence, in foreign policy decision making, disinterested internationalism
is coming a very poor second to national interest in a world of
proliferating civil conflicts far from major power centres; except when
public outrage demands action, and the prospect of unpopularity
through inactivity looms.

This is a poor lookout for the UN, dependent as it is on the
financial, diplomatic and military engagement of the Great Powers,
especially the US. Such governments are at the moment having difficulty in reconciling an outward appearance of bold decisiveness with a
risk-free policy which encompasses mediation and blue-helmeted peacekeeping but stops short of major financial expenditure, let alone ground
combat, except when a clear national interest is at stake. Even the
French deployment in Rwanda was a function of perceived national
interest, i.e. fulfilling France's idea of what she should be in the eyes of
the world in general and Francophone Africa in particular. And the
reaction of the Great Powers to the horrors of Bosnia has until the past
few weeks been inglorious, to say the least.

There is one countervailing factor which to some extent offsets this
sceptical analysis. Now that there are no built-in obstacles to consensus,
the Security Council has evolved into a kind of touchstone of legitimacy
for operations which in earlier days would have been carried out by
Great Powers without multilateral sanction. In 1983 and 1989 respectively, American forces invaded Grenada and Panama: the administration vetoed the subsequent criticism by the Council. In the 1990s, the
United States has carefully mobilized Security Council support for
action to restore the legitimate president of another country in the

American backyard, namely Haiti. In 1990, President Bush would have gone ahead and expelled the Iraqis from a position in which they threatened Saudi Arabia even if the US had been obliged to act almost alone with the members of the Gulf Cooperation Council. But the whole operation secured an indispensable measure of legitimacy from the invocation of the Security Council from the outset. In 1994 France made clear that French troops would move unilaterally into Rwanda. Even so France took the trouble to seek an enabling resolution from the Security Council. And so on: there are many more examples, the most recent being the Franco-British recourse to the Council for validation of the Rapid Reaction Force in Bosnia. By the same token the Russians have welcomed, up to the point of not getting in their way, Security Council involvement in the troubled non-Slavic parts of the 'Near Abroad'. Moscow has even acquiesced in the involvement of the Organization for Security and Cooperation in Europe (OSCE) in the aftermath of the blundering brutalities in Chechnya. Neither military superpower has needed to act in such a way except because international legitimacy is preferable to a display of naked bilateral power. This tendency is perhaps the most encouraging ingredient in the post Cold War configuration.

ANNOTATED BIBLIOGRAPHY

A vast number of books have been written about all aspects of the United Nations. Many of them are technical and academic, not the kind of literature appropriate for holiday reading.

For me, two books stand out as readable accounts of the creation and early years of the UN, namely the *Memoirs of Cordell Hull* (2 vols, London, Hodder and Stoughton, 1948) and the *Memoirs of Lord Gladwyn* (London, Weidenfeld and Nicholson, 1972). For lively histories of the main crises engaging the Security Council and successive Secretaries-General from the outset until 1985 it would be hard to beat Brian Urquhart's three publications: *Hammarskjold* (New York, Alfred A. Knopf, 1972), *A Life in Peace and War* (London, Weidenfeld and Nicolson, 1987) and *Ralph Bunche: An American Life* (New York, W.W. Norton, 1993).

Facts and figures about UN peacekeeping operations are fully set out in *The Blue Helmets*, second edition (UN Department of Public Information, 1990), and, for those interested in the machinery of the Security Council, the definitive work is *The Procedure of the Security Council* by Sydney D. Bailey (Oxford, Clarendon Press, 1975). Among recent collections of essays, I recommend *The United Kingdon – The United Nations*, edited by Erik Jensen and Thomas Fisher (London, Macmillan, 1990) and the second edition of *United Nations, Divided World – The UN's Roles in International Relations*, edited by Adam Roberts and Benedict Kingsbury (Oxford, Clarendon Press, 1993).

Researchers into the activities of the Security Council will find indispensable the *Summary of UN Security Council Resolutions 1946–1991* and the *Table of Vetoed Draft Resolutions in the Security Council 1946–1991* prepared by the Research and Analysis Department of the Foreign and Commonwealth Office. I hope that the Department will continue to bring these documents up to date every few years. The current editions are already the third in the series.

INDEX

READ MORE IN PENGUIN

In every corner of the world, on every subject under the sun, Penguin represents quality and variety – the very best in publishing today.

For complete information about books available from Penguin – including Puffins, Penguin Classics and Arkana – and how to order them, write to us at the appropriate address below. Please note that for copyright reasons the selection of books varies from country to country.

In the United Kingdom: Please write to *Dept. EP, Penguin Books Ltd, Bath Road, Harmondsworth, West Drayton, Middlesex UB7 0DA*

In the United States: Please write to *Consumer Sales, Penguin USA, P.O. Box 999, Dept. 17109, Bergenfield, New Jersey 07621-0120.* VISA and MasterCard holders call 1-800-253-6476 to order Penguin titles

In Canada: Please write to *Penguin Books Canada Ltd, 10 Alcorn Avenue, Suite 300, Toronto, Ontario M4V 3B2*

In Australia: Please write to *Penguin Books Australia Ltd, P.O. Box 257, Ringwood, Victoria 3134*

In New Zealand: Please write to *Penguin Books (NZ) Ltd, Private Bag 102902, North Shore Mail Centre, Auckland 10*

In India: Please write to *Penguin Books India Pvt Ltd, 706 Eros Apartments, 56 Nehru Place, New Delhi 110 019*

In the Netherlands: Please write to *Penguin Books Netherlands bv, Postbus 3507, NL-1001 AH Amsterdam*

In Germany: Please write to *Penguin Books Deutschland GmbH, Metzlerstrasse 26, 60594 Frankfurt am Main*

In Spain: Please write to *Penguin Books S. A., Bravo Murillo 19, 1° B, 28015 Madrid*

In Italy: Please write to *Penguin Italia s.r.l., Via Felice Casati 20, I–20124 Milano*

In France: Please write to *Penguin France S. A., 17 rue Lejeune, F–31000 Toulouse*

In Japan: Please write to *Penguin Books Japan, Ishikiribashi Building, 2–5–4, Suido, Bunkyo-ku, Tokyo 112*

In Greece: Please write to *Penguin Hellas Ltd, Dimocritou 3, GR–106 71 Athens*

In South Africa: Please write to *Longman Penguin Southern Africa (Pty) Ltd, Private Bag X08, Bertsham 2013*

READ MORE IN PENGUIN

HISTORY

The Making of Europe   Robert Bartlett

'Bartlett does more than anyone before him to bring out the way in which medieval Europe was shaped by [a] great wave of internal conquest, colonization and evangelization. He also stresses its consequences for the future history of the world' – *Guardian*

The Somme Battlefields   Martin and Mary Middlebrook

This evocative, original book provides a definitive guide to the cemeteries, memorials and battlefields from the age of Crécy and Agincourt to the great Allied sweep which drove the Germans back in 1944, concentrating above all on the scenes of ferocious fighting in 1916 and 1918.

Ancient Slavery and Modern Ideology   M. I. Finley

Few topics in the study of classical civilization could be more central – and more controversial – than slavery. In this magnificent book, M. I. Finley cuts through the thickets of modern ideology to get at the essential facts. 'A major creative achievement in historical interpretation' – *The Times Higher Education Supplement*

The Penguin History of Greece   A. R. Burn

Readable, erudite, enthusiastic and balanced, this one-volume history of Hellas sweeps the reader along from the days of Mycenae and the splendours of Athens to the conquests of Alexander and the final dark decades.

The Laurel and the Ivy   Robert Kee

'Parnell continues to haunt the Irish historical imagination a century after his death ... Robert Kee's patient and delicate probing enables him to reconstruct the workings of that elusive mind as persuasively, or at least as plausibly, as seems possible ... This splendid biography, which is as readable as it is rigorous, greatly enhances our understanding of both Parnell, and of the Ireland of his time' – *The Times Literary Supplement*

READ MORE IN PENGUIN

HISTORY

A History of Wales   John Davies

'Outstanding . . . Dr Davies casts a coolly appraising eye upon myths, false premises and silver linings . . . He is impartial. He grasps the story of his country with immense confidence and tells it in vigorous and lucid prose . . . Its scope is unique. It is the history Wales needed' – *Daily Telegraph*

Daily Life in Ancient Rome   Jerome Carcopino

This classic study, which includes a bibliography and notes by Professor Rowell, describes the streets, houses and multi-storeyed apartments of the city of over a million inhabitants, the social classes from senators to slaves, and the Roman family and the position of women, causing *The Times Literary Supplement* to hail it as a 'thorough, lively and readable book'.

The Anglo-Saxons   Edited by James Campbell

'For anyone who wishes to understand the broad sweep of English history, Anglo-Saxon society is an important and fascinating subject. And Campbell's is an important and fascinating book. It is also a finely produced and, at times, a very beautiful book' – *London Review of Books*

Customs in Common   E. P. Thompson

Eighteenth-century Britain saw a profound distancing between the culture of the patricians and the plebs. E. P. Thompson explains why in this series of brilliant essays on the customs of the working people, which, he argues, emerged as a culture of resistance towards an innovative market economy. 'One of the most eloquent, powerful and independent voices of our time' – *Observer*

The Habsburg Monarchy 1809–1918   A J P Taylor

Dissolved in 1918, the Habsburg Empire 'had a unique character, out of time and out of place'. Scholarly and vividly accessible, this 'very good book indeed' (*Spectator*) elucidates the problems always inherent in the attempt to give peace, stability and a common loyalty to a heterogeneous population.

READ MORE IN PENGUIN

HISTORY

Citizens Simon Schama

The award-winning chronicle of the French Revolution. 'The most marvellous book I have read about the French Revolution in the last fifty years' – Richard Cobb in *The Times*

To the Finland Station Edmund Wilson

In this authoritative work Edmund Wilson, considered by many to be America's greatest twentieth-century critic, turns his attention to Europe's revolutionary traditions, tracing the roots of nationalism, socialism and Marxism as these movements spread across the Continent creating unrest, revolt and widespread social change.

The Tyranny of History W. J. F. Jenner

A fifth of the world's population lives within the boundaries of China, a vast empire barely under the control of the repressive ruling Communist regime. Beneath the economic boom China is in a state of crisis that goes far deeper than the problems of its current leaders to a value system that is rooted in the autocratic traditions of China's past.

The English Bible and the Seventeenth-Century Revolution
Christopher Hill

'What caused the English civil war? What brought Charles I to the scaffold?' Answer to both questions: the Bible. To sustain this provocative thesis, Christopher Hill's new book maps English intellectual history from the Reformation to 1660, showing how scripture dominated every department of thought from sexual relations to political theory ... 'His erudition is staggering' – *Sunday Times*

Private Lives, Public Spirit: Britain 1870–1914 Jose Harris

'Provides the most convincing – and demanding – synthesis yet available of these crowded and tumultuous years' – *Observer* Books of the Year. 'Remarkable ... it locates the origins of far-reaching social change as far back as the 1880s [and] goes on to challenge most of the popular assumptions made about the Victorian and Edwardian periods' – *Literary Review*

READ MORE IN PENGUIN

ARCHAEOLOGY

Breaking the Maya Code Michael D. Coe

Over twenty years ago, no one could read the hieroglyphic texts carved on the magnificent Maya temples and palaces; today we can understand almost all of them. The inscriptions reveal a culture obsessed with warfare, dynastic rivalries and ritual blood-letting. 'An entertaining, enlightening and even humorous history of the great searchers after the meaning that lies in the Maya inscriptions' – *Observer*

The Ancient Economy M. I. Finley

One of M. I. Finley's most influential contributions to ancient history, this study examines the structure, character and operation of the ancient economy, illustrating, for example, that the Roman Empire was for centuries a single political unit operating within a 'common cultural-psychological framework'.

The Pyramids of Egypt I. E. S. Edwards

Dr Edwards offers us the definitive work on these gigantic tombs, drawing both on his own original research and on the work of the many archaeologists who have dug in Egypt. This revised edition includes recent discoveries and research.

Lucy's Child Donald Johanson and James Shreeve

'Superb adventure . . . *Lucy's Child* burns with the infectious excitement of hominid fever . . . the tedium and the doubting, and the ultimate triumph of an expedition that unearths something wonderful about the origins of humanity' – *Chicago Tribune*

Archaeology and Language Colin Renfrew
The Puzzle of Indo-European Origins

'The time-scale, the geographical spaces, the questions and methods of inquiry . . . are vast . . . But throughout this teeming study, Renfrew is pursuing a single, utterly fascinating puzzle: who are we Europeans, where do the languages we speak really stem from?' – *Sunday Times*

READ MORE IN PENGUIN

RELIGION

The Gnostic Gospels Elaine Pagels

In a book that is as exciting as it is scholarly, Elaine Pagels examines these ancient texts and the questions they pose and shows why Gnosticism was eventually stamped out by the increasingly organized and institutionalized Orthodox Church. 'Fascinating' – *The Times*

Islam in the World Malise Ruthven

This informed and informative book places the contemporary Islamic revival in context, providing a fascinating introduction – the first of its kind – to Islamic origins, beliefs, history, geography, politics and society.

The Orthodox Church Timothy Ware

In response to increasing interest among western Christians, and believing that a thorough understanding of Orthodoxy is necessary if the Roman Catholic and Protestant Churches are to be reunited, Timothy Ware explains Orthodox views on a vast range of matters from Free Will to the Papacy.

Judaism Isidore Epstein

The comprehensive account of Judaism as a religion and as a distinctive way of life, presented against a background of 4,000 years of Jewish history.

Mysticism F. C. Happold

What is mysticism? This simple and illuminating book combines a study of mysticism – as experience, as spiritual knowledge and as a way of life – with an illustrative anthology of mystical writings, ranging from Plato and Plotinus to Dante.

Eunuchs for Heaven Uta Ranke-Heinemann

'No other book on the Catholic moral heritage unearths as many spiteful statements about women ... it is sure to become a treasure-chest for feminists ... Uta Ranke-Heinemann's research is dazzling' – *The New York Times*

READ MORE IN PENGUIN

POLITICS AND SOCIAL SCIENCES

National Identity Anthony D. Smith

In this stimulating new book, Anthony D. Smith asks why the first modern nation states developed in the West. He considers how ethnic origins, religion, language and shared symbols can provide a sense of nation and illuminates his argument with a wealth of detailed examples.

The Feminine Mystique Betty Friedan

'A brilliantly researched, passionately argued book – a time-bomb flung into the Mom-and-Apple-Pie image . . . Out of the debris of that shattered ideal, the Women's Liberation Movement was born' – Ann Leslie

Faith and Credit Susan George and Fabrizio Sabelli

In its fifty years of existence, the World Bank has influenced more lives in the Third World than any other institution yet remains largely unknown, even enigmatic. This richly illuminating and lively overview examines the policies of the Bank, its internal culture and the interests it serves.

Political Ideas Edited by David Thomson

From Machiavelli to Marx – a stimulating and informative introduction to the last 500 years of European political thinkers and political thought.

Structural Anthropology Volumes 1–2 Claude Lévi-Strauss

'That the complex ensemble of Lévi-Strauss's achievement . . . is one of the most original and intellectually exciting of the present age seems undeniable. No one seriously interested in language or literature, in sociology or psychology, can afford to ignore it' – George Steiner

Invitation to Sociology Peter L. Berger

Sociology is defined as 'the science of the development and nature and laws of human society'. But what is its purpose? Without belittling its scientific procedures Professor Berger stresses the humanistic affinity of sociology with history and philosophy. It is a discipline which encourages a fuller awareness of the human world . . . with the purpose of bettering it.

READ MORE IN PENGUIN

POLITICS AND SOCIAL SCIENCES

Conservatism   Ted Honderich

'It offers a powerful critique of the major beliefs of modern conservatism, and shows how much a rigorous philosopher can contribute to understanding the fashionable but deeply ruinous absurdities of his times' – *New Statesman & Society*

The Battle for Scotland   Andrew Marr

A nation without a parliament of its own, Scotland has been wrestling with its identity and status for a century. In this excellent and up-to-date account of the distinctive history of Scottish politics, Andrew Marr uses party and individual records, pamphlets, learned works, interviews and literature to tell a colourful and often surprising account.

Bricks of Shame: Britain's Prisons   Vivien Stern

'Her well-researched book presents a chillingly realistic picture of the British sytstem and lucid argument for changes which could and should be made before a degrading and explosive situation deteriorates still further' – *Sunday Times*

Inside the Third World   Paul Harrison

This comprehensive book brings home a wealth of facts and analysis on the often tragic realities of life for the poor people and communities of Asia, Africa and Latin America.

'Just like a Girl'   Sue Sharpe
How Girls Learn to be Women

Sue Sharpe's unprecedented research and analysis of the attitudes and hopes of teenage girls from four London schools has become a classic of its kind. This new edition focuses on girls in the nineties – some of whom could even be the daughters of the teenagers she interviewed in the seventies – and represents their views and ideas on education, work, marriage, gender roles, feminism and women's rights.

READ MORE IN PENGUIN

PHILOSOPHY

What Philosophy Is   Anthony O'Hear

'Argument after argument is represented, including most of the favourites
... its tidy and competent construction, as well as its straightforward style,
mean that it will serve well anyone with a serious interest in philosophy'
– *Journal of Applied Philosophy*

Montaigne and Melancholy   M. A. Screech

'A sensitive probe into how Montaigne resolved for himself the age-old
ambiguities of melancholia and, in doing so, spoke of what he called the
"human condition"' – *London Review of Books*

Labyrinths of Reason   William Poundstone

'The world and what is in it, even what people say to you, will not seem
the same after plunging into *Labyrinths of Reason* ... He holds up the
deepest philosophical questions for scrutiny and examines their relation to
reality in a way that irresistibly sweeps readers on' – *New Scientist*

I: The Philosophy and Psychology of Personal Identity
Jonathan Glover

From cases of split brains and multiple personalities to the importance of
memory and recognition by others, the author of *Causing Death and
Saving Lives* tackles the vexed questions of personal identity.

Philosophy and Philosophers   John Shand

'A concise and readily surveyable account of the history of Western
philosophy ... it succeeds in being both an illuminating introduction to the
history of philosophy for someone who has little prior knowledge of the
subject and a valuable source of guidance to a more experienced student'
– *The Times Literary Supplement*

Russian Thinkers   Isaiah Berlin

As one of the most outstanding liberal intellects of this century, the author
brings to his portraits of Russian thinkers a unique perception of the social
and political circumstances that produced men such as Herzen, Bakunin,
Turgenev, Belinsky and Tolstoy.